FIT TO SERVE

FIT TO SERVE

Reflections on a Secret Life, Private Struggle, and Public
Battle to Become the First Openly Gay U.S. Ambassador

AMBASSADOR JAMES C. HORMEL
and ERIN MARTIN

Skyhorse Publishing

Skyhorse Publishing books may be purchased in bulk at special discounts for sales promotion, corporate gifts, fund-raising, or educational purposes. Special editions can also be created to specifications. For details, contact the Special Sales Department, Skyhorse Publishing, 307 West 36th Street, 11th Floor, New York, NY 10018 or info@skyhorsepublishing.com.

Skyhorse® and Skyhorse Publishing® are registered trademarks of Skyhorse Publishing, Inc.®, a Delaware corporation.

www.skyhorsepublishing.com

10 9 8 7 6 5 4 3 2 1

Library of Congress Cataloging-in-Publication Data
Hormel, James C. (James Catherwood), 1933–
    Fit to serve : reflections on a secret life, private struggle, and public battle to become America's first openly gay U.S. ambassador / James C. Hormel and Erin Martin.
            p.   cm.
    Includes bibliographical references and index.
    ISBN 978-1-61608-398-4 (hardcover : alk. paper)
    1. Hormel, James C. (James Catherwood), 1933–   2. Ambassadors—United States—Biography.   3. Ambassadors—Luxembourg—Biography.
4. Philanthropists—United States—Biography.   5. Gay men—United States—Biography.   6. Human rights workers—United States—Biography.   7. Gay activists—United States—Biography.   I. Martin, Erin.   II. Title.
    E840.8.H667A3 2011
    327.2092—dc23
    [B]
                        2011027074

Printed in the United States of America

To all those who died of that (still) raging virus.

Oh! what a tangled web we weave
When first we practise to deceive!

—Sir Walter Scott
Marmion, canto vi. stanza 17

CONTENTS

FIT TO SERVE

Chapter One

THEY WILL EAT YOU ALIVE

As soon as the bicycle courier arrived with the package, my office manager, Marcus, brought it to me, wished me luck, and then left me alone. I took the yellow padded envelope in my hands, knowing what it contained: a videotape—and an accusation.

Seated at my cluttered desk, just two stories above the loud racket of Market Street's trolleys, I heard nothing apart from the thump of my heart. My hands shook; they often do—owing to a hereditary muscle tremor common to the men in my family—but my anger made the shaking worse. California Senator Dianne Feinstein's mother-knows-best voice played in my mind: "Oh Jim, they will try to eat you alive," she had warned.

I freed the tape from the mailer and read the chicken scratch on its label: *Pat Robertson.*

I must have something better to do than watch this tape, I thought.

A little after eight o'clock that morning, in the bathroom splashing water on my face, I realized that it was April 2, my oldest daughter Alison's forty-second birthday. She lived in Charlottesville, with her husband Bernie, and was on a daunting mission of her own: founding a school for autistic children. She wanted her kids Harry

1

and Georgia, and others like them, to get the attention not available to them in conventional schools.

The phone rang. I answered the cordless by my bed and immediately noted a hint of agitation in the smooth voice of Ray Mulliner. A refugee of Salt Lake City, excommunicated by the Mormon Church for being gay, he had helped me manage my philanthropic and political work for more than a dozen years.

"Hey, Jim. I am really sorry to bother you, but I just got a call from the White House that you need to know about," he said, pausing so that we both could take a breath.

"Oh really?" I responded, still a bit groggy.

"Yeah. Pat Robertson did a piece on your nomination on his show this morning. It was quite ugly, apparently."

Anxiety spread inside me like spilled paint. "What did he say?" I asked.

"Well, there was a tiny protest in front of the Capitol yesterday; I mean, *tiny*, as in eight to ten people, and they blew it up into a big story," Ray said. "They made all kinds of accusations about pedophilia."

"Pedophilia?" I yelled. "What? Are these people out of their minds?"

"I know, I know. It's becoming very clear that they will stop at nothing," Ray said. "I already have a call in to KPIX to see whether we can get a tape."

"I'll be in as soon as I can," I said.

"Be prepared—the phones are ringing already," he said, hanging up.

I sat in silence, taking shallow breaths. I looked back toward my bed and contemplated diving under the covers.

After a quick shave and fast shower, I threw on a casual shirt and comfortable khaki pants—it was going to be a long day. I grabbed a banana and rushed to the office, so fixated on what had been said about me that I forgot to call Alison to wish her well.

Alone in my office, I put my dread aside, pushed the tape into the slot, and took a seat on the nearby sofa. The blue logo of *The 700 Club* filled the screen and a voice announced Robertson and his co-host Terry Meeuwsen.

The duo stood in front of a set that looked like a living room, as if all of America was being invited into their home. They stood shoulder to shoulder: Robertson, gray-haired and paternal in a tan jacket, blue shirt, and dark tie; Meeuwsen, blond and just short of fifty, perched next to him. They looked deeply into the camera, into the homes of nearly 1 million viewers. Robertson wrinkled his forehead and squinted for emphasis as he announced news on Paula Jones's sexual harassment lawsuit against President Clinton, which had been dismissed the day before. My heart quickened as they moved on to me.

"A wealthy tycoon with ties to homosexual groups that promote sex with children may soon be a United States ambassador, without approval of the United States Senate," Meeuwsen intoned, slowing at the words *sex with children.* "Are sexual politics and money driving this behind-the-scenes deal? CBN News investigates."

To me, the show had the atmospherics of children's theater, and I half-expected to see Bert, Ernie, or Big Bird sitting in the anchor's chair. Instead, the camera focused on a precisely coiffed gentleman named Lee Webb to introduce the report. Behind him, across a giant screen, was a grainy image of *me.* It was plucked from a year-old television interview conducted during San Francisco's 1996 Lesbian, Gay, Bisexual, and Transgender Pride Parade. I wore a white *Coming Out Day* T-shirt, appropriate for the sunny weather and the event but not flattering for television. Bulky headphones and a microphone stood out against my cropped white hair. I looked more like an amateur helicopter pilot than an ambassadorial nominee. The words CONTROVERSIAL APPOINTEE hovered in bold letters above my head, with smaller, fading subtitles in rows below: HORMEL, HORMEL.

Next, a written warning appeared on the screen as the pseudo-anchor tipped his head toward the camera: "A word of warning about our next story. This story may contain graphic images that you will *not* want your children to see."

Oh please, I thought. *How utterly ridiculous.*

Describing me as a "radical homosexual activist," Webb explained that I was President Clinton's nominee as ambassador to Luxembourg, and that to overcome objections in the Senate, Clinton might use special powers to bypass a confirmation vote and give me a recess appointment. Next, a reporter from *The 700 Club*'s very own *Christian Broadcasting Network* appeared on the screen.

Video rolled of a press conference in front of the U.S. Capitol, in which a group of nine protesters, identified as "a mix of ex-homosexuals and Christians," chanted: "Can Hormel! Can Hormel!" They carried signs, some of which read: *Pedophiles Go to Jail, not Luxembourg.* Speakers claimed that I had given financial support to NAMBLA (the North American Man-Boy Love Association), an organization founded in the 1970s to advocate relationships between men and boys. In his voice-over, the CBN reporter told viewers that my philanthropic work had "helped popularize homosexuality and child sex abuse."

My blood boiled. *I should have known it would come to this*, I thought.

The seemingly interminable story moved on to an interview with a Christian activist who eventually became my most aggressive attacker: Andrea Sheldon, of the Traditional Values Coalition. A bleached blonde with light blue eyes, Miss Sheldon appeared on screen in an ample, floral-patterned dress.

She stated that she had visited the James C. Hormel Gay & Lesbian Center at the San Francisco Public Library and found items that she claimed were "X-rated" and "illegal." She flipped through a fat binder of photocopied materials, several of which flashed on the screen. One was a cartoon sketch of an older man hugging a boy. Another was a vintage black and white photograph of a nude boy. Last appeared a pen and ink illustration of three nude boys diving off a sail boat. Genitalia—assuming they were in fact visible in the originals—were fuzzed out of the broadcast images.

"Hormel has denied knowing about these materials in the Center that bears his name, but there's this label with his name on it, in every publication," the reporter said, with the inflection of a prosecutor addressing a jury. The camera zoomed in on the Center's proprietary bookplate, which, indeed, was on the inside cover of every one of the thousands and thousands of items in the collection.

In case any viewers had missed the central allegation of the story, the CBN staffer restated it in his wrap-up: "The anti-Hormel forces gathered here for this demonstration said this isn't about Luxembourg. It's not about politics. It's about the sexual abuse of children."

Back in the staged living room, Robertson, seated on a stool, delivered his last word:

"Your rights as the American people are being violated on this one, and to send this, this *peed-o-phile* advocate, to Luxembourg or any foreign country, is an absolute outrage," he ranted, in his Virginia twang.

The tape ended. The screen filled with loud snow.

Frozen on the sofa, I was furious beyond words. The *audacity* of it. The *outrageousness* of presenting this slander as legitimate journalism. Dianne had been right: they *were* trying to eat me alive.

* * *

It had all started in 1992, before President Clinton had even won the election. Over dinner one night at the Fairmont Hotel, the campaign treasurer, Bob Farmer, suggested that I seek a presidential appointment. I found the idea immodest. Who was I to ask for that? Just because I had donated money to the campaign, I should expect some sort of nomination? That didn't seem right. But as I thought it over, I realized that I might have an opportunity to open some eyes, particularly if the post required Senate confirmation. That would force one hundred senators, and possibly the whole American public, to consider the experience of a gay man in America. If I succeeded, I would break a ceiling and make it easier for gay people to serve at the highest levels of government. *That* would be a big deal.

At the time, I had no idea what I was getting into.

Two years later, in 1994, I was considered as a potential ambassador for Fiji, but the government there objected to my appointment, and my name seemed to sink to the very bottom of the appointment list. For three subsequent years, I was a squeaky wheel in Washington, making dozens of visits and hundreds of phone calls to keep my name in consideration. By the time President Clinton finally nominated me to Luxembourg in October 1997—five years after my dinner with Bob Farmer—I was on an all-out crusade.

When that *700 Club* segment aired in April 1998, I was sixty-five years old and "out" for more than three decades. I had been involved with the equality movement as far back as 1977, when Anita Bryant, a Miss America runner-up living in Florida, started a campaign to kick gay teachers out of schools. In 1978, I attended my first major Democratic Party meeting, a mini convention held in Memphis. At a breakfast reception in a hotel ballroom, Cornelia Wallace, the ex-wife of Governor George Wallace of Alabama, arrived to work the room. She was planning her own run for governor. As she breezed by, her long, dark hair flowing, my lapel button caught her attention. This is my recollection of our exchange:

"My goodness, what is that all about?" she asked, in a breathy Southern accent, as she shook my hand. Perhaps she was surprised to see a man wearing something pink.

"The pink triangle is the symbol that gay people were forced to wear in the Nazi prison camps," I replied, looking deeply into her eyes. She dropped my hand as if it were burning her.

"My, isn't that interesting?" she said, spying Tennessee Governor Ray Blanton out of the corner of her eye. "Oh, Governor…," she sang out, lifting a finger in his direction and deserting me, it seemed, as quickly as possible. It was never easy to stand before someone and see horror crawl across their face as they became aware of my sexual orientation. And believe me, Cornelia Wallace, compared to some others, was polite.

To a certain extent, my skin was thick from walking so many miles along this road. The "me" who was a political animal, and who was willing to put everything aside to get the nomination, could shrug off the pedophilia allegations—they were the price of progress. *That* "me" saw *The 700 Club* show as an elaborate performance, designed to stir hatred and fear and, ultimately, raise money for Robertson's empire.

But far from Washington, in the safety of my office, I couldn't help but feel hurt. And humiliated. I had spent the last few decades refusing to be humiliated by any individual, or the world at large, but Robertson had managed to do it in a single broadcast.

Dejection and sadness slowly rose within me. They were feelings I knew well—I had been fighting them all my life. They came from an almost instinctual sense that no matter who I was or what I did, I would be neither accepted nor acceptable in a society that is relentlessly heterosexual.

Had Robertson really told 1 million people on national television that I advocated pedophilia?

Yes, *pedophilia*.

I felt nauseous, partly from my disgust over the willful fabrication, partly out of fear that the televangelist had succeeded in taking away from me what, by then, I most desired. I looked around my office at shelves populated with brass-plated plaques and cut crystal awards honoring me for philanthropy and civic involvement. What did they really mean? Did they outweigh the power of innuendo? Of outright lies? Self-doubt crept over me. My eyes drifted over assorted photos of my kids and grandchildren, and settled finally on a 5x7-inch black and white portrait of my father, Jay Hormel.

The picture was taken at the height of his career as president of Geo. A. Hormel & Co., a decade or so after SPAM and other products made the company a major international enterprise. Dressed in a checkered shirt, tie, woolen sweater, and sports coat, he leaned gingerly against a wall. His thinning gray hair was swept straight back with a dash of pomade; his thin lips stretched into a half-smile. Dashing, charismatic, and confident, he seemed to look right back at me, chiding: *Jimmy, why are you letting them get to you?*

In an instant, I was in Austin, Minnesota, a timid child in the third grade, self-consciously running from a chauffeur-driven car to the door of the school. Crossing the threshold, I hoped to fade into the crowd and be one of the boys. But that never happened. There was a sense, even among my fellow eight-year olds, that I should be treated differently. In Austin there were the Hormels, and then there was Everybody Else. And I could never, ever be Everybody Else. When that little boy—who is still alive inside me to this day—heard Robertson's accusations, he wanted to run, hide, and weep.

That April 2 blew by in a cyclone of phone calls between Washington and San Francisco, all part of a protracted conversation with White House and State Department officials and friends about whether to respond to Robertson's program, or ignore it entirely. Late that night in the office, Ray came to say goodbye and tell me that I was the last one to leave. My body was tired and my eyes ached. He didn't look much better.

"You know Jim, you don't have to put yourself through this," he said. "Maybe it's not worth it."

"I've been wondering the very same thing," I admitted.

What ate at me was my certainty that the association with pedophilia would stick. Thousands of people, perhaps, including Senators whose votes I needed to become an ambassador, would not question it. They would take it on faith. I imagined the range of people who might have watched the broadcast: retirees in their easy chairs, mothers folding laundry, a farmer eating lunch—all of them reacting to the broadcast in the same way. "That's dis*gust*ing," or, "That dirty, filthy man!" or "Typical Clinton, appointing a pervert like that guy!"

I could fight back with the facts: I *never* had and never *would* consider supporting any man–boy love association. I had nothing to do with selecting materials for the Hormel Center, many of which, by the way, also happened to be in the Library of Congress. I could point out how unethical it would be for a donor to influence a library's collection. I could open my heart and explain that I had been married once, that I was a father of five and grandfather to twelve, loving and beloved, and that nothing, absolutely nothing, made me sicker than to think of one of them being abused.

But none of that would be enough to put to rest the suspicion so carefully cultivated by the Christian Righteous that maybe, just maybe, I *was* a pedophile.

Chapter Two

COCKEYED WORLD

Two dominant smells came from the Hormel packinghouse. The first was the aroma of a smokehouse—woody and sweet and very pleasant.

The second was altogether different. It came from a dark place known as the Hide Cellar, a giant room at the lowest level of the packinghouse that was filled with thousands of cowhides. They were laid out on wooden pallets and stacked to the ceiling in endless rows until they were dry enough to be shipped to whoever had bought them, for whatever purpose. They gave off the putrid, indescribable smell of decaying flesh. When the wind blew the wrong way, the odor swept over Austin and everyone in town moaned and groaned until the breeze changed direction.

One particularly glorious spring day, as I recall—it must have been around 1940—I sat with two dozen or so other second-graders in my class at Sumner Elementary School. Our lovely young teacher, Miss Silseth, was writing spelling words on the board. She had opened the classroom's tall, wood-framed windows as wide as they would go, welcoming the sunshine and warmth that we all dreamed of during the long Minnesota winters.

Suddenly, as if it were a serpent creeping toward its prey, the rotting-flesh smell slipped into the room. It soured in my nostrils, jolting me from reverie. From where I sat, second row, center desk, I stole a glance over my left shoulder, and then my right, to see whether anyone else had noticed.

Of course they *all* had. It was impossible to miss. The sea of contorted faces confirmed that every kid in the class had gotten a good whiff. A boy who sat a few desks nearer to the window loved to play the role of wise guy, and he, of course, couldn't let the ill wind pass without a comment.

"Yep, Old Man Hormel's got his feet out the window again," he muttered, loud enough for most of the class to hear.

Snickers and giggles filled the room.

I stared ahead at the blackboard, pretending that I, like Miss Silseth, hadn't heard a word. But my heart pounded in my chest. With the subtlest of movements, I sank a little deeper into my chair. I couldn't help but feel responsible for the smell—it was my father's company, after all. And everyone in the room knew that. Everyone in the whole *town* knew it. After a few hours, the wind swung around, freeing us from the torture, but I continued to feel sorry for myself.

Late that afternoon, at home, and just before my brothers and I sat down for dinner, we went into the living room to kiss Daddy hello, as we did most days. We had a routine, almost as reliable as the seasons, that involved each of us asking, *"Can* I have *a* nut?" We posed the question in the order of our birth: Geordie, the oldest, first; then Thomas; and me, last. Daddy would pick up his opalescent glass dish of salted almonds and tilt it in our direction. Stretching his deep blue eyes over the rim of his reading glasses, he would say, with unfailing sincerity, "Okay, you *may* have *one* nut." He loved to be literal, and to make every moment a teaching moment. We went through this exchange every afternoon before supper, like a secret handshake, each of us relishing our one nut. Most days, it was the only moment we had together with him.

When we greeted him that day, Daddy was well into his rituals: reading the *Austin Daily Herald* and the *Minneapolis Star Journal*; smoking British-made Pall Malls; and drinking his first or second Old-Fashioned. The cigarettes—cork-tipped, oval-shaped, and made from Turkish tobacco—were more pungent than American cigarettes. I never knew anyone else who smoked them, but the smell was very familiar because Daddy always had one in his shaky hand. Charlie Fox, a distant relative and proprietor of the Fox Hotel, ordered them exclusively for him. When I was seven, Daddy was just forty-seven, but between the family tremor and his gray hair, he seemed old to me. I also knew, because I'd been told several times, that he had a heart condition.

Just after I got my nut, and before our nanny Madame Bougerol could shoo us toward the children's dining room, I launched into my story about the odor and the wise guy. *Surely Daddy would share in my indignation*, I thought. The instant I finished relating the tale, he looked away from me and snapped open the pages of his paper.

"Well, the next time that happens, tell the boy he should've been here when your grandfather was around," he said, from behind the newsprint.

That was *not* what I wanted to hear. I wanted comfort and reassurance, and Daddy had none to offer. His reply—inferring that my grandfather had smellier feet—was hilarious. But I was far too earnest a kid to see any humor in his comment at the time, or in the boy's original remark. I was trying to figure out how to fit in, and levity didn't seem to be the answer.

When I was a child, Austin was far less than a city but a bit more than a town. Most of its 18,000 residents descended from Norwegian, Swedish, and German immigrants who had made farms of the flat meadows and prairies in the century before. The downtown featured

an abundance of shops selling everything from chicken incubators
to ladies hats to ice cream sodas, which I can taste to this day. They
were made with a scoop or two of fresh vanilla ice cream, chocolate
or fruit syrup, and soda water, which fizzed and gave the sweet drink
a slight salty taste. In the middle of Main Street was a town square
dominated by a magnificent Victorian building of red brick trimmed
in white, with a single green-domed tower. It housed the Mower
County Courthouse. The nearest city was Rochester, about 45 miles
away, with 40,000 residents and a burgeoning reputation as the home
of the Mayo Clinic.

Geo. A. Hormel & Co., the meatpacking business my grandfather
George started in 1891, was located about a mile north of Austin's
square. It was a big operation for a small town, rising up out of the
prairie like a brick palace with a smokestack. An expansive complex
of buildings, including a slaughterhouse, a packing plant, and
business offices occupied a couple of dozen acres. More than 3,000
people worked for Hormel's, as everybody called it, hailing from
Austin or the nearby towns of Blooming Prairie, Adams, Brownsdale,
Lyle, or Rose Creek.

My family lived on the eastern edge of town on a 200-acre estate,
several miles from the neat, tree-lined neighborhoods where all the
other kids lived. Perched on the bank of a ribbon of waterway called
Dobbins Creek, our house was something like English-manor-meets-
Mediterranean-villa: brick painted white, two stories high, with a red
tile roof. The place had been added on to a few times, and to me, it
felt as if several small houses had been hooked together. From the
original section of the house, there was a wing to the left with six
bedrooms and bathrooms for some of the people who worked for us,
and a wing to the right, with a series of living spaces that connected
to a guest house. Throughout, the rooms were alive with chintz
and bright floral patterns; a mix of French and English provincial

furniture, with a touch of Manhattan sophistication reminiscent of Dorothy Draper.

In total, the house had twenty-six bedrooms and twenty-five bathrooms, including the powder rooms. I know because I counted them, making games out of navigation, traipsing from one end to the other with my eyes closed, so proficient, eventually, that I could do the six-minute trip without bumping into anything. The size of the place might have been overwhelming to outsiders, but to me it was home. It was where we lived.

Austin was probably one of the safest towns in all of America, but armed guards patrolled the estate around the clock. The 1930s was an era of kidnappings, the most shocking of which may have been the snatching (and eventual murder) of the toddler son of aviator Charles Lindbergh and his wife Anne Morrow Lindberg. The crime that caught my parents' attention, however, happened just 100 miles from home: William Hamm, the owner of Minnesota's famous Hamm Brewery, was stuffed into a car as he left his office in St. Paul one evening.

Just a few weeks later, an FBI agent visited Daddy at the plant and told him about a shootout at an Iowa diner that left one gangster dead and another in police custody. They found in the dead man's shirt pocket a list of names assumed to be kidnapping targets. The first was *James Catherwood Hormel.* I was all of six months old. From that moment, and more or less through the next decade, my brothers and I were never left alone. During the years we attended Austin's public schools, we were driven directly to the front door and met every afternoon as soon as the bell rang.

Between the security concerns and our distance from town, play dates with other children were rare. Geordie, Thomas, and I were left to create our own adventures, which was not difficult to do. The estate was a perfect place for three energetic boys—a wonderland

of skunks and rabbits, butterflies and birds, and fish just waiting for
our bait.

For several months of the year, Dobbins Creek had enough water
to accommodate a small, flat-bottomed boat, which gave life to all
my fantasies about Huck Finn and the slave Jim on a raft in the
Mississippi. My mother, who grew up in the French countryside,
loved the creek too. Wearing high rubber boots, a smart blouse, and
a light smear of lipstick, she would wade out to the middle with a
bamboo pole and catch small fish. After gutting them and removing
what few scales they had, she fried them up in butter and garlic and
ate them whole.

Beyond the creek were acres and acres of dense woods, which,
in a sense, were manmade. In the 1920s, when my father bought the
land, it was all meadow. He set aside a few acres for the house and
its grounds, and had thousands of native Minnesota trees planted in
the remaining open space. By the time we boys were around, many
of the saplings had matured into a young forest.

From the back of the house, a path meandered into the woods,
along the creek, and eventually came to an arched wooden bridge.
On the other side was a one-room log cabin with a slate terrace in
front and a tiny structure to the right that served as the kitchen.
It had a wood stove for cooking and a hand pump, which brought
up great-tasting spring water. Next to the kitchen was a barbeque,
and beyond that, a patch of garden, where we boys grew string
beans, peas, carrots, and various root vegetables. This was *our* place
to experiment, as opposed to the big garden by the main house,
which was under the auspices of a full-time gardener. The cabin
had a fireplace and two single beds, which Mamma outfitted with
cozy sheets and blankets so that we could sleep out from late spring
into the early fall. Thomas, Geordie, and I all enjoyed spending
time there, though not usually together. With no electricity, and an

outhouse equipped with a Sears Roebuck catalogue in case the toilet paper ran out, we felt as if we were roughing it. One cool morning, I woke up in the cabin to find a mouse standing up on two legs at the foot of my bed. The place was something out of a fairy tale.

Geordie, Thomas, and I got along as well as brothers do, but we certainly weren't the Three Musketeers. Part of it was age: Geordie was five years older than I, and only eighteen months older than Thomas, so the two of them made a natural pair. I was inclined to follow them around, unless they were up to something, which they often were. Neither was outrageously wild, and I was not outrageously calm, but my M.O. was to be the perfect little boy.

Thomas and Geordie were into things that made noise, like fireworks and BB guns and other items that little boys probably shouldn't have. Geordie loved pranks and always wanted to see what he could get away with. Thomas was ready to abet him, even though he was the one who seemed to get in trouble for the shenanigans. On vacation with our grandparents in Palm Springs once, Geordie decided to build a fire in the inner courtyard of the hacienda-style guesthouse where we were staying. He thought that the lone palm tree in the middle would help hide the fire. Somehow matches appeared, and he and Thomas started working on their blaze. In no time, flames shot up the trunk of the poor tree. When the guest house staff and our parents realized what was going on, they found Thomas, matches in hand, watching the fire. Geordie was nowhere in sight. I was too young to know what was going on, but the scowling faces of the adults made it clear that Thomas was in serious trouble.

Geordie had an incredible range of artistic talents. He sat at the piano and just played, without having studied a note. He easily imitated any musical style he heard. He had my father's thick, dark eyebrows, which were just a few hairs short of a unibrow. He also had freckles, giving him a devilish but cute appearance—no wonder he got away with mischief all the time. Thomas looked more like my mother. He had her almond-shaped eyes, though his were blue and hers were green. Like Geordie, he seemed to be good at everything he did, but in his case, it was the result of diligence.

Thomas studied a piece of music and learned it perfectly, even if it took him months. He taught himself to play the bugle, and then the trumpet, the clarinet, and, most especially, the accordion, which he played particularly well once he started taking lessons. He was a serial hobbyist, fearless about trying new things. He focused on something, and then, having learned it, moved on to another challenge. He started collecting butterflies, and once he knew how to identify them and mount them, he turned to model airplanes. After he made several planes that turned out pretty well, he went on to something else. Thomas had a basic willingness to take a risk, to put himself on the line without ever thinking about failure. In that respect, he was very much like my father.

I watched Thomas and Geordie, and just about whatever it was that they did made me think, *gee, I wish I could do that.* I played baseball and basketball, as they did, but with timidity. Thomas tried to encourage me. "C'mon, what are you afraid of?" he asked. I never had an answer. My hobbies were things like rock collecting, which didn't demand much imagination or risk-taking. (Let's face it: it's pretty hard to fail at rock collecting.) I had a talent for remembering bits of knowledge and expressing things in a way that made me sound much older and smarter than I was. If I said or did something that other people found amusing, I filed it away and called it up when I needed it again. I behaved this way because I desperately wanted to be liked. Not likeable, but actively liked—by everyone. Most people want to be liked, but as I was growing up—and even looking back now—I believe it was far more important to me than it was to either of my brothers. Perhaps that sort of insecurity is typical of a little brother, but in some instinctive way, I knew that I was different from other little brothers, too.

Mamma enforced several routines in the house, one of which was a family-only Sunday. The house was empty of servants. Visitors were discouraged. The only staff around were the guards.

Daddy was born Presbyterian and Mamma a Catholic, but neither went to services on Sunday. When she married outside the faith, Mamma was ex-communicated, and she spent much of her middle years trying to get back in the good graces of the Church. (She went so far as to become a major benefactor of a second Catholic church and school in Austin, Queen of Angels.) Despite this, for reasons never fully explained to us, my parents sent us to the First Congregational Church of Austin for our Sunday school.

On the way home, we often persuaded the driver (usually the guard on duty that day) to make a covert stop at Klagge's Soft Ice Cream stand. We were careful to wipe our mouths, lest Mamma or Daddy discover *our* Sunday tradition.

At home, we finished the morning by reading the newspapers with Daddy at the massive dining room table, or playing rounds of bridge or rummy. Summer afternoons were devoted to shuffleboard by the pool or croquet on the front lawn. In winter, Daddy often went with us to the rink; he loved to skate. He practiced precise figure eights, and so did we, trying to measure up to his standards. Geordie was dexterous, Thomas was zealous, and I was wobbly. At first, I kept vertical by pushing a chair around the ice. With encouragement from my father, and a lot of teasing from my brothers, I found the confidence to leave the chair behind and try retracing my father's figures in the ice.

Nobody looked at Sundays as "our" day with our father, but he spent more time with us on those days than any other. On Sunday evenings, Mamma made a simple supper, which, in wintertime, almost always included the most sinfully delicious hot cocoa you can imagine. She made it with real cream and dark chocolate. Sometimes we helped her prepare the meal that we ate together in the children's dining room. In spite of my mother's close oversight of our manners, it felt like a real treat to have them eat with us. Dinner, normally, was their time to be together.

In retrospect, I have felt that Mamma was so devoted to my father that, to the extent she was a good mother, she was doing it for him. She was going to bring his sons up as proper boys. She promoted integrity, respect, and manners. She dressed us up in shorts until a ridiculous age, at which time we graduated to knickers. Nobody wore knickers in rural Minnesota, not even the golfers.

"But Mamma, everybody else wears long pants," I complained.

"Well, you are *not* everybody else," she replied, in a French accent still as thick as it was the day she arrived in Austin.

She wasn't saying that to promote my sense of individuality. She meant: you're a Hormel—you're supposed to set a standard, not follow it. At the time, I didn't dispute her or rebel against her, but what she said didn't feel right. It was as if I was not meant to fit in.

It would be an understatement to say that I felt a little different than the other boys I knew growing up in our small town. First, there was the company, and the big house, and the guards, and the pressure of being Jay Hormel's son. Even at a very young age, it was clear to me that I could not be regarded as an ordinary, normal citizen of Austin, Minnesota.

On top of that, something else made me feel isolated from those around me. I had this sense that I was different for some other reason. As a kid, I didn't have any way of identifying the feeling, and later, as a teenager, when I began to understand my "otherness," I worked very hard to avoid it. And deny it.

There were times when Mamma was genuinely there for us, and I wonder whether I took those moments for granted. When Geordie, Thomas, and I all got scarlet fever at the same time, Mamma was the only one who came near us.

Covered with red rashes and burning with fever, we were quarantined in the children's wing of the house with the shades drawn to keep out the sunlight. Very contagious, scarlet fever could be life-threatening. Mamma brought us food, and read to us, and did whatever needed to be done. She passed the time by making an extraordinary cardboard dollhouse. Using tissues and rubber bands, she made a mamma, a daddy, a child, a baby in a bassinette, and a dog, all with painted faces and patterned clothes. Along with wallpaper, rugs, curtains, and furniture, she made tiny duvets for the beds, which she quilted—literally.

For most mothers, such attention would have been automatic. But young as I was, it surprised me that Mamma devoted herself to us in that way. Most times, she left us in the care of others.

For much of my childhood, Mamma had bouts of migraines and abdominal pain that wouldn't go away. When she wasn't feeling well, she isolated herself in her wing of the house, and we might not see her for an entire day.

Madame Bougerol, whom we called Bou, immediately took over when my mother locked herself away. She was very protective of Mamma. They were an odd couple: Mamma, stylish and urbane, and Bou, a native of Winnipeg, with her short silver hair, sensible shoes, and no makeup. I adored Bou—she was extremely attentive and loving—but it bothered me that my mother was so consistently "unavailable." The situation usually resolved itself once the doctor arrived with a heavy-looking black medical bag containing a large supply of painkillers.

Mamma seemed to have little sense of the isolation we boys endured, which was strange, because she knew very well what it felt like to be an outsider.

Germaine Dubois was born in La Vernelle, a French village of six hundred people surrounded by farms. She was twenty-one years old when my father, a U.S. Army lieutenant serving in World War I, pedaled a bike through the centuries-old town and laid eyes on her. She had brilliant green eyes, shiny dark hair, and a movie star's wide, toothy smile. With an angular face, thick eyebrows, and aquiline nose, Daddy wasn't classically handsome, but he had a glint in his blue eyes and a sly half-smile that always left one wondering what private humor he was enjoying.

In September 1918, when Daddy's tour of duty ended, they said goodbye. He returned to Austin to immerse himself in the meatpacking business. Mamma moved to Paris and took a job in a millinery shop.

Nearly four years after he left France, Daddy boarded a ship, with little or no explanation, and went to get Mamma. That was just like him—impetuous and unpredictable. We never found letters or other evidence that they kept in touch, but somehow Mamma was waiting for him. They stopped in England and married in Cheshire, depriving my grandparents and all southern Minnesota of a huge celebration. By the time Mamma arrived stateside in 1922, the *Austin Daily Herald* had already reported on the surprise marriage.

Mamma's introduction to Midwestern ways began the moment she moved in with my father and grandparents in their elegant Greek revival home. Despite marbled fireplaces, Tiffany fixtures, and intricate inlaid wood, it was modest in comparison to the mansions of Minneapolis. The atmosphere was chilly, thanks to my grandmother, a stocky, blue-eyed woman not generous with her hugs.

As Midwestern as Mamma was French, Grandma Belle grew up in Blooming Prairie and worked as a school teacher until she married my grandfather George, a struggling, small-town sausage maker. Wedding vows notwithstanding, Grandma made my parents sleep in separate bedrooms.

Daddy was extremely precious to Grandma, not just because he was her only child, but because they both nearly died at his birth. She loved her son, and he had been all hers for almost thirty years, until, suddenly, the day he came home with a bride. And a French bride at that.

By Minnesota standards, Mamma was flamboyant. Beautiful and always impeccably dressed, she had lived in Paris long enough to acquire the demeanor of a city girl. She spoke her mind and told stories and jokes constantly, even if they were a bit risqué. One of her favorites was: "What has two legs and sleeps with cats?" The reply: "Well, Mrs. Katz, of course...and sometimes, Mrs. Johnson." I heard her tell that joke many times over the years, and each time, she tossed her head, laughing.

About 1927, my father bought the 200-acre tract on the outskirts of town and began construction on the home where I grew up. The new house, however, didn't solve all of Mamma's problems.

Mamma believed that certain things were expected of the wife of Jay Hormel, but it took her some time to figure out what they were.

Out of her abiding devotion to Daddy, she did her best to play the role of the respectable and attentive wife of a company man. She learned to play golf, joined as many ladies clubs and social organizations as possible, and did crossword puzzles to expand her vocabulary. Despite her best efforts, Mamma found it impossible to fit in. Seeing my father as the heir-apparent of Hormel's, many of the ladies of Austin stood behind a wall of deference, making friendships awkward. The fact that Mamma was French didn't help; the only shade of diversity among the Northern European peoples of Austin was whether they were Catholic or Lutheran, and anyone who was different was a little suspect.

Even though people held my family in respect, they couldn't resist gossiping. And Mamma knew it.

They gawked at her stylish wardrobe, her sense of humor, and anything else that made her stand out. After several years of marriage, when no Hormel babies had arrived, they began to speculate about her fertility. (God forbid they should have suspected my father.) Mamma ended up feeling like a freak, an oddity.

At dinner one night with Daddy, consumed by tension and loneliness, Mamma burst into tears. When he asked what was wrong, she explained that she was trying so hard to do what she thought was expected of her, yet still she felt horribly out of place.

My father told her that as far as he was concerned, she did not need to belong to any club. He only wanted her to do things she enjoyed. She quit the clubs and became close friends with two women whose husbands had nothing to do with the plant: Margaret Rebman, who was married to a local doctor, and Adah Crane, whose husband Ralph owned a lumberyard. Mamma decided not to worry about what anyone thought of her, so long as my father was happy.

She realized what Daddy wanted from her. The first wish was children; the second was a social companion appropriate for the president of a major American company (which he was soon to be). He wanted a well-managed household, with fresh flowers in all the right places, where business people could come at a moment's notice, either for lunch or to spend the night, always finding a gracious hostess ready to greet them. Mamma knew she could do that. She could be the perfect wife. She stitched herself a needlepoint cushion and rested it on an overstuffed chair in their bedroom. It read: *I'll show the cockeyed world!*

Seven years into their marriage, Mamma delivered, in rapid succession, Geordie in 1928, Thomas in 1930, and me, on January 1, 1933, the worst year of the Great Depression. Geordie was named after Grandpa; Thomas for my mother's first love, a British airman killed during the war. I was named James Catherwood Hormel, with the same initials as my father, and a middle name to honor my grandfather's best friend, Judge Samuel Doak Catherwood.

I was the first baby born in Austin that year, which entitled my parents to the customary basket of cloth diapers, teething biscuits, and other gifts from local merchants. As a photographer from the *Austin Daily Herald* took pictures, my mother humbly accepted the basket and immediately handed it over to the representative of a local charity.

Dressed in the latest fashion from Bergdorf Goodman, her favorite store in New York, Mamma presided over exquisite dinners, receptions, and luncheons. The hotels in town were small and basic, so overnight guests often stayed at our house, with Mamma seeing to their every need. Daddy teased in admiration that she ran a five-star hotel. He liked it that way.

People often came to see my father, whether for business or politics, or some combination of the two. There were senators and congressmen, presidential advisors, and company presidents. I used to linger around them for as long as I was allowed, soaking up their conversations.

One of the occasional visitors was Oscar Mayer, inventor of the famous Oscar Mayer wiener, whose company was a Hormel competitor. He was friendly with my grandfather and then my father, whom he affectionately called the Duke of Austin. Another frequent visitor was Beardsley Ruml, the chairman of Macy's and the advisor who persuaded President Franklin Delano Roosevelt to establish the withholding system for federal income tax. He was a jolly, rotund man who was always willing to speak to me, not in a condescending adult-to-kid way, but in a way that respected my intelligence.

We had visits from celebrities too, people such as George Burns and Gracie Allen, who would never have set foot in Austin had it not been for a deal with the company. It was a big thing for everyone to have these actors, singers, and musicians in our little town— Hollywood was awfully far away. Bou once gave my brothers and me little autograph books to help us track celebrities at our home for a reception. My main interest in the party was a seemingly bottomless bowl of delectable potato chips homemade by a woman in Austin.

During the party, Geordie and Thomas ran around the garden getting as many signatures as they could. I stood nearby, all of six years old, looking on. One of the performers noticed and crouched down beside me, mistaking my lack of participation for shyness.

"Hey there Jimmy, do you have an autograph book? I'll sign it for you!"

"Yes, I do," I replied, "but I don't want to spoil the pages."

He laughed, and so did everyone else within earshot. As usual, I didn't get the joke.

They were just some people visiting our house, like always. I had my pretty little book with its clean pages, perfect for what I liked to do, which was drawing birds. In the midst of the crowd, my mother appeared and gave me a squeeze.

Perhaps she saw that I, too, had a sense of the cockeyed world.

Chapter Three

WAR YEARS

On Christmas Eve, 1939, over some sort of roast beast, my parents made a big announcement: five children from France and England were coming to stay with us—indefinitely.

There was no mention of bombings or food shortages—only that life was difficult where these kids lived. Just short of seven years old, I didn't have any sense of the big picture, but the prospect of more children sounded like fun, particularly since some of them were younger than me.

Shortly after the New Year, the first wave arrived, consisting of Pierre and Simone, my two cousins from La Vernelle. Pierre was fourteen; Simone was eleven. Neither one spoke a word of English, but my brothers and I had, to varying degrees, learned French from Mamma, so we had no trouble communicating with them. Thomas and Geordie easily befriended Pierre, but something about him made me want to keep my distance. He was twice my age, short and stocky, with a cocky attitude. I got the feeling right away that he liked to break the rules, and that made me uneasy.

My feeling for Simone, however, was altogether different.

She had the delightful look of a little French girl, with wire-rimmed glasses and short dark hair. At first, she greeted everything with slight trepidation, understandable given the fact that she was thousands of miles away from her mother and father, and isolated by the language. I took it upon myself to be her friend, speaking to her in French and quizzing her on English vocabulary. I explained that when someone talked about ways to skin a cat, they didn't mean to harm any furry kitty, and that "you betcha" meant that a person agreed with you. I liked being her tutor, and even though I was much younger, she seemed to appreciate me.

Simone learned English within a remarkably short time, stretching out her vowels with a characteristic Minnesota accent. After a couple of months, she was ready for the world of kids her age, but uncertain school administrators put her in my second grade class. She sat one desk away from me, her lanky, preteen body spilling over the sides of a chair sized for a seven-year old. She seemed to suffer the indignity without much pain. After a few weeks, our teacher sent her on to fourth grade. While still not the right grade for her age, it suited her better. I missed having her right there next to me, but it was edifying to see the wrong redressed.

In early summer of 1940, my godmother's two children, Nadia and Callum, and her niece, Gillian, came from England. Gill was twelve, Nadia was four, and Callum, who had the same birthday as me, was about six months old. My godmother, Irene Darbishire, was the younger sister of Thomas George, the British airman my mother was engaged to before she met my father. Mamma and Irene never met while Thomas was alive, but they wrote letters to each other after he was killed and became lifelong friends.

Irene sent along a woman to care for her children who turned out to be something less than Mary Poppins. She called herself Nanny, an unwarranted honorific given her behavior. She refused to cooperate with anyone on the household staff and seemed ready to lash out at any of us—child or adult—at any moment. Within a matter of weeks, there were whispers about whether Nanny was a tad excessive in spanking Nadia and Callum. My mother sent her back to England, war or no war. The rest of us cheered at her departure.

The refugees incorporated easily into the family. They joined my brothers and me in the children's dining room, expanding our party from three to eight. We sat around a narrow, rectangular table that took up the entirety of a small, windowed room between the kitchen and the massive formal dining room. Every meal yielded a steady banter of English and French, sometimes conducted at an unfamiliar and unreasonably high pitch thanks to Gill, Simone, and Nadia. Living with girls was a novelty for Geordie, Thomas, and me. Very quickly they became like sisters, as if they had always been a part of our lives.

Mamma developed an incentive plan to create some order around a house so suddenly filled with rambunctious children. She made an elaborate chart on posterboard, putting the name of each child in a column on the left, and seven days of meals delineated across the top. She used blue metallic stars to note good behavior and red for bad, with a single gold star for three perfect meals. At the end of the first week, only one of us had a complete line of blue and gold stars: Nadia. Little progress was made on the decibel level, and after a few weeks—her supply of red stars exhausted—Mamma gave up on the chart and surrendered herself to the unbridled energy of the expanded tribe.

I suppose that I could have resented these other children, feeling that they made it harder for me to get time and attention from my mother and father, who were difficult enough to reach as it was. Or that they just showed up and got in between my brothers and me. But I had the opposite reaction. I was thrilled to have more children to play with and someone younger to pick on: Nadia.

Nadia looked like the little girls you see in portraits at the British Museum: soulful blue eyes, straight, dark blonde hair that curled up around her ears, and skin so creamy that it must never have seen the sun. She was sweet but a little whiny. I picked up on that right away.

My mother bunked Nadia in with me for a short time after Nanny left, presumably to make it easier for Bou to keep an eye us. That was ideal—I could hassle Nadia into the last moments of her day.

Several times, when I was in the tub, I lured her into the bathroom we shared.

"Hey Nadia, can you come here a second?"

She couldn't resist. Each time, she crept into the bathroom, her face awash in suspicion. With unfailing predictability, I waited for her to cross the threshold before leaping out of the sudsy water to my feet and flashing all that I had to offer. Surely, it wasn't much, but it was enough to send Nadia shrieking down the hallway. Her screams could have shriveled cornstalks all the way to the center of Austin. I sank back into the warmth, very satisfied with my new hobby.

Even when struck low by chicken pox, I found the vitality to harangue her.

"You're going to get my chicken pox," I menaced weakly from my bed.

She didn't know what I was talking about, and the silence on her side of the room made it clear that she didn't care to learn.

I pressed on: "You're going to get my chicken pox."

Silence.

"Chickennnn poxxxx…"

She burst into tearful hysterics.

"I won't, I won't have it! And if you put it on my plate, I won't eat it," she screamed, enunciating every "t."

A few days later, the telltale spots showed up on her stomach.

The war in Europe was seldom discussed in our house. No one said, "Sshh, don't talk about that," but there was some kind of unstated, understood rule. I never asked why, and no one ever explained, but I guess it was because the fathers of the refugee kids were involved in the fighting.

It wasn't until 1941, after the Pearl Harbor attack, that the war became part of our everyday lives. I felt a special connection to the tragedy, because we had been to Pearl Harbor.

Just a few days after my sixth birthday, my grandparents took Mamma, Daddy, Geordie, Thomas, and me on a cruise from Los Angeles to Hawaii. We stayed for a few weeks at a hotel called the Moana at Waikiki, a village of shacks and banana trees. The rooms were simple, with louvered doors that let the sea air come breezing through.

Pearl Harbor was a highlight of the trip for me. We went aboard the state-of-the art, amphibious Pan Am Clipper and toured a submarine. Its compact dimensions fascinated me. There was enough storage on board for sailors to survive for weeks underwater, yet the living quarters seemed like those of my tree house, sized for kids rather than adults.

On the way home from Pearl Harbor, driving through downtown Honolulu in our rented green Plymouth, I asked our driver about the huge, loose, conical piles of metal I saw along the road. He explained that it was scrap iron waiting to be loaded onto ships going to Japan. *Our* junk was going into the war machine that Japan was quietly building to use against us.

On the day of the attack, I didn't understand exactly what had happened, or how it connected to what was going on in France and England. As I tried to process the events over time, my head filled again and again with vivid images of beautiful Pearl Harbor. I pictured myself there, bombs falling around me, fires burning, and people screaming. I could see the ships sinking into the crystalline, blue water, their sailors trapped inside. I imagined that little submarine with a gaping hole, going down.

It was terribly frightening.

* * *

I came to know every airplane in the respective fleets of the United States, Great Britain, Germany, and Japan, thanks to a deck of playing cards someone gave me. I was curious about whether our refugees had been in a bombing, or seen a Luftwaffe plane for themselves, but I never asked, and they never volunteered any information. My parents paid close attention to the radio but never seemed anxious about the war. Mamma must have been worried—her mother and sister were living in the middle of it, after all.

Like all Americans, we had ration books for meat and gasoline, one for every member of the household, including the refugee kids. We had no special privileges, despite our close relationship with the thousands of hogs processed at Hormel each week. At the estate, we had our own cows and chickens for milk, cream, butter, and eggs, and nothing went to waste.

The speed limit was reduced to 35 miles an hour, because if you drove faster than that, you used more gas than necessary and wore down the rubber tires. There was a certain practicality and conservatism about our lives then, in the true sense of the word: people were conserving. Regardless of how much money we had, we took care of our things because they were not easily replaced. The period between the Depression and the end of World War II— essentially from my birth to my adolescence—was an equalizing time. The country went from the wildly speculative days of the 1920s, when people raked in huge sums of money and fraud was rampant, to a time of breadlines, and then the austerity measures required by the war. Minnesotans used to say, "We eat what we can, and what we can't, we can." Our cellar was full of Ball jars with beans, carrots, peas, and other produce grown in the big garden during the summer. That was the character of the era.

Early in the war days, Austin's radio station, KATE, organized a broadcast of grade school kids singing songs and telling stories about foreign countries. I was one of them. There were some Germans, some Norwegians, some Swedes—many of them dressed in traditional costumes from those countries. I don't remember what I wore—my knickers, I guess. There was a boy of Chinese descent, dressed in a silk vest, who was part of the only Asian family I ever recall seeing in southern Minnesota. The show was the kind of thing that people did to emphasize that we were Americans, and that we were all connected.

What I remember most about the war years was the prevalent sense of urgency, and the feeling that every single one of us had something to contribute.

The government then, in contrast to today, raised cash to pay for the war in the form of bonds. Everyone was called on to buy them. Stars like Bob Hope traveled across the country, making appearances in major cities and small towns. We had a bond drive at the band shell in Austin, featuring Bud Abbott and Lou Costello. They spent the night at our house, and my mother, naturally, threw a dinner party, though it was a modest affair appropriate for war time.

My allowance was not lavish during those years, but like my Grandpa, I was extremely frugal. I saved. The war bonds were attractive because they were patriotic and offered a guaranteed return—unless, of course, we lost the war, which was unthinkable. The bonds cost $18.75 each and matured in ten years to $25. You could buy 25-cent stamps at the post office and put them into a little booklet. When it was full, you traded it in for one bond. I kept the bonds and stamp books in a folder in a locked drawer of my desk. I pulled them out often to remind myself how many more stamps I needed for the next bond.

Most every week, some assortment of my brothers, the refugee kids, and I went to one of Austin's four movie theaters. For 12 cents, we got previews, a newsreel, a cartoon, a serial or short subject, and a feature film. Occasionally, for that same price, we would get a double feature of sub-standard comedies or westerns.

The newsreels, unabashedly tending toward the latest Allied victories, answered much of my curiosity about the war. Even at the conflict's worst moments, the news stories were uplifting in some way. When General MacArthur and his troops pulled out of the Philippines, the event was represented as something legendary and bittersweet. MacArthur's *I shall return* became the most famous words of 1942.

Every which way you looked, we were being told that we had to stick together and do our part. The propaganda machine was grinding out all of this stuff and, boy, it had an effect. I wasn't even ten years old, but between the bonds and the little squares of blanket that I knitted for the Red Cross, I felt very much a part of the war effort.

In that window of time, I earned a place among the many patriotic citizens of Austin, Minnesota. That's what I wanted to be—included.

The irony of this period of deprivation was that Hormel thrived. Even before Pearl Harbor, Hormel had contracts with the U.S. government to provide SPAM and other canned meats for civilians in England, and, for the four years that Uncle Joe Stalin was our friend, Russia. With the onset of the war, the business grew exponentially.

Shortly after President Roosevelt signed the war declaration, the 7th Army Corps sent a telegram classifying Hormel as a war facility. Suddenly, our remote community in Minnesota was central to the war effort. I don't remember the bright white lights or the steel security fence that the War Department put up around the perimeter of the plant. Nor did I notice that Hormel workers were required to carry photo identification badges. What did strike me was that women began to work in the plant in large numbers. Over the course of the war, they replaced nearly one-third of the workforce—about 2,000 men—who were off fighting.

Most weekday afternoons, our driver, Eddie Harris, picked me up at school and then headed to the plant to get my father. Eddie took the place of our regular driver, Bob Radl, who had been drafted into the Army. We waited for my father in front of the main entrance, which all the Hormel employees used, whether they worked on the production line or in the office. Above the doorway was a huge red, white, and blue sign. It showed the number of employees in the service, and those who had been injured or killed. Every day, I looked with dread and curiosity to see how high the numbers were.

My father immersed himself in helping the Roosevelt Administration figure out how to feed its troops. He spent a lot of time in Washington working with the Commerce Secretary, Averell Harriman, and coordinating with other meatpackers, such as Swift and Armour, which were far larger than Hormel. Daddy loathed airplanes and always took the train, making his trips even longer. It seemed that weeks would go by without seeing or hearing him in our house.

On one of his visits, he took me with him. I loved every minute of it. Along with the rare opportunity to have extended, one-on-one time with my father, I was awestruck by the scores of men and women in uniform everywhere I looked. *These* were the heroes defending us from the horrors of war. I knew enough of history and civics by then to understand and believe in what Washington was supposed to be— the experience inspired tremendous patriotism in me.

The war demand doubled normal output at the plant, and for occasional periods, tripled it. Sales went from $60.3 million in 1939 to $119.4 million in 1942, and the company's net worth grew by 20 percent. My grandfather, by then living peacefully with Grandma and his golf clubs in Los Angeles, was in utter disbelief about the growth but admiring of the way Daddy managed it. In his first decade as president of the company, my father had proven himself to be an unparalleled innovator and leader in marketing, production, and labor relations. To the particular dismay of competitors, he instituted progressive labor policies, including a guaranteed annual wage and a profit-sharing plan. In 1943, that plan yielded every Hormel worker a bonus equivalent to seven weeks' additional pay.

The federal government issued guidelines for making canned luncheon meat, so whatever the troops ate, it was all the same, whether it came from Hormel, Swift, or Armour. People in the service started calling the meat SPAM, regardless of which company made it. Edward R. Murrow, during his famous Christmas Eve broadcast in December 1942, tried to point out something cheery about a family celebration in London, and said that though "the table will not be lavish, there would be SPAM for everyone." Little by little, SPAM took up residence in the American psyche.

Toward the end of the war, I saw a *Stars and Stripes* magazine in our house with a cartoon of a soldier turning his nose up at a plate of some amorphous heap of food. The caption read: *I don't care what you call it, I call it SPAM, and I say the hell with it.* It was a take-off of a famous Carl Rose cartoon from *The New Yorker* a decade earlier involving a little girl and a plate of broccoli that she believed was spinach. The company executives got very nervous because people were saying that when the war was over, they would never again eat another morsel of SPAM.

The thing about SPAM was that people liked it. It was convenient, tasty, and had a long shelf life. We ate it at home once in a while; I liked it. You could do lots of different things with it, and the company advertised it that way: put cloves in SPAM and bake it like a ham. Or fry it up with eggs. SPAM's name recognition became so big that no other meatpacking company could compete with it.

To the relief of company officials, demand for SPAM continued to grow after the war. A hungry, domestic market of consumers was eager to see products on the shelves again, and the war-weary buyers in the new, international market were happy to have anything that was meat. A longshoremen's strike in 1949 cut Hawaii off from supply lines for a few months, and SPAM soon became indispensible there.

Before the war even ended, our refugee home began to dissolve.

Nadia and Callum left to join their parents in Washington, D.C. Their father Roy, having lost part of his leg while serving in the Royal Air Force, took a desk job as a military attaché at the British Embassy. Pierre enlisted in the U.S. Army. Geordie and Thomas went off to Shattuck, a military boarding school in Faribault, Minnesota, and Simone and Gill were sent to its sister school, St. Mary's.

To my great delight, I became an only child.

I felt a bit like Eloise at the Plaza Hotel, amid housekeepers, gardeners, and kitchen staff, but more often than not left to my own devices. In the war days, worry over kidnappings disappeared. The guards were still around, but I was allowed to go out from the estate alone on my fearsome, one-speed Schwinn. It was two-toned in brown and tan, with balloon tires and a battery-powered headlight, a horn, a ring-a-dingy bell, a rack in the back, and a basket in the front. It was my very favorite possession.

My preferred route went south, past the dirt runway of the local airport on an unpaved road toward Iowa. I pedaled between the cornfields, along glens and streams lined with trees, clusters of nature amid the organization imposed by agriculture. The area was full of songbirds: red wing blackbirds, meadowlarks, bluebirds, gold finches, and wood thrushes. There were martins and swallows, all kinds of swallows. Sometimes a crane or a heron stood on the bank of the creek. With very little traffic, there was nothing to hear other than the birds, the breeze blowing through the grass, and water trickling down a stream. I was out, free, beyond the confines of the guards. It was my world and there was nobody else in it.

I was a naïve young boy, coming of age at a time when our country, pulling together and making sacrifices, seemed very noble. When I saw the sign at the plant, and thought of the Austin men who had died in battle, I felt as if I had lost close family friends. These were not Hollywood idols on a movie screen; these were people I knew. Their experience was my experience. Whether it was propaganda or something very real, I took the call to sacrifice to heart. To me, it was a mandate to protect a certain set of values that was right for the world.

Chapter Four

RHYMES WITH NORMAL

Many people find out who they are when they leave home, which I did at age thirteen, boarding a train for a two-day journey to North Carolina, home of the Asheville School for Boys.

My father's driver dropped Thomas and me at the station a few hours after supper, in plenty of time for the 10 PM departure. There was no teary send-off or other ceremony at home—just quiet goodbyes in the foyer before we got in the car and my parents turned in for the night. The little pit in the stomach that normally accompanies something new was surprisingly not there for me. I loved trains, especially sleeper trains, and this trip required two nights of travel.

Aboard the Pullman car, as the new diesel engine whistled to signal our departure, I felt a huge thrill. I was getting out of Austin.

Life was about to begin.

Rail travel in those days was well coordinated, and one didn't have to live in a metropolis to be able to get somewhere. Austin, small as it was, had two stations, each for a competing railroad company. Our Milwaukee Road train—consisting of an engine, two sleeper cars, and a baggage and mail car—went first to La Crosse, Wisconsin. Once there, the cars waited on a side track for a few hours until a train heading east to Chicago came through and picked them up.

Thomas and I had our own compartment, with an upper and lower berth, and a bathroom so ingeniously tiny that the stainless steel sink pulled out of the wall, preventing you from using the toilet at the same time. Each bunk had a reading light, as well as a blue nightlight to deter claustrophobia or other confusion in the darkness. I woke up at one point during the journey, bathed in blue, and realized that the train was still. I felt a delightful sense of being frozen in time and belonging nowhere.

The next thing I knew, it was morning, and we were pulling into Union Station in Chicago. We had a few hours before the next train to Cincinnati.

Thomas, who had made the journey many times in his two years at Asheville, had me frothing with expectation over Cincinnati's grand, art deco station. It was built a decade or so earlier, during the Depression. At sixteen, Thomas was like every other older sibling on the planet: torn between wanting to be in charge and wanting nothing to do with me. When we arrived at the station, however, he took big brotherly pride in leading me from the platform up through the grand concourse and into the station's vast, marbled rotunda.

Already about 6 feet tall, Thomas towered over me as he pointed out details of the enormous, glass mosaic murals that wrapped around the walls just below the dome. They were classic examples of WPA-style artwork with elaborate pictorial histories done in brilliant colors. While hundreds of passengers bustled to and fro around us, I stared at the giant, muscle-bound men greeting Indians, hauling cotton, sailing steamships, and hammering steel beams. There were white men and black men, and an occasional woman and child, all of them reflecting strength, pride, and determination.

Thomas took me past various shops, the movie theater, and, at last, the arcade, where we killed a few hours before getting on the overnight train to Asheville. He had a favorite machine there, called the "Metal Typer," which stamped a message of one's choosing on a souvenir coin. He dropped a nickel in a slot, punched in some letters, pulled a lever, and waited for the newly-minted token to clang into the trough below. As he fished it out and looked it over, a big smile crawled across his face. He flashed the coin in my direction.

It read: *JC Hormel Rhymes with Normal.*

In 1940, when the company launched one of its first national radio campaigns on *The Burns and Allen Show,* the advertisers didn't like the sound of HORmel. They thought horMEL was melodious and came across the airwaves more clearly. My father didn't much like the idea, but he eventually relented, and the advertising campaign was so successful that he couldn't quibble further. He resigned himself to reminding people, in good humor, that, in spite of what they heard on the radio, our name was still *Hor*mel, rhyming with "normal." The whole thing was strange for me, and apparently for Thomas as well. Some unknown person out there in the universe had, in effect, changed our name, simply to sell products.

"Daddy will *love* this," Thomas grinned, his devilish blue eyes aglow.

The following morning, in the upper berth, I awoke somewhere in the mountains outside Asheville. There were no far-reaching vistas, just crowds of trees and occasional glimpses of the French Broad River. At the station, a teacher from the school collected us.

Nestled against the mountains on the western reaches of town, the Asheville School was like a separate principality. The campus consisted of an assortment of three-story and single-story brick buildings, a chapel, and perfectly manicured lawns. The minute we unloaded our bags, Thomas was off to find his buddies on the track team. He was much happier at Asheville than he had been at Shattuck, the military boarding school in Minnesota that my father and Geordie had attended. The rigidity and discipline of the school overwhelmed him so much that he ran away halfway through his second year, and returned only after my parents promised to send him somewhere else the following year. In upending the family tradition, Thomas did me a huge favor. I would have hated Shattuck, too.

Once Thomas was out of sight, I gathered my things and went off in my own direction, determined that I would not be a pesky little brother.

There was a clear separation at Asheville between the older and younger boys, with two separate dormitories to reinforce the age division. I didn't have much occasion to see Thomas, except when we called home together about once a week. That was okay—within a matter of days, I was doing perfectly well without his guidance or company.

From my dorm room, I could see Mount Pisgah, one of the taller peaks in the Appalachian range. Coming from one of the flattest regions of America, I was struck by the mountains. They seemed *gigantic*. I used to open my window to the fresh air and the sounds of the birds, fantasizing that a hiker on the mountain could see me through the window. As in Austin, my reverie was pre-empted occasionally by an intemperate wind, this one carrying an acrid odor of sulfur from a rayon factory several miles away.

Within days of my arrival at Asheville, I became aware of the quiet platoon of male, black caretakers who served our meals, cleaned our rooms, and looked after the buildings and the lawns. Segregation was not something I had ever seen. At first, it seemed just an odd, uncomfortable arrangement, until I went to the downtown Woolworth's and realized the extent to which race ordered the universe in Asheville.

Woolworth's was a typical small town department store, or "Five and Dime," as they were called back then, consisting of one big room packed wall-to-wall with a little bit of everything. It had a soda fountain and counter after counter of sundries. On one of my first visits there—my grades were good enough that I was granted the privilege of downtown visits—I cruised the aisles and considered ways to spend my allowance. Spying a water fountain in a corner, I went over to get a drink. As I leaned in to take a sip, I felt dozens of eyes upon me. That's when I noticed a single word above the fountain, tiled into the wall as if it would be there forever: *COLORED*. I had never seen anything like it.

A small crowd encircled me. They were men, women, and children of various ages, and they were all white. No one said a word, but their stares made it clear that I had done something very inappropriate. The feeling I got was completely contradictory to what I was beginning to understand about good and evil, and God, and respect for others. I had violated the prevailing social order, and people had to let me know. I wanted to shrug off the experience but I couldn't. Those horrified faces were grotesque to me.

I soon realized that the same sign was everywhere in town—in parks, train stations, and other public accommodations. And it was the law. I didn't necessarily understand the social constructs but I instinctively knew that something was wrong.

On campus, I was surrounded by 150 white, Christian boys from families of means, literally—there were no scholarships in those days. I don't think it was until my senior year that the first Jewish student was admitted. Bill Kimberley, whose family made Kleenex, was in the dorm room next to me. One of several brothers who went to Asheville, he was pleasantly low-key, unlike many of my classmates. There were kids from Oklahoma oil dynasties and Cuban fruit plantations, some of whom went not by their names but by their initials.

Another student named J. Courtney Earl seemed an ordinary kid like me until the day his father arrived on campus driving a

General Motors concept car. It was a flashy, long, and low-riding vehicle that no one had ever seen, and would never see again, because it was one of a kind. It was then that I learned that the boy's father was Harley Earl, the head designer at General Motors. Harley Earl was a household name, the Ralph Lauren of the automobile industry.

I found myself in conversation one day with a boy whose family had founded a well-known elevator company. He and I were talking about something—who knows what—but he concluded the conversation by saying: "Well, Jimmy, you ought to agree. You're a patrician like me."

I gulped and said nothing. Asheville was turning out to be something different than I expected.

I spent so much of my childhood feeling that I would never fit in, and there, finally, I was in a society that welcomed me wholeheartedly. The trouble was that it was an exclusive society ordered by the trappings of Jim Crow. As desperate as I was to be one of the boys, I was instinctively ill at ease in a world bounded by distinctions of class and race.

I was from a town that had a nearly classless society. The people who made Austin what it was belonged to the Rotary or to the Elks Club, regardless of whether they were business owners or workers. They had a strong work ethic, went to church, and played golf. What was different about Austin was that the Austin Country Club had open membership; anyone could play there. There was no pretense of class or any sense of social inequity.

The South seemed to be a genteel society, and yet people were doing unkind things to others, and it was an accepted way of life. Although I didn't have words for it at the time, it stirred a deep feeling within me. Something about that society was inconsistent with justice and fairness. I had the feeling that we were doing harm to perfectly good, kind, hard-working, normal people who were contributing citizens.

What took place that afternoon at Woolworth's sickened me, and yet I never discussed it with anyone—far be it for me to stir up trouble. But I never forgot that it happened.

A few months into the school year, testosterone started to run through my body like sap in a maple tree. I began to feel attracted to some of my schoolmates. I did not go off to boarding school thinking about the sexual opportunity of an all-boys environment so I was surprised, but not put off, when another student cozied up to me during a school camping trip in the mountains. Some weeks later, he and I had another encounter on campus. And then I had another, with a different boy.

These sorts of exploratory experiences are not unusual among teenagers, particularly in boarding school. But I seemed to care more about them than others did. I was curiously excited by them. Almost invariably, when I saw the boy the next day in class or in the dining hall, he would not acknowledge me. No smirk, no knowing exchange of glances—it was as if the things that happened the night before came out of a dream.

I began to wonder if there was something wrong with me.

With a very limited pool of girls to draw on, a steady relationship was a sign of status. I was fortunate to meet a girl from Asheville named Catherine who called me *Jimmy dahlin'*. We dated, though it wasn't like dating at a regular high school, where you'd see your girl every day and take her to the drive-in a few nights a week. I saw Catherine five or six times a year, including the prom.

Catherine's mother was very encouraging of our relationship. She gladly picked me up whenever I had the opportunity to get away from school. She took us places or made a picnic for us or entertained

us at home. Catherine and I always had a lot of fun together. I never
thought of her as a cover for my sexual feelings; I thought I was being
like every other boy. At the same time, I never considered her as a
partner for anything more than a few kisses. There really wasn't an
opportunity for that anyway—we were chaperoned when we were
together. That took away all the pressure and made it easy for me to
ignore the incongruity of my genuine feeling for her and my "taboo"
desire for young men.

There was no frame of reference to help me figure out what
was going on inside my head and my body. How was I to know that
there was a whole universe of people who were gay? Homosexuality
then was like cancer, alcoholism, mental retardation—not to be
discussed. In class, we read Plato's *Symposium,* which was translated
and presented as if it were gender neutral when in fact the original
was a conversation among gay men about gay love. I never learned
about Oscar Wilde or his trials, or the early twentieth-century gay
movement in Germany with Magnus Hirschfeld's institute in Berlin
to promote acceptance of homosexuality. If I had grown up in New
York City or some other place with a vibrant underground community,
perhaps I would have had a different outlook, but I was sheltered to
the point that I did not even have the means to describe my feelings
toward others of my gender.

In Austin, I knew two people who were "marked" because of
their extraordinarily flamboyant behavior. One was a guy in the plant
who had a menial job—I never knew his name—but I saw people
mocking him to his face, not in an overtly cruel way, but in a way
that made it clear he was not "one of them." The second was a young
man whose mother was a friend of my parents. She was a renowned
alcoholic, someone who could be very funny under the influence,
until the influence got to be too strong and, she got sloppy. Suddenly,
she was no fun at all. Her son was extremely effeminate; there wasn't

any way he could hide it. People had a great time imitating his dramatic hand gestures and highly-inflected speech.

If that was what gay was, I didn't want any part of it. I didn't identify with either of those men, and I certainly didn't want to be ostracized the way they were.

Toward the end of that first year, just before school let out for summer vacation, Thomas and I made our weekly call home one Sunday night to find that my mother was recuperating from emergency surgery.

By then, Mamma spent a great deal of her time in Los Angeles, living in the expansive Spanish-style home my grandparents built on a hillside in Bel Air for their retirement. Daddy was there too; he joined her whenever he could.

Mamma had had one of her abdominal attacks but this time the pain was so acute that she went to the hospital. She was diagnosed with appendicitis. The doctors opened her up immediately. They found a sponge attached to the inflamed organ. It was from the Cesarean section she had when she delivered Geordie nineteen years earlier. At the time of the delivery, a nurse reported a sponge missing, but the attending doctor dismissed her, saying she had miscounted.

Mamma went home from the hospital finally free of the pain that had dogged her for years, but not the addiction that went with the painkillers.

Through four years of boarding school, my performance went from exemplary to pathetic. My hormones guided me away from my studies and toward other boys. It is already hard for a horny teenager to focus on school, but finding that your attraction is against the rules of society adds a whole new dimension of distraction. As my sexuality bloomed, so did my feelings of insecurity and confusion.

My study habits collapsed and my A average gradually shrank to middling grades. I became a student of getting by. The school had a rule stating that a senior whose grades were above a certain level did not have to take final exams. I was required to take every one of mine.

My declining performance was an obvious warning signal, but I didn't recognize it as that, and neither did my parents. Their primary concern was whether I would be accepted to Princeton, where my father had studied.

My roommate senior year, Jim Hamilton, was a Virginian blessed with a wry sense of humor. His parents wanted him to go to Yale. Our letters from Yale and Princeton arrived the same day. As we prepared to open them, he looked at me and said, soberly, "This is where they separate the Dalmatians from the Dachshunds." We tittered nervously, tore the envelopes apart, and learned that we had both gotten our wish.

What a relief, I thought. My parents would be overjoyed. It was a big deal to follow in my father's footsteps. With Princeton's acceptance, they would certainly not bother worrying about my grades or otherwise probe my adolescent angst. That allowed me to avoid dealing with it myself. And it encouraged me to keep concealing my inner feelings.

Chapter Five

DISMAL FAILURE

During my first semester at Princeton, on the Saturday after Thanksgiving, a late season hurricane was forecast to hit campus.

With the force of the storm expected that night, the last football game of the season—as always, against Dartmouth—kicked off in the afternoon as scheduled, despite the fact that the wind was already strong enough to play with the ball. That year, Princeton was undefeated, so the excitement was particularly high. I liked sports, but loathed the boozy, old boy behavior that went with the games. I thought it would be fun to see Princeton finish the season without a loss, but I didn't relish sitting in the stands for three hours in that weather. A walk in the wild gusts sounded better.

I left my dorm, a brand new brick building called Class of 1915 Hall, and moseyed among the school's Gothic buildings, with their turrets, towers, and stained glass windows. With everyone at the game, the main part of campus was delightfully ghostly in its emptiness. The lawns seemed very green for late November, but the leafless maples, ashes, and oaks, bowing in the wind, hinted that winter was just around the corner. My mind was a blank slate. The only other person I saw was a guy riding by on a bike, wearing a yellow rain poncho that seemed surreally bright against the dark sky. A moment after he passed me, an aggressive blast of wind sent him and the bike crashing to the ground. He quickly righted himself and pedaled away.

It occurred to me that the storm was a perfectly Shakespearean backdrop to what was unfolding in my life.

With as many as 2,500 young men on the all-male campus, my antennae buzzed all the time. I suspected more than a few people of having the same attractions, but no one admitted it or showed interest in any kind of intimate relationship. That disconnect made me feel like a freak. I don't know whether it was by my own design, or because of what others thought of me, but I wasn't making many friends.

My freshman roommates were Brice Clagett, a self-styled radical from Washington, D.C., and Don Robinson, a thoughtful, considerate guy who was an Asheville classmate. Brice, Don, and I shared a suite, with two small bedrooms and a common area where I slept. Across the hall, an identical set of rooms was home to a tall, friendly Texan named Wells Stewart, who became my only close friend. Our connection was sealed for life when he let me borrow his ukulele. Sometimes, Wells played hooky with me, but most days he went to class and I stayed in the dorm, perfecting my rendition of "5 foot 2, Eyes of Blue."

Princeton had none of the oversight of boarding school, and I had none of the self-discipline necessary for a strenuous academic environment. Unconsciously, I did everything possible to put myself on the path to failure. I chose an assortment of classes that met requirements, such as sociology and physics, but I had no interest in them. The only class I enjoyed and studied for was art history.

Totally at sea with myself, I did anything I could to avoid knuckling down. I went into New York City, not to a show or to visit someone, but just to hang out in the seedy Skee-Ball parlors in Times Square. When I wasn't off wandering, I was in my room smoking a lot of cigarettes, drinking far too much, and ignoring Catherine's invitations to visit her at college. The thing was that I was not having fun; I was just killing time.

I was suffering, captive to inner turmoil and without an outlet for my sexual energy. If there had been a psychiatric diagnosis for clinical loneliness, I would have been the poster child for the disorder.

Princeton was not a liberal place then, but I seemed to be surrounded by lefties, including Brice, who questioned everything about the status quo. I considered myself a moderate conservative, despite my membership in the United World Federalists, an organization that advocated global government as a means to promote lasting world peace. One afternoon, as we sparred over some issue, I unwittingly made a comment that pushed him over a precipice.

Shaking with an anger that I had never seen in him, he unleashed a torrent of invective so remarkable that it has stuck with me since. I recall him saying: "You, you, you neo-fascist, crypto-Wall Street, imperialist, industrialist, capitalist warmonger!"

I laughed at his rant, which of course made him angrier. I couldn't help it. Besides, I was just an average guy from the Midwest, wasn't that obvious?

Not to Brice. He seemed to view me as a living symbol of the excesses of capitalism.

Brice came from St. Alban's, an elite school in Washington, D.C., and his father was a judge, so he wasn't exactly a person of the masses. Still, there was a grain of truth in his tirade.

Much as I wanted to be, I *wasn't* that different from that elevator company heir or any other American kid born into tremendous privilege. Short of disavowing my family, running away from home, and changing my name, how could I escape the benefits of class and wealth into which I was born? I did not have a real choice in the matter.

Never before had anyone politicized my life the way Brice did, at least to my face, but I was so caught up in my own universe that it didn't occur to me to be offended. Still, the point was not entirely lost on me. I knew that my family's wealth was yet another thing I had to reckon with.

At the very end of that first semester, on a frigid January morning closer to noon than nine, I woke up with a start. As my alarm clock came into focus, I realized that I had slept through the oral portion of my final French exam.

I was in trouble academically. I had passing grades in art history and French but the rest were a disaster. Of the four hundred students in my sociology class, I scored the second lowest grade on the final exam. Princeton had a seven-point scale based on the average of one's grades, and I was in the failing range. After ruminating about my options all afternoon, I left 1915 Hall as the sun set and trudged through deep snow to see the French professor at his home.

In an exchange on his doorstep, I asked whether there was some way that I could make up the test. I spoke French well—thanks to my mother—and would pass, if given the chance. All I needed was a tiny little margin of a grade point to save myself.

The professor was unsympathetic. He told me that a make-up exam was out of the question and that he wouldn't change my grade. I went back to the dorm and flopped into bed, completely drained of energy.

The next morning I awoke feeling deathly sick. A doctor at the infirmary diagnosed me with pneumonia and sent me to bed. The next few days passed with alternating cycles of sweating and shivering.

When I started to feel better, I called my parents and broke the news that I had flunked out.

It was very clear from my dismal midterm exams that I wasn't doing well. Even so, I did nothing to ensure better results on the finals. When the reality of flunking hit me, I was ashamed, embarrassed, and overwhelmed by it all. I don't remember packing up my things or saying goodbye to anybody, except Wells, who gave me his ukulele.

I left Princeton in late January and flew to meet my parents in Los Angeles, where they were escaping Minnesota's punishing winter. My brothers were there, too: Geordie was getting ready to join the Coast Guard and Thomas was in his second year at Palos Verdes College. I arrived late in the evening, after my father had gone to sleep.

The next morning, I found him in the sunny dining room, a space with big glass windows overlooking a small grove of orange trees. He was about to quit the breakfast table and head to his home office. I was still in my pajamas.

He looked me in the eye, wasting no time on pleasantries. I was grateful that he spoke without emotion. He knew how I felt. Neither of us wanted to have a scene. He gave me a choice: take a job in the plant in Austin or join Thomas at Palos Verdes, a new experimental school on the peninsula several miles southwest of Los Angeles.

The choice was clear: I was going to Palos Verdes. I had a desire to rehabilitate myself academically and an even stronger feeling about the plant—there was no way I was ready to spend the rest of my life working in Austin. For my parents and just about everyone in Austin, it was a given that my brothers and I would take over the company. As my father had done, we were supposed to start working at the company, learning the business, and then eventually run it. At that point, I had little certainty about any aspect of my future, but management of Geo. A. Hormel & Co. was inconceivable. I had none of my father's talent, or his chutzpah, for that matter. If I took over, the company was sure to fall into ruin.

Looking back at that time, it is obvious that I was in crisis. I didn't see it then, and neither did anyone around me, but I was paralyzed by confusion and insecurity. Nothing in the world around me suggested that being gay was anything other than weird and perverted, and I did not want to be weird or perverted. I started fantasizing about having a twin brother so that there might be at least one person in the world who would communicate with me and understand me.

My mother made all kinds of excuses about my flunking out. "He was too young," she told people. "He wasn't ready." I resented her comments. What she was saying was probably true—I was just seventeen—but I didn't want to hear it. I wanted her to recognize that I wasn't unintelligent; I was simply unmoored.

Palos Verdes College was the kind of place where the professors lived on campus and you called them by their first names. The curriculum emphasized art and its connection to human enrichment and progress—or the lack thereof. Ironically, the commune-like learning environment was located on a former military base.

With a student population of about thirty, the teachers were impossible to escape. If a play was being performed, every student had to be in it. (Thomas and I played a pair of gladiators in George Bernard Shaw's *Androcles and the Lion.*) The closeness worked for me. It gave me a sense of being a part *of*, not apart *from*. For the first time in a long while, I started to pay attention in my classes.

We studied human rights and social justice by participating in a model United Nations session and reading books such as *Cry, the Beloved Country* by Alan Paton. Even as a closeted gay person, I had a sensibility that made me tune in to inequity. At long last, my studies started to mean something to me personally. Ideas began to percolate in my brain.

Outside of school, my brothers helped me develop a social life. Thomas and I had a lot of friends in common, and even dated the same woman briefly. He introduced me to Johnny Barrymore, an actor who lived in the shadow of his famous Hollywood family. I suppose Hollywood was like one giant Austin, Minnesota, to Johnny. Yet, unlike me, he drank heavily in public and misbehaved at every turn. Still, I had empathy for him. There was nothing sexual between us, but we understood something about each other that didn't have to be expressed. Johnny gave me a copy of a new novel, *Catcher in the Rye,* whose protagonist Holden Caulfield helped us both see that feelings of isolation and alienation were not uniquely ours.

At a party one night honoring members of Les Ballets de Paris de Roland Petit, Thomas got to know Simone Mustovoy, a tiny and bubbly ballerina with sparkly brown eyes and tight, dark curls that gave her the air of a little girl. He started romancing her right away. Not long after, Geordie met Leslie Caron, another Ballets de Paris ballerina who had left the company to star with Gene Kelly in *An American in Paris.* Before any of us knew it, the family was off to Las Vegas to celebrate Geordie's marriage to Leslie, and Thomas was soon engaged to Simone. My mother was thrilled to have two French daughters-in-law.

I look back now and laugh about the thought that I, too, might have found a partner among the ballet dancers—there certainly were plenty of gay men—but I was so busy trying to be straight that I wasn't even intrigued by them.

After finishing the two-year program at Palos Verdes with decent grades, I went back East to earn my bachelor's degree at Swarthmore

College. Like Princeton, the campus was lush and ivied, but it was smaller and less imposing. For one thing, it had just eight-hundred students, half of whom were women. I started my first semester as a sophomore and took mathematics and astronomy. After a couple of pretty bad grades, I wondered whether my poor academic history would repeat itself.

One Saturday that fall, just after classes had begun, I enjoyed a sunny, warm afternoon on the porch of Parrish Hall, a gray, flagstone Victorian dormitory that also housed the post office, the book store and the laundry. I was thinking about going to the football game, if only to show a little school spirit by chanting my favorite of all cheers: *Kill Quaker, Kill.* A crowd of boisterous, happy-looking people came past me, heading in what I presumed to be the direction of the stadium. I followed and was quite surprised to end up at the library.

Alongside the intense academics, Swarthmore, a college with Quaker roots, had an ingrained sense of social consciousness. No American college campus was a political hotbed, *yet*—but hyper-engaged Swarthmore students staged protests against the Korean War and blared Woodie Guthrie and Pete Seeger from their dorm rooms. It wasn't the knee jerk behavior or naïve politics of a seventeen-year-old kid who is feeling his way in the world. Swarthmore students were actively engaged in public service off campus, and everywhere you turned, whether in the dining hall or in the dorms, you overheard impassioned conversations on every imaginable subject. Television sets, new to dorm lounges, attracted clusters of students who sat riveted by the news and live Senate hearings. As amused as I was by peers who seemed to take themselves too seriously, I found myself increasingly interested in politics.

Like any college campus, Swarthmore had its share of self-important rich kids and I worked hard to ensure that people did not count me among them. When I could get away with it, I introduced myself without my last name or otherwise found a way to conceal my connection to the family business.

At Swarthmore, I didn't feel sexual tension the way I had at Princeton. I was pretty much closed to the possibility. It's not that men weren't on my mind, but I was determined to create a "normal" college life. Unconscious as the thought process may have been, I had finally figured out what everyone wanted me to be. I was going to prove to them—and myself—that I had grown up and that I would succeed.

I started to get "on track" that fall semester at a mixer for new students. As I leaned against a wall, enjoying a Tex Williams song, a petite, brown-haired beauty named Alice Parker crossed the dance floor with a determined stride. I couldn't help but watch her. She had a radiant presence. When she came in my vicinity, I boldly said, "Hi." She looked at me and smiled politely, but didn't say a word. Beneath the poise and charm was a distinct chill. I caught her drift and didn't ask her to dance.

I saw Alice around campus a few times and spoke to her at every opportunity, but by then, she had been scooped up by an upperclassman. I was sorry about that; there was something very satisfying about being around her. Swarthmore was nicknamed the Quaker Matchbox, and with good reason: students who went steady often ended up married. I thought that I probably had missed my chance with her.

By fall of my second year, Alice and I were in the same French literature class. I was brave enough to sit next to her. The class bored me, so I passed the time by doodling and drawing cartoons of little characters saying things in French. Alice was a serious student, generally impervious to distraction, but I managed to elicit a few big laughs from her. She eventually agreed to study with me. At one of our very first sessions, she let me know that her boyfriend had gone into the Army and that their relationship had cooled. Alice was attractive, witty, and engaging. I was so captivated by her that I was able to ignore my feelings toward men for a while.

In October, Wells invited me up to Princeton for a party. I wasn't excited to go back there but I did want to see him. And the weather was beautifully and unseasonably warm: perfect for a 60-mile drive in my blue Pontiac convertible, with a vivacious young woman by my side. As a rule, Swarthmore students were not permitted to have cars on campus, but I had a dispensation so that I could report for duty each week at my Coast Guard Reserve unit. When I invited Alice along, she said yes. On the way, we stopped for dinner in an artsy town on the Delaware River called New Hope. We traded stories about our families and our politics, and laughed a lot. It was a magical first date.

By then, I was on my feet academically. I was not at the top of the class, but I got by, and I didn't feel like a little speck, as I had at Princeton. I joined Phi Delta Theta, where boys could be boys and spend Saturday night into Sunday playing poker. When Alice and I started to date exclusively, I gave her my fraternity pin. While aware of my compulsion toward men, I felt something very special toward Alice. The essential elements of a classic relationship were there, together with a unique and beautiful feeling of commonality, affection, and mutual respect.

Part of what drew us together were debates about politics. We argued about all kinds of things: Eisenhower's policies, management-labor relations, and the United States's refusal to recognize China. We were surprised by our ability to find common ground, despite the fact that I was a Republican from a fresh-faced Norman Rockwell town, and she was a Democrat from the historic land of presidents, Charlottesville.

There was something else about Alice, too.

Years before, about the time that most of her friends were preparing for their prom, Alice was in a hospital bed, recuperating from a freak accident. During a drill at her boarding school, in which she was in charge of lowering the fire escape, the heavy metal ladder collapsed, crushing Alice beneath. Badly injured, she subsequently had more than a dozen reconstructive surgeries. Whether her experience created it, or unearthed it, Alice had a quiet, immovable strength. It pulled me to her. I found her easy to love.

Chapter Six

A ROUGH SENIOR YEAR

A few days after saying goodbye to my mother in Los Angeles, I eased my faithful, blue convertible into the long, wooded driveway of our home in Austin, arriving in the middle of a warm afternoon. En route to Swarthmore to begin my senior year, I had plotted a course via Minnesota so that I could spend a few days there with Daddy.

As I maneuvered around the circle in front of the house, he appeared in the doorway, wearing blue-striped cotton pajamas and a light wool bathrobe. After a series of heart attacks and strokes in the previous months, he was mostly confined to the house. He insisted on working, though his hours were limited. People from the plant came by in the morning to meet with him, bring him things to review, or hand him papers to sign. In the afternoon, he rested. Knowing that I was to arrive that day, he skipped his afternoon nap and waited to greet me. He was the only member of the family at home; everyone else was in Los Angeles, awaiting the birth of Thomas and Simone's first child.

Emerging from the car, I glanced around, hoping to see Berick, our shaggy, face-licking dog. All black with a white diamond on his chest, he was a Christmas gift from the Mayos in Rochester. Named after his parents, Betty and Erik, Berick spent a lot of time with us kids in the woods, chasing small mammals. Yet rather inexplicably, he became my father's dog, even though Daddy did nothing in particular to ingratiate himself. Over the years, it got to the point that when Daddy was on his way home from a trip, Berick went out to the driveway and waited, as if he'd received some communication from the universe: *Your master is about to return.* That day Berick was nowhere to be found.

Daddy welcomed me with a hug and a kiss and told me he wanted to go for a walk before dinner. After settling in, I met him in the foyer and walked with him toward the front door. His tentative steps made it clear that we wouldn't be going very far. We did a loop around the wide, bricked walkway at the entrance of the house. It was the last day of August, late enough in the afternoon that the heat and mugginess had lifted, but too early for the mosquitoes. Swallows and martins swooped in droves above us, preparing for their nightly feast.

Daddy and I chatted as we walked, speculating about the school year ahead, my plans after graduation, and my relationship with Alice. She had made a wonderful impression earlier that summer when she met the family. In the game room one evening as Alice, my father, and I sipped cocktails, Daddy stretched out his hand— shaking very badly with the family tremor—and asked her for a manicure. She retreated to her room, returned with a nail file, and took to the task with her signature boldness and enthusiasm. We were all amused, and Daddy obviously approved.

He and I came to the farthest reach of the brick path. There, a wooden gate opened on to the rest of the estate. We walked just beyond it, looking across the large green expanse of lawn toward the stables, barns, garages, and the pair of white, brick houses where two of the families who worked for us lived. Daddy seemed to take in everything—every flower, every blade of grass—very closely.

Poised at the gate was a tall wrought iron Indian with a tomahawk raised high in his hand, as if he were defending the driveway.

Normally handsome and dignified, the Indian was reduced to stiff inhumanity by a bird dropping suspended perfectly from one of his weathered nostrils. Daddy and I giggled like boys at the sight of it.

That night, after we ate, I went into Daddy's room to say goodnight. A nurse was helping him into one of the two twin beds. I sat down on the other, observing the care with which she pulled up the sheets and positioned the pillows.

I stood up and leaned over him to kiss him goodnight. He interrupted me with a warm but intense look.

"Jimmy, is there anything you want to talk about?" he asked. "Anything you want to tell me?"

His eyes reflected an air so loving and free of judgment that I felt a completely disarming sense of safety. For the instant it lasted, I basked in it. At the same time, I felt some combination of urgency and anxiety, as though I had something important to say but couldn't quite remember what.

Perhaps this was the moment I was supposed to tell my father that I was gay. But how could I? I hadn't even admitted it to myself.

"Oh, no, Daddy, nothing that can't wait until tomorrow," I said, following through with my kiss goodnight. Badly in need of a good sleep after many miles on the road, I retreated to my own bed.

At 1 AM, the company doctor, Tracy Barber, shook me awake.

A short time earlier, Daddy had woken up, feeling chest pains. He called out for the nurse, who was just outside his door. She immediately summoned Dr. Barber but by the time he arrived, there was nothing he could do.

My father was gone.

Half asleep, trying to assemble my thoughts, I got up and went to see him. He was tucked under the covers as he had been hours before, looking peaceful. He was ten days short of his sixty-second birthday.

I didn't know what to do. I felt a sense of total loss. I wanted to call my mother right away, but I had no idea what to say. On our walk, Daddy *was* seeing things for the very last time. He knew it, and yet, he seemed at ease. The thought of it made me terribly sad. I was haunted by my last words to him: *nothing that can't wait until tomorrow*. He had invited me, for the last time, to say something about myself, and I hadn't picked up on it. And for us, tomorrow never came.

Within a day or so, my mother arrived with Geordie and Thomas. Simone stayed behind and gave birth two days later to Michelle, whose arrival was a flicker of joy amid our sadness. Mamma was grief-stricken and desperately angry for not having been there with Daddy when he cried out for help that last time. I'm not sure that she ever got over that. To the end, my father was a creature of routines and habit. On that very last night, he put a few of his personal possessions on the dressing table in a neat array, as if he were going to work the next morning. There were a few coins, a pocket watch, a fob, a simple gold Dunhill lighter engraved with his initials, and a slim pocket knife.

Soon after she arrived, Mamma went into the bedroom, treating it as if it were a holy site. She scooped up all the loose items on the dresser and handed one each to Geordie, Thomas, and me. It was as if to say, *Each of you, take this reminder of your father*. I was smoking at the time, so she gave me the lighter with *JCH*—my initials, too. The odor of his Pall Malls lingered in the room, faint but unmistakably rich.

The three of us did our best to console Mamma. One of us was with her all of the time, so that she didn't have to deal with the endless flow of people who meant to be thoughtful but drew out her pain. Nothing anyone said made her feel better. By the time of the service at the Hormel Home, my grandparents' house in town, she was dry-eyed in greeting the thousands of visitors who came to pay their respects, but she did not raise a smile.

For months and years afterward, I couldn't help but wonder why I was there the night Daddy died. Why me? I had nightmares about it, in which the setting varied but the situation was always the same: Daddy in precarious health, me knowing that something could trigger a heart attack, and having no means to prevent it. In every dream, I woke up just as he was on the verge of dying, feeling helpless and incomplete.

In the early stages of my grief, I began to realize how little I understood my father. I started a mental list of the things I didn't know about him. He rarely recounted family lore and never talked to me about the nuts and bolts of company operations, even though he expected me to help manage them someday. As a father, he was often distant. The times that I did connect with him were when he'd spout some obtuse saying, purely for entertainment value. "There were two people," he used to say. "One of them learned less and less about more and more until he knew nothing about everything. And the other learned more and more about less and less until he knew everything about nothing. Which would you rather be, Jimmy?" I could only shrug my shoulders and giggle.

Yet even as I wished him back to life, I had a small feeling of release. I had always felt that I had a lot of "living up" to do. I had to live up to my father, and my image of him was so big that it would have been impossible for me to do so. When he died, my sense of obligation faded slightly. For the first time, I could envision the possibility of not returning to Austin and not being part of the company.

My mother still held tightly to the idea that Geordie, Thomas, and I would eventually run the company. Geordie had started down the path, working a few summers in Austin and then fulltime at the plant in Fremont, Nebraska, but he had found his heart in the world of music. Thomas was never in doubt—he wanted to get as far away from Austin as possible. I was ambivalent. On one hand, I didn't want to defy my parents' expectations, but I could not see myself living in Austin, either. Law school sounded good to me. Part of our disinterest was my parents' doing. They exposed us to people in positions of power, and ingrained in us standards of politesse and culture, which they believed were indispensible tools for going out into the world. Of course, their definition of "the world" was whatever revolved around the company. I doubt it occurred to them that they had set us on a course to leave it all behind.

Back at school that September, I carried on with life as usual. I was elected president of my fraternity and joined the student council. Alice and I spent lots of time together, often with friends at a favorite spot off campus, which was one of the first places I ever went that served one hundred different kinds of beer. I never sulked or cried, and seldom mentioned Daddy, but Alice knew that I was grieving, and she was there for me. My main goal that year was to get to graduation. I did not fight for the top of the class; I just wanted the degree.

One night that November, I was at Phi Delta Theta chairing a meeting of the whole fraternity when a knock came on the heavy oak door. Mine was one of five fraternities at Swarthmore, all of which were housed in a row of stone buildings with slate roofs and leaded glass windows, a bit like overgrown English cottages.

The Phi Delta Theta meetings were very private, and there would be no reason for anyone to arrive unannounced, so we were all surprised by the knock. All discussion stopped while one of the fraternity brothers went to answer the door. A moment later, he returned, saying: "It's for you Jim—someone wants to see you."

"Who is it?" I asked.

"I think it's a reporter from the *Philadelphia Inquirer*," he said.

I sighed in disgust, knowing exactly why the reporter was there. Everybody knew.

Several weeks earlier, less than a month after my father died, Geordie had been arrested in Los Angeles on charges of marijuana possession. The police said they had found a dozen or so neatly rolled joints in his car, tucked above the driver's sun visor. Drug charges were so rare and scandalous in 1954 that Geordie's arrest made headlines across the country. *The Washington Post* ran the story on its front page: "Hormel Heir Jailed in Marijuana Case."

Geordie's focus then was on a career in music, and L.A. was the place to do it. With fluid hands on the piano, and a smooth, Harry-Connick-Jr.-like voice, he had no trouble landing some big gigs. Divorced from Leslie after three years of marriage, he was seeing an actress who had been on the cover of *Life* magazine earlier that year, Rita Moreno.

Geordie maintained that the drugs were planted by a member of his band after Geordie refused to lend him money. I accepted his story, but was still angry, and for all the wrong reasons. I wasn't worried about him, or the effect of this on his career, or the prospect that he might go to jail. My biggest concern was: *how could he do that to us?* The sudden notoriety, the invasion of our privacy—particularly on the heels of my father's death—it was everything I didn't want. I was exposed as a member of the Hormel family, a relationship I worked assiduously to conceal.

With all my fraternity brothers looking on, I calmly excused myself from the meeting, and asked the journalist if we could speak outside. As soon as the door latch clicked closed, I lit into him.

"What are you doing here?" I asked, not giving him a chance to respond. "You are here in your search for some salacious material on my family, and I don't have anything for you. Please leave."

He did.

It was a horrible time for Mamma. Daddy had just died, and here, now, was her son, not only divorced but scandalizing the family with a criminal arrest as well. Still, when the trial began in early January, 1955, she was in the courtroom every day. She fainted twice during the proceedings, but she was there, as if to say: *This is my boy and I'll stand by him. He deserves to have me stand by him.*

A certain Officer O'Grady admitted that the police often used the band member to set up drug buyers, bringing the trial to a quick end. When the jury foreman announced the acquittal, Mamma burst into tears and hugged Geordie, an act that was captured by a *Washington Post* photographer. A picture ran the next day, along with a story on page 3. I realized right then, if I did not know it before, that whatever expectations Mamma had of us, her love was unconditional.

Something about Geordie's divorce, arrest, and trial made me even more determined to build that perfect life I'd been striving for.

Many of my contemporaries were either married or engaged and I knew that it was expected of me as well. It was conventional behavior, and I was—or at least was trying to be—a conventional guy. My alternative was to stay single but there I was, with a lovely woman, who seemed just the person I wanted to live with. I got along well with her family, and she with mine. Contemplating my choices, I reasoned that marriage would lock me into the mainstream, and lock me out of the *other*. I would be just like everyone else—normal. Above all, I loved Alice and I knew that she loved me.

In June 1955, just a few weeks after my graduation and the end of Alice's junior year, the two of us stood at the altar of St. Paul's Episcopal Church in Charlottesville, taking vows in front of three hundred guests. In many ways, it was a typical Southern society wedding, with bevies of bridesmaids in raw silk and groomsmen in morning coats. Thomas was my best man. I was very nervous, particularly about the protocol of the ceremony. *Oh God, what if I don't do this right?* I thought to myself.

Somehow I managed to get my "I do" out without a hitch. The next day, we boarded an Air France Super Constellation, a four-engine turbo prop plane touted as the ultimate in luxury travel. We spent five weeks visiting France, Italy, and England. We loved Paris so much we stayed six days instead of three, as planned. We spent our time in Venice charmed by the endless alleys and canals of the city. In Rome, we tried to visit the Vatican, but were turned away because Alice's elbows were sticking out of her short sleeves. En route to Paris, we stopped by the French Riviera, where I learned that the trendy blue string bikini I bought in Cannes was not inclined to stay on while water skiing. Our last stopover in France was La Vernelle.

We arrived there in time for Bastille Day, joining Mamma and the French family for a wonderful celebration. Alice met my cousin Simone, her husband Pierre Meignan, and their six-year-old son, Michele. Two nights in a row Mamma went out to the garden with a flashlight, gathering enough snails for the appetizer in a six-hour feast feting both the holiday and our marriage. The wedding and the visit to France seemed to lift, at least temporarily, the weight she'd been lugging around since Daddy died. She carried on joyfully with old friends, some of whom she hadn't seen since she had been back in 1946 for her mother's funeral.

In London, our last stop, Alice and I were surprised to see that many buildings still showed evidence of the bombings a decade earlier. For a few days, as we ambled the streets on foot, Alice didn't feel well. We first thought that she was overtired from the excitement of the wedding, and then all the travel. It soon became clear that something else was going on: she was pregnant. I was to become a father.

Chapter Seven

FEAR OF DISCOVERY

For the first several years of our marriage, Alice and I lived a picture-perfect life in Chicago, complete with beautiful, affectionate children and an expansive social circle.

I attended and graduated from the University of Chicago Law School, clerked at the Illinois State Appellate Court, and worked in a small general practice firm of about thirty lawyers. Alice, meanwhile, contended with the many challenges of motherhood, chased after our runaway dog, Barkley P. Drinkwater, and still found time to finish her Bachelor's degree at Lake Forest College.

We eventually moved to Winnetka, a northern suburb of Chicago graced with regal old homes and mansions along the lakefront. Our newer ranch-style house was nestled in a cul-de-sac away from the water, amid neighbors who were friendly and social, but not too friendly or too social. My law school classmate Frank Gerlits and his wife Suzanne lived nearby and came over often for cold beer and barbequed steaks while our kids, Alison, Anne, Elizabeth, and Jimmy, mobbed the backyard swing set with their four children, Kathleen, Karen, Mary Cameron, and Frankie.

In 1961, I went back to the University of Chicago Law School to work as its first fulltime dean of students. Like many American colleges and universities, the school was starving for students as the GI bill, which sent millions of war veterans to college, expired. The law school dean, Edward Levi, a smiley, balding man who wore horn-rimmed glasses and bow ties, was determined to continue the school's tradition of excellence. He oversaw construction of a spectacular new campus designed by Eero Saarinen, *the* architect of the day, and created the dean of students position to ensure classes were filled with the highest caliber students.

The happiest periods of my life have most always been at the beginning of something new, and being at the law school was definitely a novel experience. I had never dreamed of working at one of the major research institutions in the country and was swept up in the magic of the unexpected. The law school had all kinds of notable jurists and academic stars, including a former Nuremberg prosecutor and two future U.S. attorneys general.

Among the law school's four hundred students were just eight women and a handful of students of color—two statistics I hoped to change. En route to my office each morning, walking past a large rectangular pool reflecting the pleated glass façade of Saarinen's building, I carried a tremendous sense of mission. I felt that I owned a small share of a glamorous, exciting world.

About that time, word on the cocktail circuit was that the four-term congresswoman from my district, Marguerite Stitt Church, planned to retire.

At an after-work event, Ned Jannotta, a North Shore native who worked in a prestigious investment banking firm, chatted with me about his involvement in the search for a new candidate. This is my recollection of our discussion:

"Say Jim, have you got any interest in running?" he asked. "It's a very safe seat for a Republican."

"Well, gee, I don't know," I replied casually, as if the concept was completely new. The idea, however, had occurred to me. I did not lie around dreaming of running for Congress, but I was small-minded enough to think that I was from the right kind of family, and that it was the sort of thing that people, like Ned, might expect me to do.

"You're associated with the University…you're on the Chicago Council on Foreign Relations—you've got the right background and qualifications," he said.

As he spoke, my excitement grew. Ned was much more connected than I was. If he thought the seat was within my reach, then it must be.

"Give it a thought and let me know if you have any interest," he replied, shaking my hand and moving on to his next conversation.

"I'll certainly do that," I said, with all the grace and calm I could muster.

What an opportunity, I thought.

I was not one of those gung-ho people who ran for student body president and then spent the rest of his life climbing the electoral ladder. But I always had an eye on politics. My interest started when I was a little boy, observing my father's interactions with governors, congressmen, and cabinet secretaries, and grew when I got to Swarthmore. In Chicago, I started to connect with local Republicans.

In 1960, I volunteered for ten minutes at the Republican National Convention in Chicago. When Henry Cabot Lodge, Jr., was nominated as Vice President Richard Nixon's running mate, I paraded across the convention floor with a small crowd, hoisting a "NIXON-LODGE" placard, as if there were a massive groundswell of support for the ticket. I was not enthusiastic about Nixon but my service earned me a convention floor pass.

I was a Republican because my father was a Republican. Still, certain aspects of the party line rang true to me: Free enterprise made the country great. Labor had too much power. I was too idealistic then to catch the nuances of real life; the fact that enterprise in America was *not* so free, or that the problem with labor was not about power per se, but about union leaders who rested on their laurels and aspired to be like business moguls. The Republican Party was right for me because it still reflected the individualism of Teddy Roosevelt. It had not yet been overtaken by southern bigots disappointed with Lyndon Johnson and the Civil Rights Act of 1964.

Like many dwelling in the privileged confines of academia, I felt a psychological proximity to the events of the day. Riled by the Cold War, the Cuban missile crisis, and our stare-downs with Khrushchev, I naïvely thought that a term in Congress was an opportunity to right some wrongs. I saw myself as a conciliator, someone who could bring people together on issues. That seemed to be exactly what the country needed.

I left the event and drove my white Volkswagen beetle toward Winnetka. I couldn't wait to talk to Alice. Just thirty years old, I was puffed up with the possibility of a dream coming true. The halls of Congress did not seem far away.

The only problem was my other life.

In those days, I might have joked at a student-faculty softball game about faggots, or imitated a lisping, limp-wristed fellow to get a few laughs, while going out that same evening to seek an assignation with another man.

Encounters with men, infrequent as they were for me then, gave me the kind of adrenaline rush you get when you know you are defying society's mores. I learned, almost instinctively, which area of a given city to visit, which bar, which beach, which truck stop. It was surprising to me that I often met someone in a "legitimate" place—during the coffee break at an academic conference or on an airplane. There were code words and signs. You might slip the word "gay" into a conversation, or ask someone if they knew so-and-so, who was a "friend of Dorothy." You caught on to the code very quickly, because if you made a mistake, your life could be ruined.

I lived in constant fear of discovery.

One winter evening early in my marriage, I stopped to do research at Northwestern University's business school library, which was convenient to my drive home.

Just before the library closed, I gathered my things and went to the men's room. I put my coat on a hook on the back of the stall door and sat down. A man came in. Instead of going directly into the other stall, he peered through the crack of the door of my stall. It was creepy. He then went into the other stall and made the foot signals that gay men used at the time to reach out to each other.

I sat motionless, not reacting. I had not gone to the library looking for a rendezvous. A moment later, the guy left his stall. With one swift motion, he reached over the door, grabbed my coat, and disappeared.

My God, what just happened, I thought.

I didn't relish a cold Chicago night in my shirtsleeves but I was relieved to think there was nothing valuable in the coat. Then I remembered: my wallet. My *wallet.* It had my ID with my *name* on it. I got out of the bathroom as fast as I could and began searching for the guy, though I would have recognized nothing about him but his shoes. He had disappeared, of course.

Down the hallway, I noticed a bank of lockers, with one door conspicuously ajar. Inside, my coat draped from a metal hook, as if it had been there all day. I shoved my hands in the pocket. Empty. No wallet. Something dropped inside me. Is this guy going to blackmail me? Am I going to get a letter in the mail saying, *"Give me money, or I'm going to say that you were soliciting me."*?

At home, I climbed into bed next to Alice, hoping she was asleep. Of course she wasn't. Even if she had been, I was shaking so badly that I would have woken her up. She turned immediately to comfort me.

"Are you okay?" she asked, putting her arms around me. "What happened?"

"I got robbed. My wallet got stolen." I could barely get the words out.

"What?! Are you hurt? My God, where did this happen? Did you go to the police?" Her questions seemed endless.

"No!" I said sharply. "I don't want them to have anything to do with this. Please, I don't want to talk about it."

The situation raised more questions than I could possibly have answered.

A few days later, the phone rang. Alice picked up, only to have her "hellos" met with silence. Hearing a person exhaling on the other end, she hung up. Later that night, the phone rang again: the same wordless silence, the same breathing. I was convinced it was the man from the bathroom. Alice was unsettled, but I quickly shrugged the calls off as a prank. That was it. The calls stopped; no letter turned up in the mailbox. With a new wallet and a new ID, my panic faded.

Yet it was one of many incidents during our marriage that left Alice in a state of confusion and concern. No matter how wonderful our life seemed on the outside, my secret was always there between us.

Over the years of my infidelity, I agonized about what I was doing to my marriage—the vows I made to her truly meant something to me. I never lost sight of the fact that I violated my commitment to

Alice, or that I was a lawyer breaking the law (homosexual acts were illegal in all states back then). I lied to myself so many times: *I'm never going to do that again. It wasn't worth it. I didn't feel any kind of satisfaction. It was anonymous sex with someone who couldn't even tell me his real name.* And certainly, I could not tell him mine.

Still, I never considered the acts themselves to be immoral. I was a human being, interacting with another human being, who had feelings and an urgency to express them in a world that offered us nothing but castigation.

A private civil war raged inside me as I struggled to come up with an answer for Ned Jannotta. I found myself alternately daydreaming about campaign strategies and Washington gay bars. A seat in Congress sounded fantastic. My mother would be thrilled. But was I setting myself up for a horrible situation? These were the days of the Lavender Scare, when official Washington actively hunted down and fired gay and lesbian civil servants. Allen Drury's Pulitzer-Prize winning novel *Advise & Consent* was made into a wildly popular movie that ended in an outed gay senator's dramatic, off-camera suicide. Bang. Dead. Life over. My mind turned toward fearsome fantasies of newspaper headlines, suicides, homicides—all kinds of devastating potential outcomes.

No, no, I can't do this, I thought. *I cannot risk ruining my life or humiliating my entire family.*

I dialed Ned in covert despair. I thanked him graciously for his confidence and told him that Alice and I had decided to move out of the district, which happened to be true. We wanted to be closer to the University in a neighborhood with more diversity and less of Winnetka's air of privilege.

I later read in the *Chicago Tribune* about the Republican Party's candidate for Mrs. Church's seat. He was an energetic young man, my age, with all the right North Shore credentials. He won easily. His name was Donald Rumsfeld.

In 1962, we moved into a well-worn Edwardian townhouse in Hyde Park with an easy-to-remember address: 1234 East 56th Street.

Characteristic of its vintage, the house had ornate woodwork and stained glass windows that cast glorious colorful shadows on the white marble entryway. The rooms flowed gracefully into each other, making them comfortable for cocktail parties, dinners, and even the occasional chamber concert. The upper floors had plenty of bedrooms and a two-story playroom large enough for a trampoline and half of the neighborhood's kids, which, in combination, made the walls shake as if the subway traveled beneath the building.

Alice and I threw a housewarming on New Year's Eve attended by more than 200 people, many of whom were eager to see our new, renovated home. We loved to entertain and were good at it. I suppose many who came by that evening left feeling they had shared in the lives of a perfect couple and a perfect family. What they saw was not a false life—it was real life. I was doing my best to follow the paths that I knew, striving to be a strong, caring husband and father on an upwardly mobile career path. I was not faking it; I was trying to *be* that man.

Our reality was to the contrary, however: even as the wallpaper went up, our marriage frayed. Alice always sensed that I kept some part of myself isolated from her, and we often argued about it. By the time we moved to Hyde Park, and even after we had our fifth child, Sarah, we were no longer connecting or communicating. Alice asked again and again why I would not open up to her. I was afraid to let myself feel any emotions at all. If I let some out, how could I keep the rest in? I had all sorts of replies, increasingly hurtful, to keep her at bay. I told her that marriage didn't mean losing all of one's privacy. I accused her of trying to own my soul.

Yet, uncontrollably, perhaps even unconsciously, I laid clues for her. I encouraged her to read *Advise & Consent* and took her to see a British movie called *Victim* about a closeted gay lawyer, and *The Children's Hour* about two women accused of a lesbian relationship. Over time, the hints got more specific. One day, Alice returned from our new summer house—a breathtaking home on a cliff overlooking Lake Michigan—to find that a male friend from the law school had slept over—in our bed. I could have gone into the guest room and rumpled the sheets before she got home, but I didn't.

I had a seething cauldron of sexual energy inside me, and couldn't keep a lid on it. I had an increasingly greater need to let the feelings out but didn't know how to do it in a way that would not wreak nuclear havoc on my life. There were no resources, no role models. Even Truman Capote, as openly gay as he seemed, always appeared in public with a woman on his arm. Forget any concept of "coming out." The only eventuality was brutal discovery.

As near as I could see, the revelation of my homosexuality could only be destructive: the end of my perfect family, the loss of love from a woman I truly cared for, and the complete and total blockade of all pathways to professional success. I would not be a Congressman, or a prominent businessman, or any other sort of pillar of the community. I might even lose the job I had.

Aside from a small circle of men in the Chicago area, the very first person I spoke to about being gay was Alice's shrink. It was a disaster.

I had no idea Alice was seeing a psychiatrist until she brought it up and asked me to see him too. I agreed—anything to help us reconcile.

On the appointed day, I arrived at the doctor's office. He was like a character out of a bad novel, all tweedy and pipe smoking. With a bit of pomp, he shook my hand and ushered me into his consultation room, where I found my way to a comfortable armchair. He sat down behind his desk. I had the sensation of looking up. His seat seemed higher than the others, as if he enjoyed looking down on anyone who sat before him.

We exchanged a few pleasantries. I have no idea where I got my nerve but I came right out with what I had to say.

"As you know, Alice and I have been having difficulties for some time. We are not able to communicate the way we once were." I took a shallow breath. "I blame myself for this, because I cannot overcome the fact that I am gay."

The doctor leaned back slightly. His face contorted into a knowing sneer, suggesting that I had confirmed something he suspected for months.

After a moment of reflection, he replied, with equal directness.

"Well then, there's no hope for you and Alice. I don't see how you can continue in the relationship."

That was it; the appointment was over. He made no effort to show even a shred of understanding or courtesy. I was so very fragile, and he either didn't sense that, or didn't care about it. I am not sure which.

Deep down, I did not really want to save the marriage, but at that point, I had no ability to be honest with myself. There was something safe about being a straight, married man in a straight, married world. I didn't want to give up the security of the family that I had created or the respectability that went with along with it. It *terrified* me to think of losing that.

And then there were the kids. They were so young. The oldest, Alison, was nine; the youngest, Sarah, was just a year old. It was extraordinarily hard for me to imagine a life without them, or to conceive of what harm a divorce might do.

Alice's shrink was brutish, but he was right—there was no way that I could stay married and remain sane. I suppose, in a way, that

I was lucky that he said what he said. This was 1965: he might well have recommended electric shock treatments, a drug regimen, or one of the other horrific aversion therapies that were used at the time to "cure" homosexuality.

One summer Friday, I drove the ninety minutes from the university to our weekend home in Lakeside and found Alice waiting to talk to me. Ten years had gone by, and she had had enough of the secrecy and emotional distance. Plagued by migraines and blackouts, she couldn't take it anymore. I protested, feeling miserable and sorry for myself, and angry at her for leaving. At the same time, I could not dispute anything she said. Every word of it was true.

A few weeks later, Alice packed the kids and their belongings into the station wagon. There was no slamming of doors, no suddenness about it. They set off for Nevada, to a village on Lake Tahoe with the cheery name of Crystal Bay. The kids hiked, rode horses, and swam while Alice waited out the six weeks' residency period required to file for divorce.

Halfway through those weeks, I flew to Nevada in hopes of persuading Alice to come back and give the marriage another try. I was being very selfish. At the heart of my struggle was my desire to have it all: my engaging wife, my delightfully rambunctious children, and all the social validation that went with them. And I wanted that other life as well. I did not know exactly what that other life was, but I was drawn to it.

Alice sent me home.

Feeling very low, I traveled to Bel Air to see my mother. I felt better telling her about Alice and me in person. Mamma was a Roman Catholic, who had a kneeler and statue of the Virgin Mary in her bedroom, as well as a crucifix over her bed. She never wanted to see a divorce in our family. No one did—divorce was a scandal then.

Since Geordie had divorced Leslie, I hoped that my news would come as less of a shock. It didn't.

We were together in a sitting area just off her bedroom, where she enjoyed watching television. As I explained the situation, her disappointment filled the small room.

"When people have had the life that you've had with Alice, and then they break up, it's either over sex or money," she said. It was pretty clear to her that my problems with Alice were not about money.

She waited for a response. I said nothing. We sat in silence a few minutes more.

"I've got to go, Mamma. My plane is leaving soon," I said, rising to leave.

I was on the verge of exposure.

Chapter Eight

STEPPING OUT

My new bachelor pad at 910 Lake Shore Drive was stark and spare, as if the architect who designed it knew I needed a place without any fuss.

Only ten miles by car from our row house in Hyde Park, the apartment was light years' distance in other ways. On the seventh floor of a Mies van der Rohe glass and aluminum tower, the rooms were plain, white boxes, devoid of decorative detail. The apartment's great beauty was huge floor-to-ceiling windows that brought Lake Michigan and the sky into most of the rooms. There was an odd stillness about the place—no children clamored for pancakes at the breakfast table or set up camp under the piano.

I rattled around, feeling like a complete and utter failure. *For better or for worse. 'Til death do you part.* At the time I took those vows, I meant every word. I was stuck on what it meant to break them. I stared out of the windows for hours at a time, watching the complexion of the water change.

My thoughts were dominated by one question: *Could I be cured?*

I scoured Chicago for information that would help answer the question. In the aisle of a bookstore or library, I tried to hide my selections by piling bestsellers on top of titles such as: *Homosexuality: A Psychoanalytic Study, Sexual Inversion: the Multiple Roots of*

Homosexuality, or *The Overt Homosexual*. The bestsellers were far more enjoyable—most of the others suggested that I had a mental illness, which wasn't surprising given that homosexuality was listed then in the American Psychiatric Association's *Diagnostic and Statistical Manual of Mental Disorders*.

The funny thing was I didn't *feel* sick.

I started seeing a psychiatrist, a man in his thirties, like me, who was a great deal more sympathetic than Alice's shrink. He and I spent several months dissecting that universal question: *What is my life about?* He was very helpful, despite the fact that he had no sense of humor and was prone to answering my self-inquiry with semantic vagaries such as: "Well, Jim, that's all grist for our mill."

I wasn't seeing him in order to delve deeply into my sexuality. I only wanted to be reassured and told that I wasn't crazy, and that what I was feeling was genuine and natural. It became readily apparent to me, however, that if I were to move past my crisis, I had to go back in time.

"When did you first realize that you were gay?" the shrink asked, at one of our earliest sessions.

Images of Batman and Robin instantly popped into my head. Geordie, Thomas, and I curated an enormous collection of comic books in a nook of our cellar, and I was as devoted to the Dynamic Duo as any ten-year-old could be. I was convinced that they weren't just battling evil but also having other sorts of adventures not depicted in the pages of my comics. But did I even know about sex then? Did I fantasize about other boys? I had no clear recollection.

I couldn't put my finger on any certain moment of epiphany but I knew that from my very first moment of sexual awareness, I was attracted to other boys. The feeling was deeply embedded, not generated by choice, or prurient interest, or a desire to experiment. Homosexuality, this supposed mental illness, had something to do with my inner spirit, my soul, the person I really was.

That realization did not come to me overnight. I didn't wake up one morning and suddenly feel free—it took a while for me to recognize myself. I had spent decades living inside a shell of my own making and it was hard to break through. First, I had to deal with the immutability of being gay, and the certainty that I was born into it the same way I was born to be left-handed. The next step was about accepting myself for who I was. That process was going to take much longer. When you have spent your entire life denying your own worth, it takes some time to abandon the patterns of self-denigration and loathing, and acknowledge that maybe you are *just fine* as you are.

If anything, I came to see that being gay was not something by which I should judge myself. And I didn't want others to judge me by it, either.

Even before my boxes were unpacked, I invited men into my home. I wish I could say that we went out to the movies, or had romantic dinners in cozy bistros, but that kind of visibility was not possible for gay people then. The obvious place to go to socialize was in one of the several bars that anchored Chicago's gay underground, but one risked being caught in a raid and named in the newspaper the next day. There was also a reasonable chance that as you walked down the street, you would be harassed, perhaps by a carload of teenagers screaming "FAGGOT!" out the window as they drove by.

I always wondered: how did the hecklers know the bar was a place for gay people? Did they have a prurient interest of their own?

In that nether world, I met many fellow travelers, nearly all of them wonderful, decent people who had been driven into the shadows by society's refusal to accept their sexual orientation. One of them was a wavy-haired doctoral student in history. His name was Mort.

Like the stereotypical University of Chicago intellectual that he was, Mort went to class in collared shirts and sweaters and wore heavy-rimmed glasses. His roots were in a working-class Jewish family in Pittsburgh. The first in his family to go to college, Mort arrived in Chicago with bags packed full of his parents' pride and expectations.

Mort and I had all-night conversations and playfully combative arguments and exchanges. Alice and I had similar talks during our marriage, but something about my exchanges with Mort were more fulfilling. They lent passage to a world of intimacy and companionship, and gave me the security to think that I could tell this person anything. *Anything*. I could say, boy, *Advise & Consent* scared me to death and Mort would understand exactly how I felt. He and I communicated in the most honest and heartfelt way about the things that touched our lives. Never before in my thirty-two years had I felt that way.

The feeling gave me hope that I might be able to put my life back together.

When Mort finished his doctoral studies, he returned to Pittsburgh, where his fiancée was waiting. The picture was all too familiar. He was just like me, hiding as I had, getting married as I did, and for pretty much the same reasons. The only thing that was different about him was his blue-collar upbringing. But this difference was important to me. It helped me confirm that my sexuality had nothing to do with being a pampered child, spoiled by his mother, raised in the lap of luxury, who developed a "taste" for others of his gender. That was one of the theories the so-called experts of the day wanted everyone to believe, and I half believed it myself.

Within a year of my divorce, I was connected to a vast community of people like me. Its citizens were the whole of Chicago: people of all economic levels, races, and religions, who shared a secret that colored their behavior and their self-image. That connection gave me courage. I started to believe that I could cope because I was not alone. I had a whole new family to whom I could turn. They would always accept me.

And then there was my real family. They didn't know what was going on with me. I had offered no explanation to anyone in the family about the divorce, nor had I told them about my new "friends." I realized they would never understand me if I didn't let them into my world.

The summer after Alice and I divorced, Thomas and Simone came from Los Angeles to vacation with me at Lakeside.

I had always looked up to Thomas. He seemed to live his life without any hesitation. Married for more than a decade and the first of us three brothers to become a father, he was in many respects my role model for leading a conventional life. So far as I could tell, he seemed happy and fulfilled.

He and Simone had a free-floating, off-the-wall coterie of friends in Hollywood, including many who were gay. He seemed to enjoy their company without making the judgments that convention demanded. Thomas knew me better than anyone else on the planet. On instinct, I trusted that he and Simone would be supportive.

One breezy evening during their visit, the three of us sat down to dinner on the screened-in porch. It was a comfortable space facing the lake and offering protection from big and thirsty mosquitoes.

The tomatoes looked exquisitely juicy and delicious, the way only homegrown tomatoes can be, but I was so distracted by my own thoughts that I could hardly taste them. I couldn't keep it all inside anymore. My revelation came out in a sentence so long I felt that I was reciting the last chapter of *Ulysses*.

"Alice and I started out with this wonderful relationship but it started to fall apart and it kept getting worse and worse and I blame myself for it because I can't overcome the fact that I am gay," I said. Then I exhaled. One giant step for mankind.

"Oh," said Thomas, as if I'd said something ordinary.

Thomas and Simone silently exchanged glances and then asked a few questions about whether I was okay. Then the conversation tore off, very naturally, in a completely different direction. I didn't keel over dead, and neither Thomas nor Simone walked out the door. The next day, the sun rose, my eggs tasted fine, and most everything else was the way it had been.

The only change was that I felt accepted. I was still the same Jimmy that Thomas and Simone had come to visit. I could see that they held me in exactly the same regard, and that the love we shared was not diminished by my revelation. That emboldened me to take another step, which was to call Geordie. He responded with equal nonchalance.

"I wondered when you were going to tell me," he said.

My brothers' acceptance was liberating. I can hardly explain how I felt, except to say that I was *relieved*, in the purest sense of the word. The word *relief* comes from the Latin word *relevare*: "to lift again" and I must admit that there was an element of resurrection in what occurred. I did not realize how much pressure I was under until I relieved it by coming out. While not so direct in coming out to other people, I started to conduct myself in a way that would let them make assumptions about me. I tiptoed out of the closet and found that the more open I was, the more confident I became, and the easier it was to be out.

I desperately wanted to explain things to Alice, but I was afraid of her. I worried that she saw me as a sham, a con artist posing as a devoted heterosexual husband and parent who, by the way, could have brought home a sexually-transmitted infection. I wasn't confident that she had the ability to understand me, not because of who she was but because of the times we lived in. We married in the days before the sexual revolution, when most people would be hard-pressed to admit that sex existed, never mind that they engaged in it or liked it.

But all of that was in my head: I had no way of knowing what Alice really thought. We barely said anything to each other. We strained to be cordial and keep our emotions from spreading into the lives of the kids. A sea of negativity divided us—primarily anger on her part, and guilt on mine. She had every right to be angry. For years, I concealed an essential part of myself from her.

In the end, I waited long enough that I didn't have to tell her. She put things together herself.

As she later told me, she blamed herself for "making" me gay: she wasn't pretty enough, or sexy enough. She felt she lacked something.

In case Alice wasn't feeling low enough, her social circle in Chicago more or less evaporated. People were inclined to judge her because she divorced me. Some of our closest friends were suddenly out of communication with her and once she was no longer my wife, many in the University community didn't recognize her as belonging anymore. While fully aware that things were extremely difficult for Alice, I also felt sorry for myself, and let's face it, when people get into *poor me* mode, they don't want to have it interrupted by anyone else's problems. The unspoken truth was that despite all that we'd been through, we still loved each other, although neither of us could admit it at the time.

Several months after our divorce, Alice found a new relationship with the kids' riding instructor, a German equestrian champion named Heinz Kramp. He was a fascinating guy who came to the United States in the late 1950s to teach at Iowa State University.

Sent to a Nazi youth camp at age nine or ten, Heinz was selected to present a bouquet of flowers to Hitler at an event once. After the war, he spent many years recovering from the brainwashing of the camps. He and Alice married about 1966, and a short time later, moved to Potomac, Maryland, with the kids. I was surprised that Alice re-married so soon after our divorce, but I was happy she had found a new love, and I felt sure the kids were in good hands. Whenever I visited, Heinz went out of his way to be accommodating and friendly. Alice soon gave birth to her sixth child, Andrew, and moved on with her life. That made it easy for me to avoid ever having that heart-to-heart talk with her.

With the kids hundreds of miles away, I started to feel my tie to Chicago loosening. The life Alice and I built around university friends felt increasingly awkward for me, too. I'm sure that part of it had to do with the persistent gossip about faculty members and university staff, such as the professor in the Music Department who apparently wasn't promoted because he was gay. I don't think anyone in the law school had any information about me but my own self-denigrating, projecting condemnation led me to conclude: *I do not fit in here any longer.* It was the reaction of a teenager who looks in the mirror and sees a little pimple and can think about nothing else all day.

I went to the Faculty Club for lunch one day, which I normally enjoyed for the opportunity to sit at a round, communal table where I might find myself chatting with an astrophysicist, or with the world's leading scholar on Greek tragedy. That day, Edward Levi joined the group and, as I recall, recounted a story using the word *faggot* to describe someone. My stomach churned. His comment was in no way directed toward me, but still, I was shocked. That wasn't a word I expected to hear from a standard-bearer of academia. I could only imagine how he and other colleagues would react if they found out I was gay.

While an amazing center for intellectual discourse, the University was an institution created with human hands and tainted by the attendant human flaws. It was a mirror of the world at large. Greed, the struggle for power, the adversarial roles, the class issues, sexism, racism—it was all there, among the intellectual elite. Behavior that I thought was beyond this "enlightened" world was very much a part of it.

In May 1966, 450 students shut down the University's Administrative Building for six days to protest a new school policy that would help expand the military draft. They were saying: *Don't trust anyone over thirty.* The more I listened to them, the more I saw things their way. They were challenging the role of *in loco parentis*: we set the rules and you follow them. *"Why?"* they asked. *"Why should we follow your rules? Why should you govern our lives?"* It was my job as dean to see that law students complied with the school's policies— everything from regular class attendance to no alcohol in the dorm— and if they didn't, that they received some consequences. I started to feel funny about that.

It did not help my growing disaffection that I spent a lot of time outside work with a crazy but fun advertising executive named Bob Peitscher who had blond hair, a bouncy personality, and a love of marijuana. His rebellious spirit was contagious.

As young people in Chicago and across the country took increasingly aggressive positions in opposition to the Vietnam War, the academic world divided between the administration and the students. My sympathies squarely with the students, I made plans to resign.

Up until that point, I always believed that government was a force for good. Even in the early days of the Vietnam War, I interpreted U.S. military intervention in Southeast Asia as a matter of patriotism—

we were preventing the spread of communism. But as President Johnson led the nation into full-fledged war and race riots opened a new front at home, it was difficult to maintain that point of view. *Life* magazine and the nightly television news delivered gruesome images of people bleeding, burning from napalm, and lying dead in the streets of Newark and Detroit, making the U.S. government symbolic of something other than patriotism. I could no longer see it as a force for good.

Bob and I were together on a particular Sunday in September 1967 as I read *The New York Times* at my kitchen table. I came across a story by Andrew Kopkind, a former *Washington Post* and *New Republic* reporter who wrote highly influential opinion pieces about the war and the progressive movement. (Much later, I learned that he was a gay man.)

In the article, Kopkind spoke of the inherent strength of "the Establishment," the failure of the radical left, and the political disinterest of moderates. Bemoaning the country's oblivion to the long-term effects of the war, he called for a political revolution. I looked up, staring into space. I then re-read every word, feeling some sort of fire inside me. Just like that—as if someone snapped a finger over me—the world looked completely different. My confidence in the institutions of our society, already shaky, was torn down to its foundation.

That fall, when Bob accepted a job offer at an advertising agency in New York City, I decided to go with him. I packed up my apartment.

It was time for something different.

Chapter Nine

INFLUENCES OF THE DAY

In the fall of 1967, New York was gritty and full of crime, but the surroundings were so intoxicating that I walked everywhere, oblivious to any danger. The city was a place of radical thought and creativity, spurred by the violence of the war, the riots across American cities, and all the other extreme things that were going on.

Bob and I moved into a new high-rise on East 60th Street in Manhattan. I was on the eighteenth floor, he on the twentieth, across the hall from Allan Sherman, the comedy writer who penned campy songs such as *Hello Muddah, Hello Fadduh*. Bob spent most of his time in my apartment, so much so that he set up a second phone line for himself. I was not allowed to answer it, lest it somehow compromise his covert sexuality. The arrangement was one manifestation of how he tried to deal with the duality of being a corporate golden boy from 9 to 5, and a disco-loving "degenerate" after dark. Bob's radically shifting moods were a continual challenge for me. Today, he probably would be diagnosed with bipolar disorder. He was a talented, good-looking guy with tremendous joie de vivre who could charm and, if necessary, manipulate, his way into whatever he wanted. In those early days, all I could see was the charm.

Most mornings, after Bob put on his suit and went off to the ad agency, I headed uptown to painting classes at the National Academy at 5th Avenue and East 89th Street. Though not much of an artist, I found it soothing to lose myself in the studio for three or four hours at a time. After class, I often cut across the dusty, grassless patches that pocked Central Park in those days and set off on a marathon walk to some far-flung neighborhood of the city.

I served on the Hormel Foods board, which involved monthly meetings in Austin. Otherwise, I was not working or even looking for a job. My attraction to academia was gone, and I didn't want to go back into law. When people asked me what I did in New York, I told them I was listening to my hair grow. I was just around, open to the influences of the day, absorbing all that New York had to offer—and there was a lot.

Music, experimental dance, theater, and graphic arts—all of it was exploding with a new creative sensibility, redefining the limits of the art forms, and inspiring a whole new generation of creative thinkers.

On the extreme fringes of expression were productions such as the play *Dionysus in '69*, in which ticket holders sat on bleachers around a bare floor while scantily-clad actors tried to lure them into a simulated orgy with dialogue they seemed to make up as they went along. The Joffrey Ballet challenged dance lovers accustomed to the classical tones of *Swan Lake* and Tchaikovsky with strobe lights, sexually explicit dance, and loud, discordant music. An artist friend of Geordie's, Barton Benes, had an exhibit in a Manhattan gallery featuring works constructed of dollar bills and a set of ashtrays made from human ashes. Artistic statements like these blew away the conventions of the 1950s.

I saw the ultimate hippie musical *Hair* three times in three different incarnations. When the show came out, hair, in its various forms, had become symbolic. Even in conservative circles, people wanting to be "in" grew beards and let their curls get past the nape of the neck. I am sure if you saw a picture of Dick Cheney from 1968, you'd be amazed by his side burns. I was cautious to let go of my close-cropped brown mop, but eventually relented and found myself for the first time going to somebody other than a barber. For the shocking price of $8—about $7 more than my barber charged—I had my hair styled at Vidal Sassoon. I couldn't believe I spent so much. Eventually, my hair got so long that I started to look a little like the painting of Jesus that hung above my childhood bed in Austin.

I spent a lot of time thinking about what I might do next, but the more I experienced New York, the larger and more unexplored the world seemed. There were so many things that I didn't know, that I hadn't ever considered. Among them was Eastern spirituality.

One bitterly cold Sunday in late January 1968, the Maharishi Mahesh Yogi spoke at the Felt Forum, a 5,000-seat theater at the brand new Madison Square Garden complex. With long, stringy dark hair, and a salt and pepper beard that stood out against his brown skin, he sat alone in the middle of the stage, on a gigantic cushion, surrounded by as many flowers as I have ever seen assembled in one place. He went on for a couple of hours, saying such things as: "You have within you all of the wonders of this universe. And you have the key to unlock them for yourself."

His concept of religion was quite a contrast to what I observed, and was taught, in Austin. From what I knew, religious institutions asked you to surrender your responsibility to them: *follow our rules and don't think for yourself*. What I heard in the ideas of the Maharishi, Swami Satchidananda, and other Eastern messengers was that my strength and completeness—my wholeness—was within me, and that I had the power to make my life however I wanted it to be. The thought was mind-blowing. According to their thinking, I was in control of my life, which meant that I could no longer blame all of my problems and my frustrations on someone else. It was up to me to address my issues.

My self-directed studies coincided with a serious internal process. The initial phases of my coming out were challenging, painful, arduous, overwhelming—you name it. Somewhere in the world there is a list of the most psychologically affecting events that can occur in one's life, and job change, divorce, and moving are at the very top. Along with coming out, all these other things happened to me, one on top of the other. In their aftermath, I realized that I didn't know who I was anymore.

I had based my existence on wanting to be liked. Everything I did was toward that end. When I was ten years old, I learned cribbage and bridge so that I could sit with my parents at the table and play. Yet it never seemed to be enough; I never got the full satisfaction that I was looking for. Right after law school, at an interview with an investment banking firm, I was asked to draw a man. That was the only instruction: *draw a man*. What I created on the page was a guy in a business suit, with a tie and hat—the most conventional person I could imagine. Later, I thought that the drawing was probably meant as some psychological representation of how I saw myself. *How embarrassing*, I thought. *Is that who I am?*

It was.

For thirty-four years, I tried to be the best little boy in the world, doing what I thought would please others. I had been taught to be restrained, orderly, and considerate, and to do what society expected people like me to do. And I was very good at it. But along the way, I had sublimated many sides of myself, including the part of me that was gay. When I came out, no one abandoned me, disowned me, or threw me out of the family. I did not suffer physically; nobody ever beat me. I never had to worry about holding down a job or having money to pay the rent. Yet I was mired painfully in internal struggles of self-doubt. It was the fear of not being worthy. I wanted everyone to like me, even though I did not like myself. It was my way of meting out punishment. And believe me, the worst punishments are the ones that are self-inflicted.

Over time, I found in New York a sanctuary from my mantras on failure and guilt. The exposure to so many radically new and different people and ideas helped me put aside my fear of discovering something about myself that I didn't like. Melting into the masses, I realized that the world carried on, no matter what I did or didn't do. People didn't care what my last name was, or whether I had a job, or what I wore. I loved the anonymity. I had craved it for my entire life. New York was full of people trying to find themselves. I was just one of the many.

Another meandering personality I met was an unintentionally comical guy, Larry Noble, who lived part-time in a truck that he parked on the street and moved whenever parking regulations required him to do so. He was missing a leg, which, he confided, was amputated following some sort of accident. He told most people, however, that he lost it fighting in Israel.

One afternoon, Larry took me to a pad in the East Village, where a dozen or so free spirits were hanging out. The air inside had a familiar, friendly odor. Most everyone in the apartment was involved in busy, weed-inspired chatter except for a guy sitting on a bed, strumming a guitar. It was Bob Dylan. He was just there, in his space, and everyone left him to it.

Where do I fit into this city? I wondered.

Somewhere, I decided, because I liked the place.

After a year in New York, Bob said he had something to tell me.

"What is it?" I asked.

"I'm getting married," he said.

"What? You've already been married," I replied.

"Yes, I'm going to remarry my ex-wife," he said.

Bob had brought me into the 1960s by introducing me to marijuana and the disco scene, but I was starting to feel that we did not belong together. Once I got over my bewilderment about his re-marriage, I felt relieved. It was time for us to go our separate ways.

Even as I found more calm inside me, the world outside rumbled, and I couldn't help but feel affected by the social disarray. So many things took place within the space of one or two years, it was unbelievable.

How would the world be different if there had been no 1968: no Tet Offensive, no Martin Luther King assassination, no Bobby Kennedy assassination? And no bloody Democratic National Convention. Not to mention Europe torn apart by the Prague Spring and the riots in Paris. All of these events took place within a year of the Summer of Love, at a time when many people were committing themselves to philosophies of pacifism. *All you need is love*, the Beatles said, but a lot of people didn't listen. It was incongruous to me. When, in 1968, these violent episodes unfolded one after the other, it was as if some divine force was trying to test us humans.

That summer, like most, the kids and I spent several weeks at Lakeside. In August, they went back to Alice and I made it home to New York in time to watch the Democratic Convention on television. As coverage of the speeches gave way to video of the Chicago police beating and gassing protesters, I fell into a state of utter disbelief. One word described the situation: *bedlam*. Some 650 protestors were arrested and countless numbers were injured. A senator got hit in the head with a flying object. Mayor Richard Daley screamed and called people names. He was Mr. Malaprop, always getting his words and syntax confused, which he did when he tried to defend the city's response: *The policeman isn't there to create disorder; the policeman is there to preserve disorder*, he said. How true that seemed.

A Chicago friend, Martha Bryant, a daughter of the judge I clerked for, called me, saying she could smell tear gas from her parents' apartment on the North Side. I felt as if I should be there. I called everyone I could think of to find out what was going on. One of them was Marcus Raskin, a fellow student at the University of Chicago Law School, who had worked in the Kennedy White House. A delegate to the convention, he led a progressive think tank in Washington called the Institute for Policy Studies.

"Come see it for yourself," he said, in response to my many questions.

That was all the encouragement I needed; I got on a plane the next day.

The events around the convention underscored for me the discrepancies between the order and control of the system and the free-wheeling, free-thinking disorder of the Movement. I was angry about the state of the world and the complete and utter inadequacy of either political party to deal with it. On one end of the political spectrum, the Democrats were deeply divided between Vice President Hubert Humphrey, the status quo candidate, and Eugene McCarthy, the candidate of peace. On the Republican side was Richard Nixon, or worse, George Wallace, who was saying "segregation now, segregation forever." While not thinking consciously about getting involved, I was subconsciously rising to it.

In Chicago on the last day of the convention, I arrived in time for a post-event meeting of some 600 disgruntled delegates. The topic at hand was how to get Eugene McCarthy, who'd lost the party nomination, to run as an independent presidential candidate. Whether or not he would run, it was clear from the conviction of those in the audience that there was momentum for something big.

Perhaps more important than our collective enthusiasm was the money we had in the bank. Stewart Mott, whose father was a co-founder of General Motors, was a major contributor. His ardent support of progressive causes was interpreted by many as a response to his father's regressive politics, as if it were his life mission to serve as a counterbalance. The other supporter was Fiona Field Rust, the great-granddaughter of Marshall Field, the department store magnate, who also seemed determined to defy her ancestors by participating in the Movement, albeit with less noise than Stewart Mott. Looking back, I don't see that either was a model for me. It didn't occur to me then that I might eventually do something similar with the inheritance that would come to me over time.

As discussion unfolded on the creation of a steering committee, I sat in the audience, quiet but attentive. The committee tried to develop a strategy for Senator McCarthy's independent candidacy. As I hadn't been a delegate, I didn't even attempt to participate. I was surprised to hear an unfamiliar voice nominating me to the committee. To this day, I have no idea who it was. But I did not object. I had reached a point where I questioned all the rules, customs, and expectations that governed my life. The Movement, in all its exhilaration, offered the perfect environment for my own rebellion.

As Americans grappled with the events in Chicago, McCarthy left for Europe, making it clear he would not run. A few weeks later, when the steering committee met in Washington, we no longer had a candidate, but we did have the money, some of which had been spent already to get ballot slots in six different states. Right there, we decided to see what we could make of what we had. The New Party was formed.

With a collared shirt covered in red, white, and blue peace symbols as a mainstay of my wardrobe, I volunteered as the New Party's national director. We operated out of a meager office near

Vermont and L streets, with a few desks and phone lines, and a handful of staff members who were either volunteer or grossly underpaid. We did, however, have a mimeograph machine, the essential technology of the 1960s protest movement. Marcus and other academics from the Institute for Policy Studies formed the brain trust of the party.

We knew that we weren't going to get the Republicans or Democrats to change, but we wanted to express points of view that were nowhere to be found in the political arena. We had a few "names" among our ranks, including Dr. Benjamin Spock, whose baby book was probably the second most read publication in America after the Bible, and Gore Vidal, who was an influential if not quite so popular author. They added to the chatter about the New Party, if in fact there was any talk in the first place.

For a very brief time, I truly believed that we might generate enough support for an entirely new political entity. Unlike the Republican and Democratic parties, it would represent honesty and integrity, and concern itself with creating an equal playing field for all citizens. That's what I wanted of the New Party. That's what a lot of people hoped for in that political moment.

Without McCarthy as a candidate, the leadership threw its support behind Dick Gregory, a well-known civil rights activist who was running for the Freedom and Peace Party, a splinter group of the Peace and Freedom Party, which had Black Panther Eldridge Cleaver as its candidate. Perhaps the first African-American comedian to play white clubs, Dick's activism was characterized by hilarious, biting commentary on race relations. He wrote a best-selling autobiography called *Nigger*, and protested the Vietnam War with a two-year juice fast. Along with buttons and other materials, the campaign handed out fake dollar bills replacing George Washington with a picture of Dick. With a beard, black bowler hat, and white shirt buttoned to the neck, he looked a bit like an itinerant preacher from the Reconstruction era. The government banned the bills, as they actually worked in change machines. For a few summers, Dick brought his wife and several children to vacation with the kids and me at Lakeside, where he took me on morning runs and persuaded me to try a vegetarian diet. Dick and I, like many activists, were united by our adversaries in that righteous attitude of *us versus them*.

The "them" included the FBI, whose agents spent an unreasonable amount of time watching us. From our offices, we often saw a car parked below, with somebody in it, obviously conducting surveillance.

One day, Rennie Davis showed up for a meeting. He was an organizer for the most visible and influential of the movement protest groups, Students for a Democratic Society, and later, one of the Chicago Seven. Dressed in jeans and plain, apolitical shirts, with a curly tousle of hair, he did not fit my image of a radical. I recall our conversation:

"I'm being followed," he said to me, unalarmed, when I greeted him at the door.

"How do you know?" I asked.

"Just have a look," he said, nodding toward the window. Peeking nonchalantly at the street, I saw the sedan in question.

After a short meeting, Rennie went out the back and down eight flights of stairs to a rear exit.

About an hour passed before a very clean-cut guy came up to the office, trying desperately not to look like an agent.

"Hey, is Rennie here?" he asked.

"Rennie? Uh, Rennie who?" I responded.

"Rennie Davis," he said.

"No, there's nobody named Rennie Davis here," I answered. "Would you like to leave a message in case he comes in?"

"No, that's ok," he said, and left.

I waited until the agent was out the door before I let myself smile.

Within the span of three years, from 1965 to 1968, everything in my life changed. I went from being a model husband and father to a divorcé; from a Republican to a very left-wing Democrat; and from a timid person to someone on the verge of taking charge of his life. I was far from having a consciousness of gay equality, but I was beginning to sense my own power, starting to feel good about myself, and realizing that even as one lone soul, I had something to offer the world.

When Richard Nixon won the presidency in 1968, I had to face the reality that the New Party was over. With all the money spent, its leadership scattered soon after the elections.

I went back to New York and moved into a skinny townhouse at 190 Spring Street in Soho, which was still like any other Italian neighborhood in the city, with grandmothers keeping watch from their windows and laundry strung out to dry.

While the Movement against the war raged, the gay rights movement revved up. I kept close tabs on the episodes of resistance, including the public outcry in San Francisco in 1965 following a raid on a New Year's Eve drag ball, and the annual picketing of Independence Hall in Philadelphia, which started that same year. But no event succeeded in generating the political energy that came on June 28, 1969, when the Stonewall Riots began in Greenwich Village.

I was not among the hundreds of thousands of people who claim to have been at the Stonewall Inn that night, or in the angry street protests that took place the subsequent night. I was with my kids at Lakeside, unaware of what happened.

Out of Stonewall, an organization formed called the Gay
Liberation Front, which was intended to promote acceptance of
homosexuality. Yet in very short order, internecine warfare erupted
among the activists, and a group called the Gay Activists Alliance
splintered from GLF. We went from having no political organization
to having two, both of which seemed driven to prove the other one bad
and wrong. It was unproductive. It was not the kind of energy that
drew me.

A forerunner of a gay community center, the Gay Activists
Alliance held dances in a former city fire house two blocks away
from my home on Spring Street. I dropped by once, warily, and was
amazed. It was the first time that I saw gay people getting together
openly in public, without feeling they had to watch their backs. The
newfound openness gave me a little bit of hope that the world was
changing for the better.

Even so, I was still preoccupied with my own stuff, which
included trying to manage my relationships with my children.

I had been a good parent, but once Alice and I divorced and
lived in different places, my parenting became diluted. I'd like to
blame it all on geography but it wasn't just that. I was confused
and torn between my role as a father and my desire to explore. My
agenda did not always include being a parent. I don't know whether
I could've been a good father then; I was trying to survive and make
some sense of my own life. My kids clearly wanted my affection,
and I wanted to give it to them. When we were together, I did. Every
summer, we spent several weeks together visiting my mother in Los
Angeles and hanging out at Lakeside, and I tried to spend time with
them individually during the school year. But I wasn't there for them
on a daily basis, and when we weren't together, my guess is that they
felt a huge separation.

I never hid my sexuality from them, but also never flaunted it. So far as the kids knew, I had boyfriends and I had girlfriends. None of them were presented in a romantic or sexual context. The summer before I moved to New York, Bob was around Lakeside a lot. One day, Anne, who was about ten at the time, asked me about him. I was lying on a towel, at the water's edge, reading, when she plunked down beside me.

"Daddy, do you love Bob?" she asked, seemingly in innocence.

"Yeah," I said, unsure of where she was going.

"Well, why don't you marry him then?" she replied, with the earnestness of a precocious kid.

I answered her, saying something like, I don't love him in that way, or, only boys and girls get married. Whatever it was, I tried to prevent the conversation from going further. She may have perceived that this guy was special in my life—kids are extremely observant—but I don't think she yet had the experience to understand what our relationship was. I wasn't ready to explain it to her either.

As the kids matured, I realized that I couldn't erase the fallout of the divorce, but I could give them some basic understanding of who I was. There were so many things my parents never discussed with me, or explained to me, and I didn't want it to be that way with my children, at least on this issue.

About the time that Stonewall took place in 1969, I walked along the lake with Alison, who was then thirteen. She was old enough to know what was going on. I tried to explain that one can feel affection for somebody else, whether the person is a man or a woman, and that I happened to feel affection for other men.

Whatever she might have felt inside, Alison gave me a one-word response: "Cool." It seemed to be a heartfelt reply. She, like her siblings, never stopped loving me.

I assumed that Alison would report our conversation to Anne, and that little by little the news would spread in similar fashion to Diz, Jimmy, and Sarah. Even so, I spoke to each of them individually, over time, when they seemed ready to understand.

In fall of 1969, still hopeful about what the Movement might achieve, I went to several major protests. In October, Diz came with me to one of the largest demonstrations in Washington, D.C.

She was just ten, but not scared of the endless crowd on the Mall or the shouting of protesters. Always the observer in the family, she seemed to make a mental note of every detail. She was wide-eyed when we arrived at the White House and found it surrounded by school buses parked bumper to bumper intentionally so that protesters could not get close. To Diz, it might have appeared that every eighth grade class in the country was on a field trip to Washington, but in reality, the Nixon Administration was purposefully cutting itself off from the people.

The following month, in November 1969, I drove through the Mississippi Delta, which was closer to a developing country than anything I had seen up to that point in my life. I was there with my friend Jane, a civil rights worker whom I had met in Washington. She spent a great deal of time working in Mississippi. She was black, but so light-skinned that most people didn't realize it. In the segregated south, her color afforded her access, and white folks did not disturb her the way they might have if they had known her racial classification. We drove around in a rented car that seemed to me to be the only one in Mississippi without a gun rack. Jane told me all kinds of stories about having been run off the road, or threatened in some way by people dead-set on preserving the status quo. Against the delightful character of the little towns we saw on the drive, her stories sounded out of place, but I knew that they were true.

Jane took me to a place called Edwards, not too far from the Mighty River. It could not have had more than one thousand residents. Along the main street, we passed lovely antebellum homes, brick storefronts, and wooden churches, the kind you find in any small southern town. Within a few blocks of the center, we reached some unmarked border, delimited by a change in the quality of the road. Pavement gave way to dirt, and uncovered drainage ditches ran along the road as if the earth had split from too much strain. The buildings transformed to shacks of corrugated metal, wood, and whatever else could be strung together to create a shelter. It was obvious that we were in the black part of town.

Jane knew families living there. As we pulled into a driveway to say hello, a small crowd of kids appeared. A few of them had strangely wide eyes and bloated bellies, sure signs of malnutrition. Inside, the shack was pleasant and clean, belying the financial insecurity of the family living there. We chatted with the adults and heard about tenant farming and debt to the landowners that they could never pay off. They were stuck without any way to improve their circumstances.

I couldn't help but draw comparisons between Edwards and the small town I knew best, Austin.

As early as 1950, 80 percent of the residents in Austin owned their own homes. This was because Hormel, which probably employed more than half the town's work force, offered profit-sharing and other concrete benefits that enabled people to prosper. True, the residents of Austin were dependent on Hormel, but when it succeeded, everybody benefited. In Edwards, the system was there to keep people down. I could see no visible sign of financial concern, or even humanity, between owner and tenant.

My trip to Mississippi wasn't my first glimpse of poverty in America, but I was nonetheless overwhelmed by what I saw. Sitting in that little shack, I tried to block out images of the estate where I grew up.

Once back in the car with Jane, I thought about my obligation to the families I had just met. My immediate thought was that I wanted people all across the country to know about them, and to be aware of their hunger, living conditions, and lack of economic opportunity. My parents raised me with a sense that privilege carries with it responsibility, but it was not until visiting Edwards that I started to recognize what they meant. In those few hours, I realized that I wanted to play a role in exposing social inequities.

Chapter Ten

POLITICAL TOURIST

On the clear afternoon of March 7, 1970, I watched a total eclipse of the sun in Washington Square Park, amid hundreds of random people who lazed around there regularly, whether or not a celestial event was on the calendar.

When the moon passed in front of the sun, squirrels scooted up tree trunks, and birds roosted, thinking that night was falling. The human beings were divided between those looking up at the sky in awe, and those who carried on, seemingly oblivious to the sudden darkness. It would be nice to say, "And when the moon passed, and the sun emerged again, I could see my life clearly…" but of course that would be bullshit.

Truth told, I was feeling alarmed. The day before, a radical group called the Weathermen accidentally set off an explosion just a few blocks from the park in a townhouse on West 11th Street in Greenwich Village. Three members of the group were killed; another two, stripped naked by the force of the explosion, fled the burning house with minor injuries. According to the FBI, Weathermen operatives used the house to make bombs that they planted in post offices and government buildings around the country. I wasn't an advocate of violence in any form and didn't want to believe that the Weathermen intended violence and destruction. Surely, crazy people within our society were capable of such things, but attributing a bomb-making operation to an educated, sophisticated group of people interested in correcting injustice seemed suggestive of a paranoid government. But there had been a huge blast, and it was not caused by an overheating boiler.

Within weeks of the explosion, I got a call from the FBI.

A quietly insistent man on the phone informed me that agents had found my name and number in a house in Washington, in a phone log kept by a member of Students for a Democratic Society. The log indicated that someone called me on Halloween night, 1969. Vague about the details, he wavered between tones of chumminess and menace. "Would you be willing to meet with us? We just want to check this story out and put it to rest," he said. "We would be happy to come by your house anytime it's convenient."

I was slightly disoriented, the way you are when you randomly encounter an acquaintance from one city in another and can't remember his or her name. Who could have possibly called me from D.C.? And from an SDS house? Nothing came up for me. I wracked my brain, trying to recall that Halloween.

Though suspicious, I decided that refusing the meeting would only add to the FBI's interest.

"I'll meet with you, but I prefer to come to your offices," I said. We agreed upon a time and he gave me the address.

Shortly after, that particular evening came back to me. I had seven people for dinner in my Spring Street apartment, at which I served a chicken dish cooked in a pumpkin shell. It was so unforgettably delicious that I never made it again—it could never be as good. But I had no phone call from D.C. and no recollection that anyone else had received one either.

The morning of the FBI meeting, I was a little nervous. I chose a plain white oxford over my shirt with the peace symbols. I briefly considered a suit and tie, but thought that might be going overboard. I wondered exactly when the FBI put me on their watch list. Perhaps they had seen me in the audience at the Chicago Seven trial the year before.

The FBI offices were on East 69th Street in a high-rise building. The entrance featured a big display of the wonders of FBI history, including the arrest of Al Capone and the killing of John Dillinger. Two white, clean-shaven agents met me in the reception area and took me to a large cubicle, where they invited me to take a seat at a table. One agent sat opposite me while the other paced behind me. This is how I remember the conversation:

They asked again about the phone call from the SDS house in Washington.

"It seems to me that I was home that night, and that I may even have had a dinner party," I said. "I don't remember any phone call."

It was the truth.

"Well, you must have some contacts, based on what you've done during the last year in Washington," the seated agent said.

"Yeah, you must know some important people," the pacer said, in a weaselly sort of way.

"Yes, I know some people," I replied, realizing instantly where they were going.

The phone call story was a ruse to ask for my cooperation. They wanted me to spy for them.

"It would be very helpful for us if we knew what some of those people were up to, if we knew what transpired at their meetings," the seated agent said.

"Oh, you mean you want me to be an informer?" I asked.

"Oh no, we didn't say that, we just wondered if you'd be willing to go to some of the meetings and let us know who attended, what they said," he said.

"Yeah, you want me to be an informer," I replied. "Well, the truth is that I know a few people distantly but I don't have contact with anyone you're looking for."

"Well, you may not know who you know," the pacing agent insisted, with an air of desperation.

A bomb factory had exploded on their turf, and they were crazed over the possibility that there might be others. I got the feeling that they were grasping at any possible straw to figure out what was going on in the counterculture. For all they knew, Bob Dylan might have been involved. He did have that line in "Subterranean Homesick Blues": "You don't have to be a weatherman to know which way the wind blows…" The conversation continued:

"Besides, I would not want to work for an organization that practices discrimination," I said.

"What do you mean? We have black employees," the seated agent replied.

"I was referring to gay people. How many gay FBI agents are there?" I asked.

Neither man responded. My question was enough to end the meeting.

I left, making it clear that I had nothing to offer them, and went home. I never heard from the agents again.

Disgusted as I was by my FBI encounter, the Weathermen incident had contributed to my ebbing enthusiasm toward the Movement.

When I first got involved, everything seemed black and white, us versus them. Yet despite the relentless wave of public protests, the poetic power of its music, and its occasional moments of inspired leadership, the Movement wasn't making much progress. An incredible number of mind-boggling events had taken place, just about everything short of another nuclear bomb, and the ship of state sailed right on. Was the Establishment just too big, or as Andrew

Kopkind put it, "pervasive and ubiquitous?" Or was the Movement itself—this wonderful, dynamic force, which was supposed to promote the general welfare—really just a small cabal building its own empire?

Everywhere I looked it seemed that people at the top were making noise, looking for attention and power, for the sake of attention and power. Beneath all the daisies and idealism, the Movement was like any other structure of the time—full of racism, sexism, and homophobia. Bayard Rustin, for example, was a phenomenal thinker and organizer who led the planning of the march that landed Martin Luther King, Jr., on the steps of the Lincoln Memorial for his *I Have a Dream* speech. But Bayard got limited credit for the things he did because he was a gay man. I was having trouble reconciling what the Movement claimed to be, and what it was in reality. The hypocrisy was inescapable.

Just a few weeks after the eclipse, an out-of-the-blue experience helped me to resolve my political restlessness.

It started with a phone call from Thomas with a proposal for a great adventure. He had signed on to a seven-country tour of Asia, primarily because the trip included tickets to Expo '70, the World's Fair, in Osaka.

We became fans of the worlds' fairs at an early age: my parents took all three of us to the fair in New York in 1940. Growing up with a grandfather whose favorite business mantra was *Innovate, Don't Imitate*, we couldn't help but love the ingenuity on display.

When a space on the Asia trip came open at the very last minute, Thomas thought of me, knowing that I could drop everything and go. Tall and shaggy at ages thirty-seven and forty, we were sure to stand out amid the gaggle of retired teachers on the tour, but the package was cheap and the World's Fair tickets were nearly impossible to get otherwise.

The fair in Osaka was like most anything that happened on an international scale between 1946 and 1990: an impressive demonstration of Cold War tension. The question seemed to be: *Who's Got the Biggest Pavilion?* The United States had a major space exhibition that included a moon rock, and relatively small countries in the Soviet sphere had disproportionately significant displays, including Czechoslovakia, which featured a 13-ton glass sculpture entitled, "The River of Life." I was struck by how technologically superior Japan seemed with its high resolution televisions and bullet trains.

The most memorable events, however, happened at the very end of the journey, when we arrived in Bangkok.

Bangkok, in May 1970, was not exactly a place to seek refuge from the world's troubles.

It was a huge, sprawling city, busy and polluted. And full of hustlers. It was a destination for U.S. soldiers on leave from Vietnam, and the city and its entrepreneurs had risen to the occasion with endless numbers of nightclubs, "massage" parlors, and other places of entertainment. If you wanted sex, heterosexual or homosexual, or drugs, or even a plate of spaghetti the way your mother made it, someone hustled to provide it for you.

The GIs were out of uniform but you knew them by their haircuts. There were two kinds of kids there, and I do mean kids: those from a cornfield and those from the ghetto. On our first night, Thomas and I were in a nightclub surveying the huge dance floor from the bar when a soldier walked toward me. In contrast to his buzz cut, my wavy brown hair was almost to my shoulders, like a long Prince Valiant. I might have been wearing my favorite shirt, a white, billowy cotton tunic that reached my thighs. As the guy approached, I looked the other way, trying to ignore him. But he came right up to me.

"Hey, you look familiar," he said, with puppy-like enthusiasm. "It's nice to see somebody looking so free, at least free from the military."

I had a barely resistable urge to shout at him: *Why are you taking part in the massacres in Vietnam?*

Instead, I shrugged and mumbled, "Yeah, sure, free…"

He looked at me a moment, furrowed his brow in confusion, and then walked away.

I had no desire to carry on a conversation or connect with him in any way. As far as I was concerned, he was a living, breathing instrument of war. I did not recognize the fact that he, like many of the troops—in fact, most of them, maybe even all of them—did not want to be in Vietnam. They were drafted. My favor was with people who avoided the draft, those who went to Canada, or to jail.

Within moments, I looked back at my exchange with the soldier with shame. He probably had had some horrible, traumatic experiences, and yearned for the day when he could let his hair grow. Yet in that moment, I did not see him as an individual, or acknowledge the humanity in him.

The next day, a Bangkok newspaper advertised a new Air France flight to Siem Reap, Cambodia, the gateway to Angkor Wat. I showed the ad to Thomas, knowing full well that between the photo opportunities at ancient temples and the respite from our slow-moving fellow travelers, he would wrestle me for the last seat on the plane.

Several weeks before, Prime Minister Lon Nol and the National Assembly, in a peaceful but illegitimate maneuver, had deposed the king, Sihanouk, and declared Cambodia a republic. We knew about the coup before leaving the United States. Yet from what we could gather, life there was as it had been before the turnover. If not, we surmised, Air France would not have opened the new route.

Our flight the next day was unremarkable, which is always positive commentary when it comes to air travel. Taxiing down the runway, I could see from our plane that the aircraft of the national carrier had on their fuselages a big smear of paint, followed by the off-center words: *Air Camboge*. The word *Royal* had been erased. Throughout the trip, we saw similarly conspicuous blobs of ink or paint, just about the only overt sign of the transition.

In the shed-sized terminal, we were greeted cordially in English and French by immigration officials, even though we did not have the required entry visas. In the wake of the coup, the officials were so glad to see any tourists that they waived the visas and sent us on our way.

We dropped our bags at our dingy hotel before heading to Angkor Wat for the afternoon and early evening. At first sight of the temple complex, Thomas began snapping away. Scaling walls and peering into crevices, he captured incredible images of stone gods in fading light, lichen-covered walls, and reflections in the temple's double moat. I walked around in awe, as did the only other visitors we saw: a handful of Buddhist monks in saffron-colored robes. In the light of dusk, the Wat, with its craggy towers, looked a bit eerie. But rising as it did from a huge clearing in an otherwise voracious jungle, it had a certain magic and majesty.

The next day, before we were to fly back to Bangkok, Thomas and I took a jaunt to the fishing villages on Tonlé Sap, an enormous puddle of a lake that quintuples in size during the monsoon season. We traveled there in motorized bicycle cabs that looked like rickshaws but sounded like lawn mowers. As we zipped along in our individual cabs, we each shot shaky photos of the other. We toured the lake by boat, admiring the brilliantly adapted lifestyle of the people, who built their houses on stilts to accommodate the rising and falling waters.

Back in our bike cabs, the air blasting pleasantly in my face, I was in the state of bliss that comes from seeing with your own eyes something spectacular and unimagined. My euphoria slipped away as I became aware that the scene on the road was markedly different than it had been that morning. The thoroughfare for scooters, bicycles, water buffalo, and the occasional car had become an artery for military transport vehicles.

Troops were moving into the area.

Our cab drivers showed no sign of nervousness, but they raced to the hotel. As we sped past the lumbering trucks brimming with troops, I could find no markings on the uniforms, nor flags on the vehicles. I had no idea whether they were government or Khmer Rouge. It sure seemed a good time to leave.

At the hotel, Thomas and I gathered our bags in haste and found a taxi. We saw no military presence along the road, but at the terminal, soldiers surrounded our car. They trained their automatic weapons on us. A soldier shouted in Khmer and used the tip of his gun to motion us out of the vehicle. We looked pretty grubby, and I wasn't sure whether that was a good thing. We deduced that he wanted to see our passports and tickets, and turned them over. I get nervous any time someone else has his or her hands on my passport, but I was not nearly as frightened as I would have been if I had known what had prompted the uproar. While his cohorts remained frozen with their guns in our faces, the soldier methodically scanned each page of our documents. I remembered that we didn't have entry visas. This could be trouble, I feared.

After a seemingly eternal silence, he handed each of us a passport, as if he were dealing cards, and made a sweeping motion with his gun and his head toward the plane on the tarmac.

I looked at Thomas, as if to say *phew*! We moved toward the plane, a soldier on each side, stepping off with such a sense of

urgency that eventually all four of us broke into a trot. Thomas and I
dashed up the staircase and into any seats we could find. Breathless,
sweaty, and disoriented, I don't remember even showing our tickets
at the door.

I sat on the plane, in silence, wondering what on earth had just
happened.

The previous day had been mesmerizing. I had been absorbed
by Angkor Wat and ruminations on the community and culture that
had constructed it 800 years earlier with mysterious archeological
techniques before dwindling and leaving the temple and its
neighboring city to the vegetation. I loved the graceful quality of
daily life around Siem Reap and the lake, where people lived a very
basic life but without the outward expression of hopelessness or
despair that I had seen in Edwards, Mississippi. Cambodia felt like
an island of serenity in a universe full of chaos.

But in an instant, my illusion faded, as the island, too, was
consumed by chaos.

Back in the comfort of our Bangkok hotel that night, I got my hands on
an English-language newspaper and found out what had happened.

That day or the day before, President Nixon announced that U.S.
and South Vietnamese forces had launched a ground incursion into
Cambodia and confirmed that the United States had been conducting
an extensive, covert bombing campaign in eastern Cambodia for the
preceding twelve months.

I was furious. The Nixon Administration had repeatedly told the
American people that Cambodia and Laos were neutral territories.

The way I saw it, we had been lied to once again, by a president
who won the Oval Office with the claim that he had a secret plan to
end the war. People called Richard Milhous Nixon "Tricky Dick,"
a nickname I found too kind. To me, he was despicable. I couldn't

believe I ever voted for him. Unlike George Bush, who initiated the Iraq War, Nixon inherited Vietnam from Lyndon Johnson. But so far as I could see, he had no trouble perpetuating the systematic deception of the American people. We had no idea why we were fighting that war, and the Administration would or could never clarify our strategic interest.

I was not alone in my outrage over Cambodia; students at home demonstrated across college campuses, including Kent State, where Ohio National Guardsmen shot and killed four young people and wounded nine.

The newspaper story mentioned one final detail of Nixon's announcement, which was that Americans were banned from traveling to Cambodia.

That's when the meaning of the experience hit me. Thomas and I just happened to be in Cambodia at the precise moment of escalation. Within the space of forty-eight hours, a hearty welcome from immigration officials turned into a threatening goodbye from excitable soldiers who may have been as surprised by the turn of events as we were. We had unknowingly, perhaps naïvely, placed ourselves in a very dangerous situation. To this day, I wonder what the Cambodian soldier was thinking when he looked at our passports and saw the eagle and the gold letters of "United States of America." Perhaps my stringy hair, wilted in the humidity, made it clear that we were tourists and not military operatives. Perhaps he had orders to get all the foreigners out of the country, regardless of their country of origin. Perhaps he had no orders at all. Whatever it was, it was no small miracle that he let us go.

Looking out my hotel window, I felt extremely frustrated. Outside, U.S. soldiers on leave from Vietnam filled the streets, looking for some nightclub, some call girl (or boy), or a drug that would help them to forget the horrible things they had experienced in combat.

Several hundred miles away, Cambodians were being sucked into a conflict that would eventually claim more than a million lives. The reach of the U.S. government felt huge at that moment. Our government was everywhere.

I couldn't help but feel powerless, as I had so many times in recent years.

Our close call with the soldiers at the airport was disturbing, but then again, almost everything about the late 1960s and early 1970s was disturbing. The Establishment was too big to tear down. It couldn't be dismantled, and it didn't seem that the progressive movement was even chipping away at it. Apparently, it did no good to create new political parties, or camp out at the Washington Monument, or boycott grapes, as the union organizer Cesar Chavez encouraged us to do. Or at least, not enough good. I wanted to be angry with the leadership of the Movement, the way I was angry at Richard Nixon, but many of them had good intentions. Perhaps I was blinded by my own idealism. I went into the Movement thinking it was all wheat, when, in reality, it was like anything in life, wheat and chaff. My experiment with radical politics had reached its end.

In spite of my disillusionment, I was politicized for life, with a perspective and motivation that shaped everything I did after that. Whereas for so long I had perceived myself to be separated from everything going on around me, I felt wholly connected to my surroundings. I was drawn to the experiences of people directly and negatively affected by the system, such as those Cesar Chavez spoke for.

The thing I had learned, though, was that change had to come from inside the system. I was sure of it.

A year or so after the Asia trip, when an electrical fire ravaged my house on Spring Street, I took it as a sign from the universe that I should move on. In 1973, with the country's bicentennial approaching, I sold the house and moved to the Hawaiian island of Kauai. My intention was to write a series of essays on economic and cultural inequities, and other aspects of colonialism that would be overlooked in most of the 1976 celebrations.

With endless rainbows and air scented by plumeria and pikake, Kauai seemed like paradise on earth. My essay writing quickly stalled as I gravitated toward the various self-development and self-awareness experiments of the 1970s, including *est*, Erhard Seminar Training.

I became so dedicated to *est*, with its tidy formula for inner peace, that I persuaded many friends to take the seminars. I even recruited Alice and sent my kids to *est* teen camp. The kooky pillow-smashing exercises and restricted bathroom breaks aside, the seminars and lectures helped me find my own humanity and my innate caring for other people. *Est* led me to a point of self-acceptance. After years of self-loathing, I was able to say *I like myself just the way I am*—and really mean it.

I might have continued living happily in Hawaii, but on a 1975 trip to Minnesota for a Hormel Foods board meeting, I had a love-at-first-sight encounter that blossomed into a relationship. Larry Soule was blond and cute and funny. We spent one of our first days together walking through Minneapolis in a blinding snowstorm, oblivious to the weather. He was just starting out as a graphic artist, and San Francisco seemed an ideal place for him to find work. We decided to move there. It turned out to be perfect for me, too. Almost from the day we arrived, I found much to do.

My parents, Jay Hormel and Germaine Dubois Hormel, shortly after their wedding in 1922. They met and fell in love during World War I, when my father served in France, but when his duty ended in 1918, he returned alone to Austin. Four years later, without explanation, he went back to get her. They eloped in England.

My grandparents, George A. Hormel, left, and Lillian "Belle" Hormel, second from left, together with my parents. We sailed to Hawaii in 1939, where we visited Pearl Harbor and toured a submarine. Eight years old when the Japanese attacked two years later, I imagined terrible scenes of the ships sinking.

My mother had strong opinions about how we dressed, even as young boys. She loved to put us in knickers and jackets though no one in Austin, not even the golfers, wore knickers. Thomas is on the left, I am in the center, and Geordie is at right.

My mother in her mid 30s. Although born in a rural French village of six hundred people, she had the demeanor of a city girl when it came to her vivacious personality, love of high fashion, and risqué sense of humor.

My father invites Hollywood celebrities George Burns and Gracie Allen to sample SPAM to kick-off Hormel's sponsorship of their weekly radio show. Such famous people would never have visited Austin, Minnesota, a town of 18,000 people, were it not for Geo. A. Hormel & Co.

Dubbed "the Duke of Austin" by rival Oscar Mayer, my father was first in his industry to offer workers a guaranteed annual wage and profit-sharing. During World War II, he oversaw the tripling of production at Geo. A. Hormel & Co. and the global rise of SPAM.

My cousin Simone and my godmother's niece Gillian—two of five French and English children escaping the war in Europe—enjoyed some sun with me by our pool, about 1942. We had plenty of room for "refugees" at our house, a twenty-six bedroom, twenty-five bathroom estate on two hundred acres.

In 1951, my parents with Geordie, right, Thomas, center, and me, left. As the Korean War heated up, my father encouraged us to join the Coast Guard Reserves. He spent little time on the front during World War I, but he knew the horror of war and did not want us to experience it.

A picture of me when I was a freshman at Princeton University in 1950. Paralyzed by my attraction to men, I flunked out after one semester. I was in crisis but I didn't see it, and neither did anyone around me.

After my father died of a heart attack on August 30, 1954, thousands of people turned out for his memorial service. It was held at the Hormel Family Home, my grandparent's house, which they had donated to the Y.W.C.A. in 1929.
Photograph used with permission of Hormel Foods, LLC.

Thomas, Geordie, and me, left to right, the afternoon of my father's funeral.

Me dancing with Leslie Caron, Geordie's first wife, shortly after she filmed *An American in Paris*. She, like Thomas's first wife Simone Mustovoy, was a ballerina with Les Ballets de Paris. My mother was thrilled to have two French daughters-in-law.

Alice and I leaving the Charlottesville church where we married in June 1955. Attractive, witty, and engaging, Alice was easy to love. In the early days of our relationship, I was able to ignore my feelings toward men.

Me, reading to Diz, Jimmy, and Alison, left to right. Alice and I appeared
to have a perfect marriage, complete with five beautiful children and
an interesting circle of friends in the University of Chicago community.
Meanwhile, I was secretly pursuing assignations with men.

My mother and I at
Geordie's wedding to
Nancy Friedman in
1968. In those years,
my conventional life
changed in a dramatic
and disorienting way
as I divorced, moved
to New York City, and
started to live openly as
a gay man. Although I
never directly came out
to my mother, she fig-
ured it out over time—
surprise, surprise!

Geordie, Thomas, and me, left to right, at Thomas's studio in Los Angeles around 1969. We had no hesitation in adopting the styles of the 1960s and 1970s.

In 1970, Thomas and I took a tour of Asia that included a stop in Japan for the World's Fair in Osaka. Still taking incremental steps to come out of the closet, I saw this sign in Kyoto as the expression of how I wanted to live.

Moving to San Francisco in 1977, I was amazed by the feeling of freedom—the city seemed to have room for everyone. One evening, this collection of gay men gathered to read Plato's *Symposium* in its original form, where love refers to love among men.

I found a dear friend in Jerry Berg, right, a charismatic lawyer who helped San Francisco's LGBT community organize into a political constituency. Jerry's dedication to building a better world helped catalyze my own commitment to a life of activism and philanthropy. He died of AIDS in 1991.

Wary that an appearance at a gay political event might hurt his presidential bid, former Vice-President Walter Mondale, right, nonetheless agreed to speak at the Human Rights Campaign Fund's first dinner in 1982. I am pictured with him here at a different event.

Nancy Pelosi and I became friends through the Host Committee for the 1984 Democratic National Convention in San Francisco. When Nancy ran for Congress in 1987, I stirred controversy by supporting her over Harry Britt, a gay man, but I had no doubt that she would be effective in making AIDS a national policy issue.

At the 1992 Democratic National Convention in New York City, the same
year I served on the party's national platform committee, I was unabashed
about my hope for equality. My service on the committee was significant:
at that time, the Democratic Party rarely awarded high-level policy positions to openly gay people. My then partner Larry Soule is seated at left.

I joined many protests
during the Vietnam
war era, but none was
as gratifying as the
April 1993 March on
Washington for gay
rights. Hundreds of
thousands of people
took part, including
scores of gay and les-
bian service members
who risked their jobs
by going public.

In August 1993, at a California event, President Clinton admired my cheetah tie. I yanked it off and handed it to him as he laughed and promised to wear it within a week. Seven days later, newspapers published a photo of him enjoying his birthday cake, sporting the tie.

In 1996, as an alternate on the U.S. delegation, I addressed the United Nations General Assembly. After my unsuccessful Fiji bid, I pursued presidential appointments in hopes of keeping my name in consideration for what I really wanted: an ambassadorial post.

The reading room of the James C. Hormel Gay and Lesbian Center at the San Francisco Public Library, one of my proudest philanthropic ventures. Opponents of my nomination as ambassador to Luxembourg cited materials in the center in an attempt to associate me with pedophilia, even though some of the same items were in the Library of Congress. *Photo courtesy of the San Francisco Public Library.*

My seven-year fight to become the first openly gay U.S. ambassador provided ample fodder for editorial cartoonists. This spoof by Paul Berge ran in the *Seattle Gay News* in January 1999.

President Clinton gave me a recess appointment in June 1999. Here, Secretary of State Madeleine Albright swore me in as U.S. Ambassador to Luxembourg as my former partner Tim Wu held my father's bible. At that moment, I was the highest-ranked openly gay government official in American history.

I shared a laugh with President Clinton at an event. Between 1997 and 1999, when the Republican-controlled Senate refused to bring my Luxembourg nomination to a vote, the President remained steadfast in his support of me.

Nearly all of my family, including my ex-wife Alice, my brother Thomas, my children, and their spouses, along with my grandchildren, attended the swearing in. Their support was unwavering during my fight to become ambassador.

Me with my partner Michael Nguyen, a dancer, choreographer, and musician whom I met in 2006. Our relationship, which initially challenged my own ageist preconceptions, taught me once again that being true to myself brings great rewards; this time, in the form of unconditional love.

Chapter Eleven

A NEW LIFE

It wasn't the gay scene that lured Larry and me to San Francisco. It was the city itself: its culture and art, the natural beauty, the mild weather, and the easy hop to the mountains, the redwoods, or Los Angeles, where my mother seemed to be aging more quickly. Yet the first inkling of home did not come from enjoying the Golden Gate Bridge, red rust at sunset, or a fog sneaking in from the sea. It was the sight of men walking down Castro Street, holding hands.

I first laid eyes on San Francisco when I was an eighteen-year-old Coast Guard trainee living across the bay in Alameda, and from that first moment, it held an air of intrigue for me. There was something fresh and beautiful about it. Twenty-five years later, the decision to move there and set up housekeeping felt like a big adventure. Larry dreamed of a graphic design business, and while I had no particular expectations or plans, I felt sure that a completely new path awaited me.

We rented a handsome floor-through in a cozy neighborhood on the edge of Pacific Heights. The apartment had high ceilings and Victorian trim, with rooms flowing railroad style off of a single, long corridor. In a city renowned for its views, our large and lovely living room looked across Jackson Street to a schoolyard. The day we moved in, after hours of arranging furniture and unpacking boxes, our landlords, Pam and Richard, invited us upstairs for dinner with their two children. It was novel for Larry and me, as a couple, to be welcomed into the home of a straight family with kids.

We arrived in San Francisco at the tail end of the social revolution, when the Grateful Dead, Santana, Jefferson Starship, Boz Scaggs, and other local musicians fed the lingering afterglow of the Summer of Love. The energy of the city blew me away. It was full of people who had migrated from places that were hostile—if not outright threatening—and found refuge and personal freedom, which they may never have tasted before. No one seemed to dwell on the social, economic, racial, or sexual differences that meant so much everywhere else in the country, affording us new arrivals a sense of identity and a tentative feeling of acceptance.

Slavish about my newspapers, I subscribed to the *San Francisco Chronicle* right away, and got hooked on Armistead Maupin's "Tales of the City." A decade before the *New York Times* was bold enough to use the word *gay*, the *Chronicle* gave it prominence in Maupin's stories of 28 Barbary Lane, where a pot-growing landlady and gay, straight, and bisexual neighbors romped. Among the characters was the lovelorn Michael Tolliver, who, one February 14, made a Valentine's Day resolution to never refer to anyone as "butch" or "nelly" unless, of course, that was his or her real name. Maupin played with the lingo of the underground in a way that made its secrecy seem anachronistic.

Socially, the blue collar neighborhood of Eureka Valley was the place to go. Near a long-standing establishment coincidentally-named Gay Cleaners, bars, restaurants, and shops owned and operated by gay men and lesbians opened for business. The bars were recognizable and easy to find—a far cry from the underground days of only a decade or so earlier, when same-sex meeting places were scattered inconspicuously in various neighborhoods and owned by straight people who collaborated with the police on raids and overcharged for watered down drinks.

The dress code of the Castro in the 1970s ran the gambit from leather to macramé, flannel to satin, with lots of bare skin to be seen. It was relatively safe; people felt that they could go there without fear of harassment. That was not the case with Polk Street, the Castro's predecessor, where I found myself one night in the late 1960s with my friend Jerry Berg. As we wandered through the seedy area, checking out the gay locales, a young man tripped me as I walked by him. Regaining my footing, I turned toward him and glared. Before I could say a word, Jerry restrained me. He knew that if I responded to the taunt, a gang might emerge from the shadows and beat us to a pulp. That sort of menacing never went away entirely—in fact, even through the 1980s, gay men commonly carried whistles to summon help—but in general, Castro Street felt much safer.

Jerry's behavior that night was typical: he was a natural conciliator. I had met him years earlier, at Stanford, while recruiting for the University of Chicago Law School. A shade taller than me, with a buzz cut and penetrating, hazel eyes, he said hello in the courtyard of the school's sandstone Quad, instigating a deep conversation about law schools and U.S. politics. The exchange was academic, but the personal connection was magical and profound. He became an instant influence in my life.

In spring 1964, Jerry asked me to be a groomsman in his wedding to Janet, another striking Stanford student. Not long before the ceremony, we spent an evening together dissecting the commitment he was about to make. I knew that Jerry was gay, just as he knew that I was, but I was still so attached to the thinning reality of my marriage that I didn't try to talk him out of it. The ceremony took place in a Carmel church just a day or two after Sarah was born. Alice and Sarah were still in the hospital but I left for the wedding after asking Frank Gerlits to bring them home. When I returned, I suggested to Alice that Jerry be Sarah's godfather. Although hurt that I had left her in the hospital, she agreed.

Jerry and I stayed in touch over time and miles, even after he and Janet moved to Malawi, where he helped the government of the newly independent African country draft its constitution. No matter how long it had been, he and I picked up where we left off. Whenever something major happened, Jerry was one of the first people I thought to call. It was the same for him. He was the one who persuaded me to check out *est*.

By the time I arrived in San Francisco in 1977, Jerry was a highly-regarded lawyer, long-since divorced, with a head of thick, salt and pepper hair and a mustache. He had made a name for himself representing a young British citizen wrongly drafted by the U.S. government during the Vietnam War. After that, draft dodgers, people wrongfully arrested—basically anyone with a cause against the government—went to Jerry for help. He had a tremendous legal mind and a strong belief that a lawyer's role was to promote peace between his clients and their adversaries.

Jerry invited me one night to a black tie dinner at his home for twelve gay, male guests, who together read Plato's *Symposium* in its original version, the one in which the conversation about love refers to love between men. Through Jerry I met an unbelievable number of smart, dynamic people, a new generation of western pioneers trying to build a community out of the 100,000 or so gay refugees living in the Bay Area.

One of them was a prominent magazine publisher named David Goodstein, a short, overweight, and arrogant man who nonetheless had unparalleled insights and ideas for the gay community.

Known for turning *The Advocate* from what was essentially a newsletter into a profitable national gay magazine, David had been a successful banker, sought after for his management innovations, up until the day that Wells Fargo discovered his sexuality, demoted him, and eventually fired him. David was also an *est*hole, as we used to say, and so opinionated that he often tried to impose his views on others. Determined to help build a strong, healthy gay community, he didn't hesitate to put his own money on the line to make that happen. He funded and led the creation of an *est*-like program specifically for gay people.

The Advocate Experience was much more user-friendly than *est*, thanks to Rob Eichberg, a bright and assertive psychologist from Los Angeles whom David hired to design and facilitate the weekend-long programs. Ever soul-searching, I took part in the first official Advocate Experience, held at a union hall. I was relieved to discover that the program did not mimic the *est* boot camp element, or the sometimes-judgmental tone used by the *est* trainers to move people out of their comfort zones. The Advocate Experience was for people who had been judged too often. Still, there were strict ground rules about showing up on time and following basic directions for maintaining order. The dynamic was like that of a classroom in which the teacher calls whispering students to the front of the class to share their chatter, with the purpose of creating an absolutely safe space that allowed people to participate without feeling exposed.

The forty or so participants, nearly all of them men, did a series of exercises intended to foster recognition and acceptance of their self-worth. Perhaps most emotional was the task of writing a letter to one's parents, living or not, coming out to them. Even for those few who had already come out to their parents, the act of writing helped unleash important emotions. We were encouraged to share the letter in a small group, which most of us did, catalyzing sobs and floods of tears. On Sunday evening, as the session adjourned, we were left to decide whether or not to send our letter. The weekend concluded with the whole group speaking about their experiences. As if the tears had succeeded in washing away their pain, at least for that moment, the feeling in the room was one of elation. I left the union hall with a sense of relief, a desire to be kinder and gentler to myself and others, and a feeling of community.

I never sent my letter. I was afraid it might confuse Mamma or otherwise undo the mutual understanding we had achieved over the years. Bedridden most days, her mind cloudy, her condition provided an easy excuse. At the same time, she was of a different generation and not inclined to undertake extensive contemplation of what it meant to be gay. A few years after I came out to my brothers, I gave Mamma a book of poignant biographies of gay men in New York City called *Familiar Faces, Hidden Lives* by Howard Brown. She was disdainful at first, questioning why she should bother to read it, but she later admitted that the ranging stories of loneliness and abandonment, first love and self-discovery, had moved her. From then on, I never felt the need to discuss my sexuality with her. In later years, her acceptance of me was evident in her acceptance of Larry, whom she called occasionally just to chat. In her own way, she made it clear that she loved me for who I was. And I loved her for who she was.

My personal situation aside, the Advocate Experience session convinced me that coming out was the single most important thing a gay person could do to affirm his or her integrity.[1]

Shortly thereafter, David asked me to serve as president of the Advocate Research and Education Fund, a nonprofit set up to run the Experience. I didn't hesitate. I was ready to be part of things again. I worked briefly with the fund before agreeing to run the San Francisco office of the Experience, where my responsibilities

---

[1]That was the outcome sought by Rob, who later founded *National Coming Out Day.*

amounted to managing a troop of volunteers, coordinating with the New York and Los Angeles offices, and ensuring that thirty-two to 120 bodies filled the chairs every weekend.

Over the next several months, I learned about gay people. That may sound funny, but it was the first time I had been exposed to gay people on such a scale. New York had a *live and let live* atmosphere, but the community there was subsumed by the mammoth city. Hawaii had a gay-friendly environment (at least up until the early 1990s, when the Mormon Church started spending its money to prevent the state from being the first to allow same-sex marriage) but there weren't many gay people around. San Francisco offered a gay-friendly atmosphere that was *also* heavily populated by gay people.

Participants in the Experience voluntarily filled out a question-naire that captured what was going on in their lives. I learned of military veterans simultaneously reckoning with their sexuality and their actions in Vietnam. I met a traumatized man whose recently deceased father concealed his own homosexuality all his life, even after the son came out to him. I met a transgender woman born male on a Minnesota farm whose botched sex-change operation left her in chronic pain and self-doubt. People had their stories, and every one of them reflected the personal injury caused by a society that refused to accept us.

Every time I sat in on an Experience session, I thought of someone who would be very interested in participating: Alice.

For her doctoral dissertation, Alice studied and wrote about attitudes toward homosexuality in the Episcopal Church, developing an intimate understanding of gay and lesbian people. Her work was one of many things that encouraged our abiding love and respect to re-emerge. Alice accepted my invitation to a session, bringing along her new love, Jim Turner, another Charlottesville native who was soon to become her husband.

I was comfortable with Jim immediately. An obstetrician who was part of a University of Virginia medical team working on sex change operations, Jim had helped make educational films for high school students, including one called *Rolling With Love* about two gay tennis balls. He and Alice fit right in with the small crowd at the Experience seminar. They left as teary-eyed and emotional as every other participant.

In the end, several thousand people went through the Advocate Experience, and David Goodstein succeeded in mustering a small army for the cause.

The year I moved to San Francisco, Anita Bryant, a Miss America runner-up and Florida orange juice spokeswoman, led a successful effort to overturn a Miami-Dade County ordinance protecting gay people from discrimination. I, like much of the nation, watched her "Save Our Children" campaign, fully aware that she would embolden zealots in other parts of the country to launch their own assaults. As a singer and entertainer, Anita Bryant's stock in trade was a good girl persona grounded in Christian evangelism. She published a cookbook called *Bless This Food: The Anita Bryant Family Cookbook*, which mixed Christian prayers and musings with frequent mentions of Florida orange juice.

Shortly after Bryant's win, a California acolyte, State Senator John Briggs of Orange County, declared war on gay civil rights. He proposed a state ballot initiative known as Proposition 6, which set out to bar gay people from teaching in California's schools.

Prop 6 called on the state Department of Education to take on a function akin to a secret police, gravely violating individual privacy. It was extremely threatening.

I started thinking one day, *Wouldn't it be fascinating if all people who were gay woke up green one morning so that they couldn't hide anymore?* You'd walk out the door and the cop on the beat would be green. The maitre d' at your favorite restaurant would be green. You'd go into your bank and the teller would be green, and then you'd see the vice president in charge of loans, and he or she would be green. Would John Briggs find out that his favorite high school teacher was green? What would he say then? The crazy notion behind Prop 6 was that gay people wanted to recruit young children, which San Francisco Supervisor Harvey Milk turned into a big joke, starting his speeches with, "I'm Harvey Milk, and I'm here to recruit you." To me the biggest joke of all was, when are these heterosexual couples going to stop producing gay people? After all, that's where we come from.

In early 1978, I went to a Prop 6 fundraising dinner in my neighborhood at the home of an investment banker named Lou Hermes, whom I had met through Jerry. The idea for the dinner came from Lou, Jerry, David Goodstein, a textbook publisher named Bob Sass, and several close friends who commiserated together one weekend in the wake of Anita Bryant's victory. The guest list included people who could afford to contribute $1,000. My Hawaii-inspired wardrobe did not include the requisite jacket and tie, so I showed up that evening in borrowed clothes to meet a doctor, a lawyer, an importer, a real estate investor, an advertising CEO, and a resort owner, among many other accomplished guests.

As we finished a succulent meal, one of the hosts, Bob Hunter, pulled closed the pocket doors separating the dining area from the paneled living room, with its dramatic view of the Golden Gate Bridge, as if to say, okay, it's time to get down to business. In 1978, $1,000 was a huge donation, even for that successful crowd. As the hosts launched into the "ask," a chilly reluctance arose. It had nothing to do with the amount of money. The problem was that several of the men, still closeted at work and even with their families, were terrified of being connected publicly to the fight against Prop 6.

As the dinner guests realized that writing their name on a check symbolized another major step in coming out, the conversation became very emotional. By the end of the evening, every guest found his courage, resulting in a $22,500 contribution to an emerging statewide campaign called "No on 6." To me, the individual acts were a measure of the growing strength of our community.

Briggs' initiative represented a major erosion of Californians' civil rights. Despite this, our "No on 6" poll showed that as many as 70 percent planned to vote for the measure. Even though we had several months to organize and educate, Prop 6 seemed a sure thing. The idea of defeating it was audacious, to say the least, particularly given the lack of cohesion among the burgeoning gay political groups in California.

Ever since Election Day 1961, when an opera-singing drag queen named José Sarria ran for city office on a whim and got 6,000 votes, gay people in San Francisco knew that they had some muscle to exercise. Not long after that election, Sarria and others formed the Society for Individual Rights, or SIR, and began organizing the base that eventually made Harvey Milk San Francisco's first openly gay elected official and the second in the nation.[2] In subsequent years, several other groups popped up, including the Stonewall Democratic Club and the Alice B. Toklas Democratic Club, which was created in 1971 by Jim Foster. (A year later, Jim became the first gay person, along with New York lesbian activist Madeline Davis, to address a national political convention, speaking to the Democratic Convention

---

[2]The first was Elaine Noble, elected to the Massachusetts State Legislature in 1974.

in the wee hours, presumably when America was safely sleeping.) A friend of mine said once that the only thing the gay Democratic clubs could accomplish was adjournment, and while Jim and others were among the finest minds in the constituency, I was not inspired to participate.

Harvey Milk was perhaps the biggest personality of the grassroots movement. Brash and aggressive, he had performed as a clown in New York and knew how to act like a one to get attention and win affection. When he moved to San Francisco in 1972, he opened a camera shop in the Castro, where enthusiastic, gay hippies met to talk politics. Many people, particularly those who had been working for years to move equality issues forward, did not take Milk seriously. They had been toiling in the fields, as they say, when Harvey came dancing in, organizing in the streets, and gathering a pretty immediate following. He struck some people as a political accident. I'd only met him in passing, but I thought he was very shrewd. In each of his three failed runs for city supervisor, Harvey built name recognition and created for himself a place in the firmament of gay political leaders.

David Goodstein, by contrast, was representative of the gay political establishment, nascent as it was. He believed that a person fighting for esteem and dignity must project esteem and dignity. In his eyes, men who kissed for the cameras and women on motorcycles who stripped to the waist were not advancing the movement. He derided struggling advocacy organizations with office spaces defined by grungy broken furniture and overflowing ashtrays, saying that they were like "toilets," and that nobody should work in a "toilet." David's idea was to persuade the masses that we gay people were washed and clean and just like them. Harvey's approach was to get to those who were not political, especially young people just hanging around, and inspire them to be involved. He used a bullhorn to rally them into the streets, to take part in protests and marches or whatever else it took to get attention to our issues. For the well-being of the constituency, David put on a front after Harvey was elected, but I don't think they cared for each other.

What both leaders had in common, though, was their message and their desire to get people off their asses. In their own ways, they were both saying: *How can we expect anyone to show us our due if they don't know who the hell we are? Come out*! The 1970s was a period of self-empowerment, and David and Harvey capitalized on that, albeit in different ways. For better or for worse, Proposition 6 was big enough for both of them. Harvey traveled around California debating Briggs on television and in public forums, and regularly rallying his base. David, who had contributed $5,000 the evening of Lou Hermes' dinner, put his bankroll and his brain behind "No on 6." For the first time, the various political organizations across Northern and Southern California set aside their rivalry. Briggs helped the disparate personalities and political wings of California's gay movement coalesce in defense of their rights.

I was involved in "No on 6" as a funder and strategist. Our principal argument was about protecting individual privacy: if the government was given permission to peer into the bedrooms of one group, what would stop them from going after others? A key element of the strategy was to kindle support among straight Californians, such as the very popular Los Angeles city attorney Burt Pines, who was a breath of fresh air to gay people at a time when not many in the straight world were being nice to us. Notable straight people sent a message that the issue went well beyond gay men and lesbians; Prop 6 was about everybody.

One of the great political ironies of the battle was that former Governor Ronald Reagan, who earned the wrath of the gay community a few years later by refusing to acknowledge the AIDS pandemic, played a crucial role in the debate. The privacy argument appealed to Reagan, a conservative and professed advocate of small government, who was warming up for a presidential run. Sometime in October, organizers from a benignly-named but powerful gay organization, the Metropolitan Election Commission of Los Angeles, or MECLA, went to see him. MECLA was one of the first gay groups to attract straight politicians to its events. A week before the November 7 vote, the candidate-in-waiting released a statement on the letterhead of *Citizens for Reagan,* criticizing the Briggs Initiative as an infringement on individual rights. I remember watching a news broadcast of a Reagan speech. At its end, he said, "Thank you very much," and started away from the podium. Suddenly, he stopped and leaned back toward the microphone, saying: "And don't forget, vote no on 6."

From then on, momentum turned against Prop 6. The measure lost by 1 million votes, failing even in Briggs' home district in Orange County. Against all odds, we won, and it felt good.

There were so many events in those days—some of them good, some of them horrible—and we took to the streets either way. On this occasion, dancing started in the Castro and moved down Market Street to City Hall. Even as we reveled, we knew that Bryant, Briggs and others of their ilk were consoling themselves by devising even more creative ways to prevent gay people from enjoying basic civil rights. But that particular moment of victory was ours.

The party didn't last long.

Less than two weeks later, on November 18, hundreds of Northern California residents died in a mass suicide in the Guyanese jungle. A charismatic minister named Jim Jones, who had established a highly-visible, active church on Geary Boulevard called the People's Temple, had lured followers to Guyana to establish a village he named Jonestown. When Congressman Leo Ryan of San Mateo arrived in Jonestown to investigate claims that some church members were being held against their will, a few of Jones' followers opened fire, killing Ryan and a few journalists and staff members who had accompanied him on the trip. Jones and the 900 or so people in the compound drank a poison-laced punch, which killed them within minutes.

It seemed as though everybody knew somebody tied to Jonestown, including me. My friend Frances, a friend in New York who helped me sort out my Soho apartment after the electrical fire, lost her son and mother.

The second event, on November 27, was the assassination of Mayor George Moscone and Supervisor Milk in City Hall, by another supervisor, Dan White. Initially, people feared some connection to Jonestown since Jones had been politically active and knew Moscone well. As it became clear that Dan White had acted alone, the anger was uncontrollable. People rioted, burning police cars and smashing windows. Dianne Feinstein, then chair of the board of supervisors, and as emotionally devastated as the city around her, was sworn in as mayor. The events gave rise to the same sort of horror and sadness I experienced over the assassinations of President Kennedy, Martin Luther King, and Bobby Kennedy, except that the violence and White's surreal small-town pettiness were products of the place where I lived and breathed, the city I chose to call *home*. And Harvey Milk was a hell of a lot more than just Harvey. To put it simply, he was *my* man. He was *our* man. He was standing up for us. And standing *in* for us.

Much of San Francisco spent hours, days, and weeks trying to register the events—it all seemed so unreal. Larry and I had just moved into a contemporary house in the Glen Park neighborhood, which looked toward the TransAmerica tower and the other buildings of downtown San Francisco. I remember surveying the city and thinking, *how could these horrible things have happened here? Is this some sort of a nightmare?* There were lots of services and candlelight vigils, and I avoided them all. I didn't want to go out.

During the last month of 1978, San Francisco reeled from its tragedies. Milk, who had anticipated that he might be assassinated one day, told people while he was alive that his untimely death should not be a cause for anger but a catalyst for change. And so it was.

In demanding equality, the early pioneers of the gay civil rights movement tried to be nice. Brave souls such as Frank Kameny, a government astronomer fired in the mid 1950s over his homosexuality, organized polite pickets of gay men in suits and ties and lesbian women in suburban-looking dresses at the White House and Independence Hall in Philadelphia. The gracious requests for change had a limited effect, though they did catalyze responses from people like Anita Bryant, calling us "human garbage."

Just as whites in the 1960s refused to give rights to African-Americans, no one was going to hand equality to us. We had to demand it.

By the late 1970s, the gay movement was aligning its forces. Two young organizations, the National Gay Task Force in New York and the Gay Rights National Lobby in Washington, tried to influence policy and generate attention to our issues. The gay movement was making small inroads—Jimmy Carter, for example, invited a delegation of gay men and lesbians to the White House for a first-ever meeting with his senior staff—but the fervor of anti-gay rhetoric in the growing evangelical movement made it clear that we needed to ratchet up our game.

When Steve Endean, a boyish and peripatetic Minnesotan, came to me with a detailed proposal for a political action committee to support candidates for federal office who were supportive of gay rights, I was intrigued. As executive director of the Gay Rights National Lobby, Steve knew how Washington worked, and he brought in some talented people to help him set up an organization. They included Jim Foster, the Toklas Club founder and leader of Ted Kennedy's Northern California presidential campaign, and Larry Bye, a respected political scientist and researcher.

My experiences in the Vietnam War era taught me that we would make more progress competing as equals against Christian groups such as the Moral Majority than by throwing stones at them from the outside. That meant raising money. David Goodstein offered to go on a fundraising campaign across the country and Jerry volunteered to help run the new venture. I agreed to serve as a board member and eventually became a major contributor.

The new group, the Human Rights Campaign Fund, was launched in 1980. In the temper of the time, the name intentionally omitted the words *gay* and *lesbian*. From a philosophic point of view, we wanted to keep the focus on what we stood for: a simple extension of civil rights and basic fairness. Practically, we knew that the inclusion of those words would decrease our ability to raise and dispense funds at a time when we needed to engage as many supporters as possible. We wanted to steer clear of titles that might incite the *Swiftboaters* and *Birthers* of those days, or cause people to withdraw rather than participate. We established a twelve-person board that was as politically correct as any board of the time, with male and female co-chairs and three people of color. Jerry became a co-chair, together with Kerry Woodward, another Minnesotan.

At the top of HRCF's agenda was a lesbian and gay civil rights measure along the lines of the 1964 and 1965 bills that enshrined equal rights for African Americans. The bill was intended to deliver to our constituency basic protection, so that a person couldn't be fired for being gay, denied an apartment, or otherwise discriminated against.

We knew that our constituency had money; the big question was whether people were brave enough to put their names on a check. The fundraising strategy was based on direct mail and dinners in private homes in cities such as San Francisco, Los Angeles, and Washington, D.C. The first solicitation letter went out in 1981, signed by the playwright Tennessee Williams. He had never before done anything political for gay people. He was apparently a bit soused when a handsome, young activist went to see him and persuaded him to put his name on the letter. It was, nonetheless, very effective in bringing in the dollars. The dinners, too, were showing results.

We decided to have our first public dinner with a big splash in New York, with a speaker who commanded attention in the mainstream political world. We invited Walter Mondale, the former vice president and Minnesota senator who planned to run for the White House, and courted him for months. With the help of Dianne Feinstein and her husband Richard Blum, I met Senator Mondale. Later, I arranged a meeting with him and Steve Endean, Kerry Woodward, Dan Bradley, and myself. Dan was a former Carter administration official considered one of Washington's most eligible bachelors until the day he shocked the socialites by coming out. With three of the four of us from Minnesota, how could Mondale refuse the invitation?

We met over breakfast and then headed to the former vice president's very simple and sensible Georgetown office. In a small conference room, with Mondale and a staff person sitting across the table from us, we discussed HRCF's mission and the reason we needed a political organization to focus on civil rights for our constituency. Mondale was an egalitarian, but like so many people of the time, he wasn't fully aware of the level of discrimination gay people faced. He asked detailed questions about our goals, our members, and what we stood for. We were new and without a track record. Out of the White

House for two years, Mondale was trying to attract attention to his candidacy and wasn't sure whether dinner with HRCF was the right way to do it. Obviously weighing the risks, he told us that he would *try* to be there. It was clear that he was uncomfortable.

The HRCF dinner was to take place after Labor Day, at the beginning of the fall political rush, in the grand ballroom of the Waldorf Astoria, a venue we chose deliberately for its first-class reputation. We were so determined to have Mondale as the principal speaker that we didn't contemplate what might happen if he said no. And he didn't say yes until almost the final hours. That evening, he easily waded through a handful of picketing Hasidic Jews, the only protesters to turn out. Although Mondale did not use the word "gay" in his speech that night, his presence alone was a statement of courage.

In the 1981–82 election cycle, the eight-month-old HRCF raised about $600,000, gave twenty candidates contributions of $4,500 each, and made smaller donations to another one hundred candidates. Of those HRCF supported, 81 percent won, giving us a new crop of co-sponsors for our bill, which, years later, became the Employment Non-Discrimination Act.[3] HRCF, which was later re-named as the Human Rights Campaign, was getting the attention we wanted.

Every time I got involved in something, my appetite to do more grew. When I was asked to chair a committee raising money for the Pride Center, a lesbian and gay community center on Hayes Street, I agreed. Not having the vaguest idea of what to do, I reached out to San Francisco philanthropists such as Cissie Swig and fundraisers such as Florette Pomeroy, who gave me ideas of how to manage the

---

[3]The bill has still never been approved by both houses of Congress.

campaign. When Jon Sims, the mastermind of the San Francisco Gay Freedom Day Marching Band and Twirling Corps, approached me for support, I agreed. Jon was a versatile musician straight out of Kansas who knew how to strut with boots and a baton. He also started the San Francisco Gay Men's Chorus, and organized its first national tour. It was so successful that more than a dozen gay men's choruses popped up immediately in small cities across America. It was unbelievable—who would have thought that Lincoln, Nebraska, in 1981, would be home to a gay men's choir?

At lunch one day with Sam Puckett, a friend I'd met through the Advocate Experience, we discussed the ways in which a collective lack of confidence held the community back. We had been told over and over, by those we loved and the society around us, that we were not worthy, and many of us believed it. For some, the almost impenetrable sense of low self-esteem surfaced in incidents of alcoholism, verbal and physical abuse, and even suicide.

Together, Sam and I came up with an idea to honor people in our community who were making a difference. We finished our sandwiches with a commitment to keep talking, and eventually put together a committee of ten people, several of whom had come through the Advocate Experience. One of them was Zohn Artman, a cheerful and mischievous sprite of a man who worked for the concert promoter Bill Graham.

Discos were just getting to be a big thing, and Zohn, a public relations genius, knew of a brand new place south of Market Street called Dreamland that was eager for publicity. Zohn also recommended that we ask the San Francisco Volunteer Bureau to be part of our event. The Bureau's executive director was receptive immediately, and our event had the validation of a well-respected city organization. We recruited some straight people from the non-profit community to be on the host committee.

The evening was called "GayCare." Admission was set at $5 so that people couldn't say we were playing to the elite—anyone could find $5. We packed the program with popular entertainers such as Linda Tillery, and snuck in a few short speeches. One of the honorees was Dorrwin Jones, a roly-poly, openly gay man who started the local Meals on Wheels program. Dorr, who had had several heart attacks, probably outlived his life expectancy by at least twenty years, powered by sheer enthusiasm and effervescence. The volunteer bureau set up tables at the door and registered about half of the 750 attendees as prospective volunteers, apparently the best single recruitment day they had to that point.

My financial contributions to "GayCare" were anonymous, as were most all donations I made to community organizations in those days. The judging voice inside me had decided: *I don't deserve this wealth; I didn't do anything to get it. And I certainly don't deserve attention for giving it away.* At some level, I didn't feel the need for any public recognition. The donations gave me an incredible return: a counterweight to my guilt. Instead of feeling sheepish and awkward about having means, I began to think about a strategic plan for giving. I realized, finally, that my inherited resources gave me the power to touch people on a broad scale. With my fiftieth birthday on the horizon, I had the feeling that I had found the right path.

That was roughly the time that gay men in America started to die en masse.

Chapter Twelve

DEATH AND BIRTH

Within a matter of years, San Francisco's haven of freedom devolved into a world of pure terror. Arriving out of nowhere, a plague spread with no end in sight.

The first person I knew who died of AIDS was a casual acquaintance, an editor at *The Advocate* named Brent Harris. Around 1980, he got a type of cancer that wasn't familiar to most people. Not long after, other friends said they knew somebody who had the cancer, or a strange, severe pneumonia, and it seemed that just a short time later, I was hearing that those same people had died. We, along with the rest of the world, were baffled by the fact that more than a few gay men were getting a cancer almost exclusively associated with old men in the Mediterranean, and the persistent, recurring pneumonia. As the links between *Kaposi's sarcoma* and *pneumocystis pneumonia* were identified, the emerging plague was named *gay-related immune deficiency*, or GRID.

At first, GRID hit people outside of my circle, so I didn't have an immediate sense of how horrible it was. I assumed the medical establishment would figure it all out. Time passed, with few answers, except for the theory that GRID was sexually transmitted and had nothing to do with the amyl nitrate poppers, which people commonly snorted then. That's when I started to think about myself. I was sexually active—if there was something out there that people were being exposed to, I was being exposed as well. I wondered: *Am I going get sick? Or one of these days, will one of my good friends get sick?* I didn't want to consider such possibilities.

By 1982, as the understanding of transmission developed, GRID became AIDS, the acquired immune deficiency syndrome. Perhaps the name change had something to do with the fact that a handful of other demographic groups, including Haitians, were becoming infected rapidly. Still, it was something nobody wanted to talk about. When people died of AIDS, their obituaries never said so. The cause of death was "cancer" or "pneumonia" or a "long illness."

On December 30, 1982, I set off on a three-day cruise from Miami to Nassau to celebrate my fiftieth birthday. More than 100 of the people who meant the most to me in the world came along, infusing the atmosphere of the 1,000-person ship with clannish enthusiasm. My brothers and their wives, my kids, Alice and Jim, my grandchildren, and several nieces and nephews were there, along with a huge crop of friends from San Francisco and my college and law school days. It was Austin meets Chicago meets San Francisco. The celebration was another step for me in the constant process of coming out: if anyone there hadn't realized that I was gay, they certainly knew by the end of the trip and apparently loved me all the same. The experience was so rich, so satisfying for me. Yet within a decade or so, at least a dozen of the guests were dead, most of them killed by AIDS. That's a lot of people to lose when you're speaking of your close friends.

One morning in the New Year, I drove down Market Street to my office—a modest, three-story structure between Van Ness and Franklin—in what I hoped was an up-and-coming neighborhood. The building had a recording studio supposedly used by some of the more famous Bay Area artists, though we could never figure out exactly which ones. There, a small team helped me manage my affairs.

When I walked up the stairs to the second floor reception area, I saw that Craig Applewhite, an articulate man from the Deep South who worked as office manager, was not in his chair. He was out sick, *again*. Craig was as fit and strong as any thirty-year-old but he'd been missing work regularly. Soon, I learned that he had AIDS. As Craig got progressively weaker, Larry and I spent a lot of time by his side, telling jokes to distract him from his pain. Even as he became so frail that he could not sit up without help, Craig managed a few cracks of his own.

About that same time, my friend, Mark Feldman, who I knew through the Advocate Experience, started getting the terrible sores characteristic of Kaposi's sarcoma. Even so, his attitude was: *we're gonna lick this thing*. "Phooey on AIDS," he used to say. He got out of bed on a Saturday that June to be in the gay pride parade, but his valiance was not enough to stave off the inevitable. The deaths of Craig and Mark made AIDS all too real for me.

In retrospect, the epidemiology of the disease progressed fairly quickly, but at the time every day was like a year. It seemed like forever between those first cases and the conclusion in 1984 that the illness was caused by an identifiable virus.

Part of the alarm about AIDS was that there wasn't any predictability about it. Some people got sick, and then well, and then sick again. Others were diagnosed and gone three weeks later. A friend who ran a successful public relations firm, Jim Graves, became very ill just as he finished a monumental campaign for one of the city's museums. Within weeks, he was gone, just like that. Jim, Craig, and Mark were only in their thirties.

When it became clear that our community was under siege, people tried to find ways to help. There were dance-a-thons and other fundraisers, and glass jars and tin cans in bars and restaurants across the city. They filled up with tens of thousands of dollars in coins, which the AIDS Emergency Fund doled out to people with HIV/AIDS. Debilitated and unable to work, AIDS sufferers often ran out of money to pay their rent, health insurance, and other basic living expenses. Sam Puckett launched one of the very first initiatives, the StopAids Project, an outreach effort modeled along the lines of the Tupperware party. Hosts invited anywhere between ten and twenty people into their homes to hear an expert talk about AIDS, and each guest, in turn, was asked to host a gathering for another group. The house-to-house approach caught on because people could discuss intimate matters in a somewhat private environment, and the fact that an AIDS diagnosis meant almost certain death, and an agonizing death at that, was a great motivator. StopAids reached more than 2,000 people within two years, slowing San Francisco's rate of infection. But unfortunately thousands of gay men were already HIV positive.

The federal government seemed not to recognize the urgency of what was to become the plague of our lifetimes. The city and county of San Francisco, however, set out to become a national model for treatment, prevention, and education. Even so, as AIDS reached pandemic levels in the mid 1980s, the scale of sickness and death defied their resources. That's when things really started happening. All kinds of local organizations jumped in to help fight the disease and support those suffering from it. One of the first hospices was a fifteen-bed facility called Coming Home, which some people thought would be too big. They were wrong. Men kept dying, and the hospices proliferated, as did organizations delivering groceries, meals, or otherwise checking in on patients too weak to get out of their homes. Anyone in the gay community not sick in bed was most likely doing something to help those who were.

Along with StopAids, The Shanti Project was among the first efforts I supported. Founded in 1974 by Charles Garfield to assist terminally-ill cancer patients, Shanti expanded to include AIDS sufferers in the early 1980s. Another group was the San Francisco AIDS Foundation, a second Sam Puckett initiative started in 1984 to prevent transmission. I funded the California Pacific Medical Center Foundation, which supported the hospital that treated most AIDS patients. And Project Open Hand, a food delivery service, began when a woman named Ruth Brinker, who had worked with Meals-on-Wheels, started preparing food for AIDS patients in a church basement. amfAR, the American Foundation for AIDS research, started in 1985 when a research group led by New York doctor Mathilde Krim merged with a like-minded West coast organization. Elizabeth Taylor, who lost her dear friend Rock Hudson to AIDS, became amfAR'S founding chairperson. Elizabeth was the first person of any real public profile to take a stand in support of people suffering from HIV/AIDS. A pioneer, she made it safe for other people to start caring about the disease.

As we tried to open a front on AIDS, what I feared as a possibility manifested as a reality: friends in my inner circle started to get sick. Jon Sims, founder of the Gay Freedom Day Marching Band and Twirling Corps, called one day to announce that he was leaving to visit the graves of famous musicians all around the world. He returned several weeks later, feeling unwell, and died soon after.

The patterns became painfully predictable. Within a matter of months or years of diagnosis, depending on that friend's fortune, he started losing weight, no matter what or how much he ate. Then he either developed the horrible cancer, which attacked him inside and out, or he got bouts of pneumonia, which further weakened him with each recurrence. Or both. Then he ended up confined to a hospital bed in Ward 5 of San Francisco General Hospital, with tubes and oxygen, as I and others of our tribe sat there, holding his hand while he gasped for his last breaths.

Each day of that decade was one lived with more fear than I had ever known. I woke up many mornings and wondered, *What am I going to find out today? What horrible news is coming my way?* I wasn't the only one who was frightened. Once, when Jimmy arrived for a visit, he balked when I tried to hug and kiss him. He wasn't sure that it was safe to touch me but he put his arms around me, anyway. I knew he and other members of the family were worried for me. I heard their concern in the way they asked so seriously, *How are you?*

In the midst of the death and mourning, I began to feel tired and weak. I woke up in the middle of the night in an icy sweat. I had a cold and hacking cough that seemed to hang on forever. I went immediately to see Tom Waddell, a friend who was a doctor.

Before I was tested, Tom and I had more than one conversation about what might happen. What if I got a false test result? What if I found out I was positive? I knew people who were diagnosed and then dead a month later—would that happen to me? And what if the test results were exposed? There weren't reliable protections to guarantee the privacy of the information, and there was justifiably great concern over that. Ryan White, a teenage boy who contracted HIV through a blood transfusion, was expelled from school and his family driven from their home in Kokomo, Indiana, after someone fired a bullet through their living room window. That's how fearful and irrational people were when it came to AIDS.

I decided to be tested, even though my cough and fatigue seemed to make the result inevitable. It didn't occur to me that I was exhausted and emotionally wrung out from countless bedside vigils that ended, every single time without exception, in death.

My test came back negative.

I was in total shock. Why had I been spared?

AIDS was an unavoidable, everyday concern in San Francisco, but not so in Washington.

Barbara Boxer wanted to change that. About two months into her first term in Congress, in the spring of 1983, I was surprised to be invited to meet Barbara in her San Francisco office. I did not know her and had openly supported her primary opponent, Louise Renne. When I asked how much time I could have, the staffer said we'd have about an hour. Rather audaciously, I asked how many people I could bring. A little taken aback, the staffer said there should be no more than four of us.

When the day came, I walked through the doors of the office with Martha Bryant, my Chicago friend, Jerry Berg, and Tom Waddell. Martha had moved to San Francisco and taken a job working with the homeless and aged in a dicey city neighborhood, the Tenderloin. In his law practice, Jerry saw how discrimination, bankruptcy, probate, and other legal issues affected AIDS patients. Tom was essential to the discussion: he knew everything that was then known about AIDS from the medical point of view.

Tom was a wunderkind. An epidemiologist who served as an Army paratrooper, he competed in the decathlon in the 1968 Olympics. He was well known in the Bay Area for trying to found the Gay Olympics, an effort that catalyzed a protracted legal battle with the U.S. Olympic Committee over use of the name. There were Crab Olympics and Special Olympics and God knows what other Olympics, but the idea of a Gay Olympics was something the USOC could not tolerate. Tom agreed to rename the competition the Gay Games but the USOC continued to litigate the copyright infringement, practically bankrupting him. Nonetheless, 1,350 athletes came to San Francisco in 1982 to compete in eleven different sports.

Congresswoman Boxer spent not one but two hours with us. She did a lot of listening and asked many questions. On the way out, the four of us talked about what a useful meeting it had been, if only as a step toward raising awareness. Yet the very next week, Boxer went to the House floor, requesting what resulted in the first major commitment of federal funding to HIV/AIDS research and support. She was the first at the federal level to do anything about AIDS in terms of public policy.

Through my work on the Pride Center and my service on the San Francisco Chamber Orchestra board, people in philanthropic circles were getting to know me. In 1984, I was approached to participate with several people associated with the San Francisco Ballet, Symphony, and Opera on an AIDS event directed at raising money from the mainstream philanthropic community. I agreed to do so and became painfully aware of the extent to which AIDS had scared people senseless.

Given the caliber of the performers, anyone remotely interested in those arts should have been thrilled to attend. But it was like pulling teeth to get people to be there. When volunteers and fund-raisers called their regular patrons, trying to sell tickets, the patrons sometimes hung up on them. One woman said, "I'm sorry, I couldn't possibly go. I don't have anything to wear—I don't have a gas mask." It was as if leprosy had returned.

The night of the event, I wandered through the hallways of the Opera House, recognizing many gay men and lesbians. Straight people, as far as I could tell, weren't there in any significant number. I went home and climbed into bed, crestfallen. *What a shame, what a shame*, I thought, over and over. AIDS was just one more vehicle for rejection.

The experience reinforced my notions of how quick people are to make judgments based on their fears and their lack of knowledge. They treated others as pariahs because they were infected with something that scared them. By 1984, it was pretty widely known that AIDS was not transmitted by shaking hands, pecking on the cheek or drinking from the wrong wine glass. It seemed that the extreme reaction went beyond a simple fear of contracting AIDS. It had something to do with abhorrence. Gay men were seen as carriers of death, perhaps deserving of our fate.

As I reflected on the disappointing response to the Opera-Ballet-Symphony fundraiser, I began to see that my anonymous giving didn't really serve any purpose. It didn't make me any nobler, except in my own head. To the contrary, my name often helped to attract other donors. It wasn't simply about wealth. It was more subtle than that. It had to do with my family's name, and the sense of class that many people attach to "old money." I was raised in a household where I was taught politesse; I learned how to hold my fork and to make polite conversation, to conduct myself in way that made it easier for me to move in certain circles and get ahead in this world. For years, I deliberately overlooked those advantages. But now, the family name and the trappings I disdained for so long were things of tremendous value. They were a commodity, which I could trade upon.

That's when I started attaching my name to every gift. I tried to be more visible. Anytime I wore a jacket, the pink triangle pin was in the lapel. It was very important to me that people saw me and knew that I was gay. It felt good to let people know who I was and what I stood for. It took away the power of others to define me. In 1988, I made a grant of $100,000 to KQED, the Bay Area's public broadcaster, toward its new building. When it came time to inscribe the names of donors on a plaque on the wall, I requested that it read *James C. Hormel and Larry Soule.* I was trying to say, *hey, you people who have all these rights and privileges, including marriage, you have to recognize that we are not a counterculture; we are all a part of the same culture.* From then on, I customarily made my philanthropic donations in my name *and* that of my partner.

Out of sadness, loss, anger, bitterness, and guilt over my good health, I hurtled myself into nonprofit work. From the day in 1983 when I gave Shanti my first donation of $250, through the early 1990s, I gave more than $4 million to more than forty organizations working on AIDS-related initiatives ranging from medical and social services to arts performances including *Angels in America* and John Corigliano's *Symphony No. 1.* I helped raise funds for three or four capital campaigns, including the Coming Home Hospice. Eager for platforms at which I could highlight the needs of the gay community, I joined more than a dozen boards between 1984 and 1994, including those of KQED, amfAR, Swarthmore College, the San Francisco Chamber of Commerce, the San Francisco Performing Arts Library and Museum, (now the Museum of Performance and Design) National Gay Rights Advocates, 18th Street Services (later called New Leaf), and the visiting committee of the University of Chicago Law School.

Several times during the years of the pandemic, Larry and I went to Hawaii for a break. Each time, as I marveled at emerald peaks, sparkling seas, and daily rainbows, the thought occurred, *I should just stay. It's so nice here. I can pick up the phone and call back to San Francisco, and say: Sorry folks, I'm done. I'm not playing anymore.* On one visit, I learned that a friend started a volunteer agency in Kauai for people with AIDS, confirming what I knew in my heart: there was no escaping AIDS. Even a Pacific island 2,400 miles from California, with a population about 40,000, could not duck the HIV virus. The truth was, though, that I didn't really want to escape.

All the new commitments were tiring, draining, and sometimes overwhelming, but at the same time, something about the work was revitalizing and gave me a limited sense of accomplishment. I was part of the operation to provide services and resources to those in need, and that felt a lot better than sitting back while people were dying.

Alongside my support for AIDS groups, I continued to seek out organizations in a position to enhance the community's political empowerment. During the course of the 1980s, nearly all gay interest groups were absorbed by AIDS and unable to create a sense of forward motion for LGBT civil rights policy. But the pandemic created political opportunities because it made gay people visible in a way they hadn't been before. Those who before had said they didn't know anyone who was gay realized that, in fact, they did. Even the most closed-minded of congressmen were forced to admit that they had gay constituents. That awareness opened a channel to advance gay rights. I made a concerted effort to donate to gay and straight candidates who supported LGBT equality as well as groups focused on rights and education, such as HRC and the American Civil Liberties Union, which started its Lesbian and Gay Rights Project in 1986 with my assistance.

Funeral by funeral, AIDS gave me and many others a new life. Death on such a scale made people realize that we weren't just a few dozen queers on Castro Street. We were brothers and sons and, yes, fathers. And we weren't just male. Gay men and lesbians, many of whom became care givers to their gay brothers, together began lobbying for health care, medical research, protection in the workplace, and other basic human rights. We were no longer just a *community*—we were a political *constituency*.

In 1983, Nancy Pelosi asked me to serve as a member of the Host Committee for the Democratic National Convention, which she chaired. I had met her several years before through Jerry Berg but didn't know her well. My committee responsibilities involved, among other things, hosting a reception in my home for the South Carolina delegation, which was led by the then-Governor Richard Riley, later President Clinton's Secretary of Education. Over the course of planning the convention, Nancy and I got along well. We connected right away over the fact that we both had four daughters and one son, and a love of dark chocolate. In her frequent calls to see how things were going, I sensed her dedication, her ability to focus, and her breadth of understanding of the issues. She was very loyal to the party and eager to see it represent the best in terms of people's motivations and ambitions.

The year before the convention, Congressman Phil Burton died of heart failure. He was a lion of a man, one of the most impressive people ever to serve in the U.S. Congress, and he did roar from time to time. Phil's brilliance was reinforced by his chief of staff, Bill Krause, an openly gay man with remarkable political acumen. Phil's wife Sala, a very caring and dedicated person born in Poland, won a special election for Phil's seat in early 1983, and was reelected twice before being diagnosed with colon cancer. In her last days, Sala apparently asked Nancy to run for her seat, as if she were anointing her. Phil might have been able to get away with that, but not Sala, and in fact, not most people in San Francisco. Voters were ready to oppose Nancy just on the basis of the way she came into the race.

In the gay constituency, a sense prevailed that our time had come. Harry Britt, who filled Harvey Milk's seat on the board of supervisors, was the guy to carry the banner.

Harry had been a minister, and he could speak like one—he was a very good orator. But he presented himself as a socialist on the issues and seemed reluctant to compromise, which made me wonder about whether he could make an impact in Washington. His experience in government was limited to the board of supervisors, and I wasn't sure he had a sense of how to make things work in a bigger arena. I was with him once at a MECLA dinner in LA, an event packed with hundreds of high-powered people. It was the kind of audience that makes politicians salivate. I walked him around the room, introducing him to people I knew, but it was like pulling a mule. He was terribly uncomfortable. If LA was difficult, how could Harry move around Washington? With Ronald Reagan in office, refusing to utter the word AIDS, we needed a strong personality to establish networks and garner support.

As the campaign unfolded, a third candidate, city supervisor Doris Ward, siphoned off votes, turning the race into a nail-biter. Both Harry and Nancy came to ask for my support.

Harry stopped by first. When I asked him why he was running, he responded: "This is our big chance, Jim." And he didn't say much else.

When Nancy came, I asked her the same question.

"When I get to Washington, this is what I'm going to do…" she began, and went on for the next several minutes with a lengthy list of policy objectives. At the top of her list was AIDS funding.

While she had never held elective office, Nancy had several leadership roles in the state Democratic Party. She went to her first national Democratic Convention when she was twelve with her father, Thomas D'Alesandro, the mayor of Baltimore, and later, a congressman. In the course of our conversation, it became very clear, how can I not support Nancy? How could I support Harry?

It was one thing to back Nancy, but when she asked me to be one of three co-chairs on her campaign I had to think about it. I really did. I came to the conclusion: *Yes, of course*. If I'm going to support her, I need to support her all the way. If this is what she wants from me, this is what I'll do.

To be a gay man supporting Nancy Pelosi was equivalent to selling state secrets, and the peer pressure was on. *You have to support a gay man*, I was told several times. Bob Ross, the founder of the *Bay Area Reporter*, a San Francisco paper catering to gay readers, was so furious that he didn't speak to me for years afterwards. Most of my friends supported Harry, including Jerry Berg. I tried to talk to him about Nancy, and he refused to consider her.

The political dynamic in San Francisco was such that the attention went to the person perceived to be the most progressive candidate. Harry, calling himself a socialist and living in humble circumstances, became that person. Nancy, with a home in Presidio Terrace and an investment banker husband, immediately became the establishment candidate. That made *me* an establishment figure, which translated into not caring about the poor, or street people, or transportation, or job opportunities, or education or health care, or what the *Contras* were doing in Central America, for that matter. I'm not sure there's another place in the country like San Francisco in that regard. Our board of supervisors probably has passed more resolutions on foreign policy matters than any comparable city government in America.

People were dying right and left, and those whom I felt closest to politically felt that I had betrayed them by supporting Nancy. Privately, it was easy, because I felt that she would be very effective and true to her word on HIV/AIDS. It was apparent to me then, as it still is, that the movement for gay rights wasn't going to go forward without non-gay allies. Five percent of the population wasn't going to move 95 percent. I just had to accept the fact that people weren't going to like it.

In the end, the outcome was close. Nancy won by about 3,000 votes.

Her very first act as a member of Congress was to introduce legislation seeking funding for HIV/AIDS research and treatment.

Rob Eichberg. Zohn Artman. Sam Puckett. Tom Waddell. Jon Sims and 257 men of the gay men's chorus. Steve Endean. Jim Foster. Bill Krause. Dan Bradley. Many of the men at the Lou Hermes dinner.

My first boyfriend Mort. My brother Thomas' brother-in-law. And so many more. Between 1981 and 1995, I knew hundreds of men who died, most of them in their thirties and forties. I lost more than half of my friends—literally.

These were people very dear to me, and many of them were powerful leaders. They had devoted themselves, in different ways, to bringing gay people out. Not just as sexual beings, but as people who could feel whole, and confident in themselves, and participants in a larger community.

The thing was that they were not supposed to die. They were young men, with careers, aspirations, and energy to make the world better.

In January 1991, my mother passed away in Los Angeles. My brothers and I buried her in Austin, next to my father in Oakwood Cemetery, on a day so cold that the membranes of my nose froze. As the priest from Queen of Angels Church conducted the rite, I scanned the three generations of family gathered there. No one was crying.

Despite the countless string of funerals I had attended, Mamma's passing should have stood out to me. But unlike my friends coming to painful and premature ends, her quiet death at age ninety-four came in the natural course of things. She was so drained of vitality that living was more tragedy than blessing, and we had not been able to talk for so long that I was accustomed to living without her.

Just as we never openly discussed my sexuality, we never discussed the drug addiction that dogged her into her seventies. She kept that part of herself locked away from my brothers and me, perhaps not wanting anyone to perceive her as vulnerable. For years, without a close understanding of the power of addiction, I was willing to make the doctors all wrong, to blame them. But Mamma was such a forceful personality—it was hard to think that she couldn't have broken the habit if she wanted to. Perhaps I wanted to believe that she was that strong—people with big personalities are often the most devoted addicts. However, I suspect that loneliness had a lot to do with her drug use.

Later that year, I learned more about the human heart's capacity to bear pain when Jerry passed away.

His experience was like all the others. He started getting colds, and coughs, which wouldn't go away. He got a little weaker and started working from home more than in the office. Don't tell me Jerry is sick, I thought. He and his partner Jim Proby, a delightful Australian who spoke fluent Danish and designed clothes, went to Germany for treatments intended to cleanse toxins and strengthen their immune systems. Jim actually got sick first, but Jerry got sick faster.

As his days waned, Jerry and I had a series of conversations focused on where he was going, if anywhere. For his whole life, more or less, Jerry sought enlightenment. He did *est*. He traveled to India. He befriended the holistic health guru Andrew Weil. He read voraciously about life and afterlife. The illumination that came to him in his final days was that the act of passing on was an important part of the human experience. He didn't explain it in terms of theology or psychology or any other formalized idea. He had concluded, simply, that death was something humans were meant to experience.

The last time I saw Jerry, he was slipping into a coma. He was at his new home, just outside Santa Fe, with Jim and Rob Eichberg. Jerry looked small in the double bed, his chest heaving with each labored breath. Every four hours or so, Jim or Rob gave him a morphine pill to alleviate his pain. When I said hello, he nodded slightly, without opening his eyes. I took his hand and he gave a little squeeze back. At dinner that night, Rob and Jim, themselves in various stages of HIV, were exhausted. I had to go to New York early the next morning but wanted to help somehow. I volunteered to stay up on watch with Jerry. After dinner, I lay down next to him in the bed, listening to every pained breath. I rose at the appropriate time to give him his pill.

The next morning, I left for the airport at 7 AM. When the plane stopped in Chicago to make a connection, I called from a pay phone. Rob answered and told me, very matter-of-factly, that Jerry had passed on about an hour before. I knew when I said goodbye that I was seeing Jerry for the last time, but still, I was disappointed in a way that I wasn't there when he took his last breath.

"We found the pill that you gave him," Rob said. "He spit it out. He did the same thing with the last one that I gave him."

I was sure that Jerry had done that deliberately. He wanted the full experience of dying.

Even though I had been through so many deaths, his passing nearly paralyzed me. Our relationship was, in some ways, the most important in my life. He had known me through so many phases, going all the way back to the days of my marriage, and he had helped me find my way. He gave me courage; he gave me a sense of possibility. There's a wonderful scene in the movie *Gandhi* set just after the title character comes back from the long salt march, a monumental victory for basic rights in India. Gandhi tells his wife he feels like a failure. As focused and successful as Gandhi was, he still had feelings of inadequacy. Jerry had those moments. He had done so much, inspired so many people, but he still had feelings of self doubt and weakness. And he shared them with me. And I shared mine with him, without any fear of judgment.

Now I had to carry on without him.

Chapter Thirteen

FIT TO SERVE

The first time I met William Jefferson Clinton was in March 1992, at the Fairmont Hotel in San Francisco, where he gave a campaign speech to the business core of San Francisco's Democratic Party. Amid a sea of men and women in dark suits, with the occasional cocktail dress in the mix, I fit in well, particularly since few people there were younger than forty.

The only thing I knew of Clinton at that point was his atrocious introduction of Massachusetts Governor Michael Dukakis at the 1988 Democratic Convention in Atlanta. Although not a delegate, I borrowed a floor pass to join the California delegation for the acceptance speech of the presidential nominee, who was a classmate of mine at Swarthmore. Clinton made no small task of the introduction, droning on for thirty-three minutes. When he finally broke through the increasingly loud chatter rising from the floor to say, "In conclusion..." the delegates cheered wildly. Just about the only thing people remembered about his speech the next day was its length.

When he showed up four years later to speak in the elegant Venetian Room at the Fairmount, the Arkansas governor's oratory sensibility had improved considerably. Even so, his candidacy was floundering, thanks to the revelation of an extramarital relationship with an Arkansas woman named Gennifer Flowers. He was third in the polls behind Massachusetts Senator Paul Tsongas and California's former governor, Jerry Brown. Undeterred, Clinton was out on the campaign trail, like a reincarnation of the Unsinkable Molly Brown, grinning and plugging away for votes.

Clinton spoke that day, as Democrats always do, about putting education and health care at the center of his presidency. He spent considerable time on his plan to improve middle class prosperity by "growing" the economy. But on top of these issues, Clinton, to that straight audience, went out of his way to make a statement about the unacceptability of discrimination based on sexual orientation. *That* caught my attention.

After speaking, Clinton left the podium and weaved his way through the maze of clapping listeners, who were receptive, even friendly, but certainly not effusive. As he came in my vicinity, I stuck out my hand.

"Hello Governor, I'm Jim Hormel," I said.

"Hi Jim, glad to meet you," Clinton replied, with a warmth that made me feel like I was the most important person he had met all day.

I mentioned a friend from Little Rock, Jean Gordon, who had helped Clinton raise money for his congressional campaign in 1974. I knew Jean through an informal network of philanthropists.

Aware that the moment was fleeting, I got to the point: "I deeply appreciate your references to sexual orientation. The equality issue is very important."

Looking me deep in the eye, and nodding, he said, as I recall, "It *is* very important."

As quickly as it had brought him to me, the momentum of the crowd whisked Clinton away, leaving me with something I hadn't anticipated: a sense of awe. Clinton was taller and broader than I had realized, and he seemed to establish a genial rapport with everyone he met. Familiar, without being insincere, he communicated a genuine sense of caring. With many voters hungry for the sort of charm that Ronald Reagan had, Clinton's charisma was an invaluable political asset.

He's hard to resist, I thought.

My curiosity stirred, I called a few Democrats who knew Clinton well. They told me about the Governor's efforts to improve Arkansas schools, his welfare-to-work innovations, and other initiatives later cited as the hallmarks of his "New Democrat" philosophy. The consensus among them was that the scandal ended with Gennifer Flowers; no more dirt lurked beneath the carpet.

At that point in the campaign, many Californians backed Jerry Brown, who, in his third run for the presidency, finally seemed to be a viable candidate. I had met him years before through Jerry Berg and supported his campaigns. I liked him a great deal. He was smart and independent, and uncompromising in his support of LGBT equality issues. Jerry Brown defied political definition, but he wasn't always pragmatic and had a tendency to detach easily from public opinion, which led to his infamous, if somewhat unfair, nickname: Governor Moonbeam. I had an intuition that he wouldn't be the nominee.

The more I was exposed to Clinton and his campaign, the more I saw something very different and appealing. Even as the underdog, he used tactics that made him look stronger without belittling others in the field. The Gennifer Flowers exposé would have caused others to say, *I'm not gonna go through with this*, but Clinton was absolutely determined, and Hillary was there for him—she was a very stout campaigner. I made my first donation about a month after the San Francisco speech, and made several others to him and the Democratic Party. At the July Democratic National Convention at Madison Square Garden, when the California delegation split between Clinton and Jerry Brown, I went with Clinton.

That year, before the convention, I was a member of the National Platform Committee, which was responsible for drafting a document on the party's positions. At meetings that loosely resembled congressional hearings, I was among three dozen or so Democrats who visited cities like Cleveland, Philadelphia, and New York City, listening to experts testify in front of large audiences.

Our platform was typically progressive on social issues, such as pro-choice, gay rights, middle class tax relief, and environmental protection. It steered away from things that might carry the negative connotations of liberalism that loomed over, and eventually doomed, Michael Dukakis, instead stressing, as Clinton did, the importance of smaller government, family values, and individual responsibility. Participating on the committee expanded my contacts with political movers and shakers; it was even more important because, in 1992, gay people were seldom, if ever, given a visible policy position in the Democratic Party. The election took place in a year in which AIDS deaths in the United States climbed precipitously, and the active involvement of an openly gay man on the committee set an example, making clear that the party had room for our constituency.

On the eve of the November elections in 1992, as Clinton took a strong lead, a few of my friends began to rib me: "You know, you could be an ambassador or something."

Over dinner one night—coincidentally, at the Fairmont Hotel— the national party treasurer, Bob Farmer, encouraged me to pursue a presidential appointment. An old friend, Bob made his name as national treasurer for John Glenn's 1984 presidential campaign. He also happened to be gay.

While Bob's suggestion intrigued me, I didn't take it all that seriously. It didn't seem realistic: I had contributed, but I didn't go to any great lengths to stump for Clinton. I couldn't imagine that I was very high on the totem pole. Besides, the idea of seeking an appointment seemed immodest. Who was I to ask for that? Just because I had donated money, I should expect a nomination? That didn't seem right. And then, of course, there was the cringe-inducing thought of entering the national political arena, where San Francisco Democrats were treated with the same affection as rabid raccoons.

Bob suggested that I get my hands on a copy of the coveted Plum Book, a congressional directory of the seven thousand appointed political positions within the administrative structure in Washington. Officially titled the *United States Government Policy and Supporting Positions*, it is the kind of book that a Senate staffer, once upon a time, kept secure in a drawer, lest a colleague see it on the desk and walk away with it. (Now, of course, it's available for all to read online.)

I skimmed through the Cabinet jobs, the senior level department appointments, and the presidential commissions. There was assistant secretary of this and undersecretary of that and memberships on commissions relating to every aspect of public policy. In most cases, my qualifications weren't suitable for a given position, or else I knew of someone higher in the pecking order than me. The best fit, it seemed, was an ambassadorial post.

Some ambassadors are career diplomats who rise through the ranks of the Foreign Service to earn their nominations. Others are political appointees who have distinguished themselves in some way or been very supportive of the President, either by bringing voters or dollars to his campaign. I was in that latter category, doubtless one of dozens of white men on the list who had done the same thing. The only thing that truly set me apart was the fact that I was openly gay.

That was an important difference at the time. The country was a mess, having just endured eight years of Reagan and four years of Bush Senior, and the gay constituency had been overwhelmed by a pandemic. My philanthropic work had grown significantly, owing to both the expansion of my resources after my mother's death and the enormous needs created by AIDS. But public service of any kind was an opportunity to demonstrate that the constituency could make a contribution. Something else nudged me too: I knew that I could afford the risk. It sounds like noblesse oblige, and I don't mean it that way, but the truth was that being open about my sexual orientation was not going to cost me a job. Or get me kicked out of my house. Or destroy my family. I lived in a place of privilege from which I could speak and act without fear of any other retribution than a bruised ego, and increasingly, I felt compelled to make use of those circumstances. As I mulled it over, a presidential appointment seemed a golden opportunity.

To me, the most important aspect of all of this was that the nomination required Senate confirmation. That would oblige one hundred U.S. Senators—and, in all likelihood, the media and the American public—to decide whether a gay person was fit to serve as a direct representative of the President of the United States. If the Senate opted not to confirm me, its decision would call into focus the discrimination gay people face in this country. Either way, a national conversation would mean something for the whole LGBT constituency.

The possible benefits began to outweigh my personal misgivings. And besides, how bad could it really be?

I tested out the idea with a few people, including Senator Alan Cranston and Congresswoman Pelosi, both of whom were encouraging. There was consensus that a nomination process would be challenging, even with Democrats in power in the White House and both houses of Congress. But the regressive social politics of Reagan and Bush were riding out of town, and Clinton's boundless optimism was contagious. I felt confident I could be confirmed.

Following protocol, Senator Cranston sent a letter recommending me to Warren Christopher, the head of Clinton's transition team, who later became Secretary of State. On December 24, 1992, I sat down at the computer to write to Christopher myself. As if shooting off a last minute note to Santa, I asked for an appointment to Norway, a country very accepting of same-sex relationships, where my youngest daughter Sarah was head coordinator of master's degree and foreign exchange programs at the Norwegian School of Management. I mailed the letter and waited for a reply.

The New Year came and went. I heard nothing. Spring arrived, and still no letters, no phone calls.

As summer flew by, I received an invitation to a small reception with President Clinton at the navy base in Alameda. He was coming on August 13 to tour the visiting aircraft carrier *USS Carl Vinson*, and offer his rationale for closing several military bases around the country, including the one in Alameda.

My friend Don Angus and I arrived at the base that day and joined forty to fifty other non-military guests assembled alongside nearly six thousand members of the *Vinson*'s crew and another seven hundred sailors from the *USS Arkansas*. While cordoned off in our own area, I was close enough to the sailors that I was able to strike up a conversation across the rope divider with a nineteen-year-old Texan. Among other things, I asked him what he thought about Clinton's plan to lift the ban on gays serving openly in the military.

"When this ship is out at sea, we're out there all together," he said. "To make things run, we have to work together. I can tell you that there are gay sailors on this ship, and many of us know who they are, and I've never seen a situation where it made any difference."

After Clinton spoke, the small group of civilians, most of whom I assumed to be party contributors, was ushered to a nearby building for a meet-and-greet. The room had a windowed wall, with two doors on either end of the solid wall across from it. We shuttled in through one door and clustered around it, assuming that Clinton would come in that way too. Having gone in the room first, Don and I were pushed to the back of the pack. Suddenly, the other door opened. In burst a beaming Clinton, wearing a bright but tasteful blue tie. As everyone pivoted toward the other door, Don and I found ourselves positioned at the front of the crowd. Clinton was accompanied by Marsha Scott, a very attractive, gentle, and forthright aide from Arkansas whom I'd met several times. She was at that point head of the office of presidential correspondence, a position that belied her influence.

"Hello Jim, it's good to see you again," President Clinton said, shaking my hand and taking note of my neckwear, a red tie decorated with cheetahs. "Nice tie."

"Thank you, Mr. President," I said. "I think yours is very nice, too."

After greeting Don, the President moved on through the room. As Marsha walked by, I collared her. I briefly considered raising my nomination effort but decided that it might be inappropriate. Instead, I asked whether I could give the President my tie.

"Why, he'd just love it," she said, with a smile.

When Clinton began making his exit a short while later, we shook hands again.

"I'm glad you like this tie," I said, tugging at the knot with my left hand.

"Oh no, no, don't do that," he said.

"Oh, Mr. President, I really want you to have it," I replied, handing it over.

With a wide smile, he took the tie, folded it up, and put it in his jacket pocket. "I will wear it within a week," he said.

Exactly seven days later, on August 20, Don called.

"Jim, have you seen the *Chronicle*?" he asked. "You've got to get it immediately."

The paper's front page carried a color photo of Clinton on Air Force One, smiling over a little birthday cake. Around his neck, bright against the white icing and his white shirt, was my cheetah tie.

The spark of that moment passed, along with the rest of the summer, and still I heard nothing. My contacts at HRC monitored White House press releases and scoured *Roll Call,* the Capitol Hill newspaper, which tracked even the most insignificant of appointments. My name was nowhere to be found. Two weeks after seeing Clinton in Alameda, Tom Loftus, the Speaker of the Wisconsin State Assembly, was nominated to be ambassador to Norway. I was dismayed but not surprised: like many people from Wisconsin, Loftus was of Norwegian descent. I made periodic calls to John Emerson, a friend from Los Angeles who served as deputy director of presidential personnel. He had nothing to report, except to say: "You're still on the list."

As important as the nomination fight was, most waking moments those days were devoted to other things, including my most significant philanthropic project to date: the creation of a gay and lesbian center at the new $134 million public library at the San Francisco Civic Center. The idea was to include in the library complex four affinity centers and a meeting room, dedicated to groups that had shaped the history of the city. (The others were: African Americans, Chinese, Filipino Americans, and Latino/Hispanics.) In the early days of the AIDS epidemic, I thought a lot about history and its preservation. A gay and lesbian affinity center was an unprecedented opportunity to preserve LGBT literature, history, and culture, and to do so within a community institution of tremendous stature. Excited to be part of the effort, I donated $500,000, the largest individual gift I had ever made, and involved myself in fundraising efforts thereafter.

As 1993 dragged on, with the nomination process simmering on the back burner, some sort of reverse psychology seized me: the

longer an appointment eluded me, the more I wanted it. Whenever
I contacted John Emerson or others in Washington, they assured
me that I was still in consideration, but as the available posts were
filled, my name seemed to wither on the list. In a way, I felt like
the awkward, uncoordinated kid waiting to be picked in gym class,
except that the kid always gets picked in the end, and I wasn't sure
that I could count on that.

One of the people I checked in with was Senator Dianne
Feinstein. As we discussed my frustration one day on the phone, she
planted a seed in my head. "If you really want this Jim," she said,
"you're going to have to wage your own campaign."

Dianne is right, I thought later. *No more polite reticence, like
with Marsha Scott in Alameda. If I am going to do this, I have to go
all out.*

From then on, I went regularly to Washington. I made myself
seen at events, met with everyone I knew, and pursued as many
new contacts as possible. I'm not much of a salesperson, and am
particularly bad at it when *I* am the commodity being sold. Yet, I
knew instinctively that Dianne's advice was appropriate. To keep my
name in circulation, I had to build a circle of supporters.

In November 1993, Larry and I were lucky enough to be among
140 people to receive an invitation to a state dinner. The first such
event the Clintons had in the White House, the dinner was in honor of
President Kim Young Sam of South Korea. Diplomatically speaking,
it was not an official state dinner, but it all had all the trappings of
one. Washington was abuzz about the guest list, particularly with the
Clintons' Hollywood connections.

The invitees that evening did make for quite a who's who: there
were members of Congress, Supreme Court justices, university
presidents, CEOs, and a healthy contingent of celebrities ranging
from Gregory Hines to Beverly Sills to Walter Cronkite. The ambient

giddiness in the gilded State Dining Room was inescapable, as were the diamonds and other precious gems dripping from the ears, necks, and fingers of various guests. I worked the room, pressing my card into the hand of anyone who would take it. I sought out Warren Christopher, who was then Secretary of State, and let him know that my interest in an appointment remained keen. I also wanted him to be able to put a face with the name.

When the time came to sit for dinner, Larry and I went to our table, where we, like all couples, were separated. I took up my assigned seat next to a Korean-born woman from Chicago, who was grossly overdressed, which is hard to do at a black tie dinner. I tried to speak with her, but her English skills were sparse, and my Korean was non-existent. Next to her was General John Shalikashvili, the Georgian-born Army general who had become the Chairman of Joint Chiefs of Staff a few months before. Over beef tenderloin, with our dinner companion trying vainly to follow along, the General and I had a very cordial and open discussion on sexual orientation and the military. He told me that it was a matter of time until gay men and lesbians were allowed to serve openly in the armed forces.

The very next week, under great political pressure, President Clinton made a decision that delayed the open service of gay men and lesbians, giving effect to the heinous *Don't Ask, Don't Tell* ban.

At the very end of the 1980s, the government was on the verge of doing away with the regulation barring gays from military service. Lawrence Korb, an assistant secretary of defense, authored a report describing the policy as counterproductive, unrealistic, and keeping good people out of the service. Coming from a man appointed by Ronald Reagan, the report had a powerful punch. The trouble was that no one knew about it.

In 1989, during President Bush's term in office, Congressman Gerry Studds, an openly gay man from New Bedford, Massachusetts, made the report public. It was one of the most important acts of his political career.

With his report out in the light of day, Korb started making public appearances. He was particularly persuasive because he had been responsible for enforcing the ban when he was at the Department of Defense. Ted Koppel and other journalists reported the stories of people such as Joe Steffan, a Minnesota farm boy who was dismissed from the U.S. Naval Academy a week before he graduated. Articulate, serious, and attractive, Joe was at the top of his class. He had sung the "Star Spangled Banner" at two Army-Navy football games. Yet when the Academy found out that he was gay, they kicked him out. The press attention catalyzed an air of inevitability; it appeared that the regulation was going to collapse under its own bad weight. Then the Persian Gulf War flared up, and presidential elections came along, and the issue faded into the background.

The controversy had not escaped Clinton, though, who mentioned it a few times on the campaign trail. I believe he honestly and truly saw the issue as a matter of fairness.

Even though he had minimal experience with official Washington, and had been labeled a draft dodger during the campaign, Clinton revived the issue very early in his administration. He might have called the generals and admirals together, pointing to Korb's report, and said, "This is what I'm going to do, and this is why." If Clinton had been as authoritative as Harry S. Truman was with desegregation of the armed forces in 1948, he might have gotten away with it. But Clinton didn't have the same credibility as Truman, who had led the United States out of World War II. By comparison, Clinton seemed to spring the issue on everyone, without having laid the political groundwork. The military leadership resisted immediately, and both Republicans and Democrats erupted in opposition.

"Don't Ask, Don't Tell," or DADT, was conceived of as a way of moving out of the rigid regulation of the time. I can understand how Clinton might have thought that the policy, which included the elimination of explicit questions about sexual orientation, was a step in the right direction. But from the outset, it was disastrous, codifying deception and secrecy—the very practices the gay constituency was trying to overcome. The policy had no positive value whatsoever.

As each day passed, the possibility of an appointment seemed more remote. I stopped dwelling on it. Then, in the spring of 1994, Nancy Pelosi phoned me from Washington.

"Expect a call from the White House," she said.

I was jarred into primary alert. "Really?" I wondered aloud. "Is something really happening?"

She assured me that it was.

For the next several days, I waited expectantly, but the call didn't come. I began to feel a bit like a Tantalus, longing for the delicious-looking grapes just out of my reach. I hoped that I wasn't waiting for the impossible.

Three or four weeks later, I called Nancy back.

"Nancy, I haven't heard from anybody," I said. "Do you know what's going on?"

"Let me see what I can find out," she replied, surprised.

She got back to me a few days later with a tale of twisted political machinations. The White House apparently had planned to nominate me as Ambassador to Fiji, until Governor John Waihee and Senator Daniel Akaka, both of Hawaii, began to discuss the post with the White House. One of them was probably going to be nominated, she told me.

Both Governor Waihee and Senator Akaka were in stronger political positions than I was. I stopped waiting for the phone to ring.

But several weeks later, in June, a call came out of the blue. For some reason that I never clearly ascertained, the White House had reverted to its original plan. According to the staffer who phoned me, I had been *designated*, a technical term that meant the nomination was not public and still subject to vetting.

I immediately set out to learn everything I could about Fiji, starting with a resource I had on my book shelf: a guide to gay-friendly travel destinations. Within five minutes, I knew the thing I most needed to know: Fiji had a sodomy statute in place.

Enacted during British colonial days, the law wasn't enforced, but it was still on the books. Right away, I called a contact at the State Department to ask whether the statute would be of concern. A week later—presumably the amount of time it took to check the traps—the officer from State called back. The statute would not deter Clinton from making the nomination. While encouraged, I only shared the news with a handful of people, including Larry, who dreaded the thought of a public fight. He was an introspective person who preferred quiet nights with friends to glad-handing at events.

When I set out on the journey to become an ambassador, the matter of my sexual orientation never came from my lips. Not once did I raise the subject or speak of it, not in correspondence or conversations, or any other public utterances. When I learned about the Fiji sodomy statute, I spoke directly to State Department officials about my sexuality and my concern, but otherwise, I never proactively raised the matter. If asked, I replied briefly and specifically. I never concealed the fact that I was gay, but I didn't want to tout it or use it as a manipulative device that would overshadow my credentials or qualifications. In the end, *The Washington Post* put the topic in the public domain.

Al Kamen's "In the Loop" political column was so highly regarded that many Washington politicos read it with their first sip of coffee. A few weeks after I was designated, in July, Kamen's column ran with the headline, "Pacific Isle for an Activist?" The first few sentences summarized what had happened to date, mentioning me, my sexual orientation, and Fiji. I suspected that the White House leaked the information to test the waters. A line in the story reeked of our collective naiveté: "Sources say there was some concern inside the administration about exactly where to place Hormel so as not to turn this into a big deal."

There was no visible reaction to the story around Washington, and the political establishment went into August hibernation.

Not so in Fiji.

In September, the week before I was to return to Washington for briefings, I rolled out of bed one morning and found in the bathroom mirror that one end of my moustache pointed south. In fact, half of my face was drooping. When I tried to speak, my lips were heavy, and a lot of "zhu zhu" sounds seemed to come out of them. I saw a doctor and found out that I had Bell's palsy, a temporary paralysis of the facial muscles. He assured me that there was little I could do but wait it out. Odds were that my face would go back to normal with time.

Figuring that I would be calling on people with a certain level of maturity and sophistication, I proceeded with my plans to go to Washington. It didn't occur to me that my affliction was an omen of the political paralysis to come. I arrived at the State Department, anticipating a few days of briefings. A young officer from the Fiji desk greeted me in the cavernous, flag-filled marbled lobby, making no remark about my sagging face.

He said, somberly: "There's been a complication."

Upstairs in his office, he showed me the front page of a recent *Fiji Times*. "Gay Activist to be Next U.S. Ambassador," the headline screamed. The story itself was innocuous—it mentioned the Kamen column and a bit of my experience—but the headline alone was enough to generate all kinds of hostile reactions in Fiji. Apparently, the Fijian ambassador to Washington had been instructed by his government to ask President Clinton not to make the nomination.

The news surprised me as much as the Bell's palsy had. Two months had passed since the Al Kamen column, and nothing indicated that there might possibly be this level of objection—here or abroad.

That week, an attaché from the U.S. Embassy in Fiji happened to be in town. He shared his views with me over lunch across the river in Virginia, saying that he thought I would be well-received in Fiji.

"First of all, if the Fijians deal with this in their way, they will pretend you are not gay," he said. "There is a member of cabinet who is gay. He pretends not to be. He is married and has a family, but everybody knows."

The attaché said that although the President and Prime Minister of Fiji were not happy, they would give their approval if President Clinton asked for it. He said he described my background to them in this way: "I told them that you are an activist, the same way Elizabeth Taylor is an activist."

The president's response, he said, was: "Well then, send us Elizabeth Taylor."

We both broke into laughter. It was one of few light moments during the entire process.

The midterm Congressional campaign that year was turning out to be very heated. The bloom was long off the Clintons' rose. They were bogged down with the Whitewater real estate scandal, among other things. Seemingly turbo-charged, Republican Congressman Newt Gingrich worked his way around his adopted state of Georgia and the rest of the country, waving a document he called *Contract with America*.

The Republicans' momentum carried through to Election Day. Democrats lost control of the Senate, and the House, where they had been in the majority since 1954. When I visited Washington a month later, I went to Capitol Hill to say hello to people I knew, such as Nancy Pelosi, Barney Frank, and Gerry Studds. The scene at the Congressional office buildings resembled the evacuation of Paris in World War II. I'd never seen so many downcast faces. The halls were full of boxes. Democratic staffers were leaving in droves.

As a result of the handover of power, Republican Senator Jesse Helms of North Carolina, notoriously antagonistic to the gay constituency, became chairman of the foreign relations committee. My discouragement morphed into near hopelessness—and with good reason.

A staff person in Helms's office let it be known, in the whispering way of Washington, that as far as the Senator was concerned, my nomination would never see the light of day. That, I was told, was an exact quote.

Some people offered condolences, but I refused to pronounce my nomination dead. I was so heavily invested that I could not imagine bowing out. I was after something much larger than a post or a title—I was seeking to break a barrier kept in place by the *Fiji Times* with its screaming headline, and by Jesse Helms's staff person with his menacing comment.

Sixty years old, with a law degree and a thirty-five-year career as a businessman and philanthropist, I decided that it wasn't too late to work on my résumé.

Chapter Fourteen

WORKING ON MY RÉSUMÉ

Between 1994 and 1997, I was a squeaky wheel in Washington, at least behind closed doors.

Self-promotion was something I did not enjoy or do well, but once I decided, *Yes, I'm interested,* and *Yes, I might make a difference,* then I had to accept that putting myself on the line was the only way to get where I wanted to be.

I made continual phone calls to the Office of Presidential Personnel and the State Department. I stayed in close contact with Marsha Scott, who had moved up to deputy director in the personnel office; she always seemed to have Clinton's ear. I regularly consulted Dianne Feinstein, a new member of the Senate foreign relations committee. And the lobbyists at HRC were constantly on the lookout for new intelligence on a possible nomination.

The Administration had a lot going on during those three years. The Republican takeover of Congress had put Congressional Democrats out on their asses and changed the whole complexion of Washington. Paula Jones, an Arkansas state employee, had filed a sexual harassment suit against the President, and Republicans were spending God-knows-how-much taxpayer money on that and Whitewater, trying to find something actionable against the President. I'm sure Clinton was worried about how the hell to survive the 1996 election. Sympathetic as he or anyone else in the White House might have been, the big question was: could the President afford to pursue my appointment? The failed nomination processes of Lani Guinier, Zoe Baird, and Kimba Wood were evidence that he couldn't.

Trying to spend as little political capital as possible, the White House sought to appease me with other opportunities. One was an appointment to a U.S. delegation led by Vice President Al Gore to the UN Summit on Social Development, a global poverty conference in Copenhagen in March 1995. The fact that Gore was delegation leader said something about the summit's significance, but I didn't see how participation would enhance my qualifications for an ambassadorial post. Delegate to the United Nations Human Rights Commission in Geneva seemed more appropriate. When I suggested that to a contact in the White House, I was rebuffed.

"Wouldn't you rather go to Copenhagen with the Vice President for a week in early spring than suffer through six weeks of winter in Geneva?" asked a chuckling staffer in the White House Personnel Office.

The remark was made in humor, but I couldn't resist a little dig.

"I'm not looking for a vacation," I replied. I was looking for a way to maintain my credibility as an ambassadorial candidate.

The Geneva assignment interested me because it centered on human rights, an area in which I had some expertise. Working under the auspices of the State Department with career diplomats, I would get a sense of how a U.S. mission operated. The appointment didn't come with Senate confirmation but it would keep me on the right track.

With my steady cajoling and nudging, the White House eventually came through with the appointment.

My term of service to the Human Rights Commission coincided with the fiftieth anniversary of the UN, which was cause for pageantry celebrating its past and polemics on its accomplishments. Much as the UN aspired to the ideals of the *Universal Declaration of Human Rights,* it was too often used by super powers and tiny countries alike to promote their domestic and international agendas.

The Human Rights Commission, with fifty-three countries each serving a three-year term, was a venue for the political games. Any member state of the UN, regardless of its human rights record, was eligible to participate. Anyone with a modicum of experience could predict with almost 100 percent accuracy the events of the annual meetings: verbal battles between India and Pakistan; a monumental effort by the United States to introduce a resolution on China; and a proportionally mammoth effort by the Chinese to prevent that resolution from coming to the floor. Smaller countries formed voting blocs, as they did in the General Assembly, enabling them to exert disproportionate political power.

Commission meetings took place at the Palais des Nations, an elegant, classical building on a hill facing Lake Geneva and the French Alps with peacocks roaming free on its front lawn. The interior was a ramble of meeting rooms, offices, and open spaces used for coffee-drinking and networking. The debates, which were held in a huge, sunken assembly room, centered on human rights violations in Libya, Burma, and several other countries, along with women's rights, racism, xenophobia, and abuse of indigenous peoples. In a heartening moment, the Commission formally ended years of battle over Apartheid in South Africa.

Our delegation had no staff; each member took turns reporting back on the sessions, whether morning, afternoon, or evening. Led by former New York congresswoman and vice presidential candidate Geraldine Ferraro, the delegation met every morning at 8 AM and reviewed happenings of the day before and schedules for the day ahead.

I didn't know Gerry before I went to Geneva but found her very personable and active in getting to know members of the delegation. She and I took a brisk walk along the lakefront most evenings after dinner, during which we discussed politics, family, and even the ongoing O. J. Simpson trial, which was covered as much in Europe as it was in the States.

Gerry assigned me the task of preparing and presenting a statement on HIV/AIDS and human rights, which was, to my knowledge, the first speech on the subject before the Commission as a whole. I was thrilled to do it. My cynicism aside, the Commission had as its audience the governments of nearly all countries of the world, along with their national media, making it an ideal forum for raising the profile of any global issue. World Health Organization scientists, who worked in their own headquarters up the hill from the Palais, gave me access to all the latest data. They told me then, in February 1995, that 40 million people would be infected with the AIDS virus within a decade—a fact I used in my speech, even though it seemed too apocalyptic to be true.

Right after I spoke, I returned home to San Francisco for the weekend, where I was the principal funder of a concert called "Stand Up To Be Counted." It was part of an ongoing effort to focus attention on AIDS as a matter of broad public concern. We organizers wanted the world to see the virus as a universal health issue, like polio and malaria, and not a "gay" disease. Hosted by Carol Burnett, the concert attracted a diverse group of San Francisco's socialites and donors, who, by then, had begun to give full support to AIDS initiatives.

Our efforts to build awareness were not enough to prevent WHO's predictions from coming true. And the majority of those who died were not gay. They were heterosexual men and women from Africa.

Not long after I returned home from Geneva, in April 1995, the San Francisco Public Library dedicated the James C. Hormel Gay & Lesbian Center.

When the campaign for the LGBT affinity center began, library fundraisers hoped to raise $1.6 million including my contribution. Almost immediately, money streamed in from all over the country. A fund-raising dinner at the Hyatt Regency drew more people than the ballroom could hold; we needed an overflow room for an additional three hundred people. The final tally defied all expectations, including my own. Some three thousand individuals donated about $3 million—double the original goal.

When Chuck Forester, a city planner who was a driving force behind the center, approached me about naming the center in my honor, I graciously declined. I felt uncomfortable; the library project was much bigger than one individual, particularly one still living. He argued that the center was a landmark for all time and that it would mean something to the collection and the constituency to have it designated in my name. Eventually, I relented, feeling humbled and honored.

On the evening of the official opening, the library was decked out for a party with balloons, a DJ, and dance floor. Any semblance of library silence was overtaken by the ebullient chatter of hundreds of guests. My friend Jeffrey Leiphart, a psychiatrist who for many years worked with AIDS patients, roamed around with a video camera and microphone, asking attendees their reactions to the center. Contrary to my usual jacket and tie, I wore a bright, canary yellow shirt and multicolored vest, which I bought earlier that day. I wanted to be flamboyantly festive, to be "gay" in every possible nice connotation of the word. I spoke from the middle level of a staircase that rose up through the atrium of the library.

While the Center's expansive collection is housed in the library's stacks, the center itself is a nicely paneled and warmly lit corner room. Above walls of shelved books and various reading and study spaces is a round ceiling painted with an allegorical mural entitled *Into the Light*. The work by Mark Evans and Charley Brown features Michelangelo, Florence Nightingale, Vasco da Gama, and dozens of other influential writers, artists, and historical figures known to have had same-sex relationships. I'm depicted too, next to a stack of books, hopelessly inferior amid such accomplished figures. Another of the center's powerful statements is the list of donors etched into a glass wall at the entry way. Many of them are gay couples who might never before have seen their names in print together. They are there for the world to see as leading citizens, as contributors to the community, in one of the most elemental of American public buildings: a library.

It was an enormously gratifying evening for me.

One of the ironies of that night, however, was that it was one of the last big events that Larry and I attended together. After eighteen years, we were splitting up. Ours was not an atypical situation. It was the story of two people discovering themselves and moving in different directions. We tried couples counseling and worked at resolving things that seemed to be keeping us stagnant, but our relationship had become comfortable and convenient in a way that was not good for either of us. Perhaps the loss of so many friends kept us together longer than we might have otherwise. Fortunately, we parted on good terms and remained friends.

Better prepared after the Geneva experience, I went back to my badgering role in late 1995 and early 1996, sure that several Washington officials prayed each day for me to go away.

As much as the appointment was a bête noire for them, it held potential for political gain. Democrats, and the President in particular, realized that the concerns of the strengthening LGBT constituency were consistent with the broad, social concerns of the

Democratic Party. In purely pragmatic terms, doing something for me might reinvigorate progressives and restore a few friendships on the eve of the elections.

Somewhere along the line, it occurred to me that I should press for the position of U.S. delegate to the UN General Assembly, which required Senate confirmation. According to the particular procedure for that post, delegates were appointed and presented as a group for Senate confirmation *after* their service. If confirmed once, I thought, the second time should be easier. As part of the delegation, I would learn a lot more about diplomacy.

Initially, the White House was reluctant. What confused me was that they offered me other appointments for which I was less qualified, such as a seat on a high-level trade commission that any CEO would envy. I could only guess that the UN slots were on hold as a political reward for someone else.

It was clear to me that while the White House didn't want to engage Republicans in a confirmation battle, I was never completely removed from the list of possible ambassadorial appointments. There was enough movement to make me feel that the President cared to do something, but hadn't yet figured out how or what. For example, whenever I called Bob Nash, Director of Presidential Personnel, asking for a meeting, he always made time for me. An African American, Bob let me know that he understood from personal experience what minority representation meant. He had a sense of what I was battling against, and what I was battling for.

After what seemed like an endless wait, the appointment finally came through. I accepted right away and was off to New York in September 1996 for the fifty-first session of the General Assembly.

The United Nations Secretariat building, home to the General Assembly and the Security Council, was impressive, even with its dated décor and lack of regular maintenance. Inside, I felt as if I had walked back into the 1960s, and that Nikita Kruschev or Adlai Stevenson might walk through the door at any moment and make me party to an international incident. Perched on the western bank of the East River, many rooms had huge windows overlooking the water, with its steady traffic of tugs, including one with a big banner shouting TAIWAN. I had never spent any time at the UN and was struck by the vibrancy of the people: the European women with elegant suits and scarves tied close to their necks; the West African men in colorful damask and linens, South Asian representatives in silken saris, and every language imaginable arriving in snippets to one's ears. During my time there, Kofi Annan took over from Boutros Boutros-Ghali as secretary general. The difference between the leaders was sharp: Boutros-Ghali carried himself with an air of aloofness and entitlement and moved around the building surrounded by body guards. Annan greeted everyone in the hallway with handshakes and warm smiles.

Normally, I walked to the UN from a pied à terre on 55th Street that I acquired in 1992. In my obsessive way, I figured out the traffic lights so that I could do the twenty-five-minute walk at a steady pace without ever having to stop. The U.S. Mission was across the street from the UN Secretariat, in a twelve-story building with space for more than two hundred staff members and an ambassador. The General Assembly delegation included five alternates: two Senators and three members of the public, whose task was to be everywhere the U.S. Ambassador and other senior officials could not be. The delegation's senators, Democrat Claiborne Pell of Rhode Island, who had been a staffer at the UN at its birth in 1945, and Republican Rod Grams of Minnesota, spent most of their time in Washington. We three public members shared a secretary and a suite of bland offices. Our windows offered a glimpse of Dag Hammarskjold Plaza and the famous sculpture of the knotted gun, a gift from Luxembourg to the UN.

In the General Assembly chamber, where the UN does much of its day-to-day business, each delegation had the same amount of space, whether the country was as large as India or as small as Kiribati. During important sessions, Ambassador Albright sat in the U.S. delegation chair. On lesser occasions, when given the chance, I happily took her place. While the task normally involved listening to boring speeches, I spoke on behalf of the United States several times. I never knew what I was going to say until a staff person handed me a statement. Once I was given Speech A and Speech B, and it wasn't decided until the last minute, when we knew what had happened in the Security Council, which I would give. I loved the bustling marketplace feel of the UN and the immersion in policy debates but the experience was tantalizing—I wanted to do more.

About that time, a small, brave group of gay and lesbian UN staff members came together to form a solidarity organization, despite the fact that they may have risked prison terms and even execution if their sexual orientation was known in their home countries. I met with members of the group in Geneva and New York but did nothing official or public with them, lest a perception develop that I was using my position to promote an agenda other than that of the U.S. government.

Sitting at my desk at the U.S. mission one morning, I received an unexpected call from Sally Morrison, a friend who worked with Elizabeth Taylor. She said that Elizabeth wanted to address the General Assembly on World Aids Day, December 1. I loved the idea.

"How exciting it would be to put that program together," I told her. It was just the sort of opportunity I had been looking for.

Ambassador Albright gave her support immediately and assigned a staff person to work with me, who, by coincidence, was a Swarthmore alumna.

Following protocol, we contacted the President of the General Assembly, Razali Ismail of Malaysia, to ask permission for Elizabeth Taylor to speak.

The reply from his office came back quickly: NO.

I was shocked—who could draw more media and public attention to AIDS than Elizabeth Taylor? We called the President's office, asking for an explanation. The assistant who dealt with our request was quite fluent in bureaucratese. Our phone conversations went something like this:

"Only members of delegations are allowed to address the General Assembly," he said.

"Well, Stevie Wonder was here a few weeks ago addressing the General Assembly on some children's issue," I replied.

"That wasn't an official session," he said.

"Well, this doesn't have to be an official session either," I said.

"I'm afraid that if we let her speak, it would look as if we were showing favoritism to the United States."

"But Elizabeth Taylor is an international figure. She was made a Dame by the Queen, and she has a British passport," I explained.

"Nonetheless. She will be identified with the United States. If you were going to present a program, you'd have to have a panel with four or five people from around the world, people *like* Elizabeth Taylor," he said.

"Well, there really isn't anybody *like* Elizabeth Taylor," I said.

"Nevertheless. We simply can't allow her to appear by herself in this context," he said.

My Swarthmore colleague and I did a little brainstorming and decided a five-person panel would still work. We deliberately sought out women—powerful women—believing they would be persuasive in conveying the universality of the fight against HIV/AIDS.

We recruited a high caliber group: Marina Mahatir, daughter of the Prime Minister of Malaysia and head of the Malaysian AIDS Foundation; Noerine Kaleeba, a Ugandan woman who helped develop a national plan to fight AIDS in her country; Martina Clark, a San Francisco woman living with HIV; and Cristina Saralegui, the "Oprah" of Spanish language television. And then, lastly, Elizabeth Taylor.

World Aids Day fell on a Sunday that year, so we held the commemoration on Monday, December 2. The day dawned rainy and windy. The airports had closed periodically over the weekend but somehow all the panelists arrived in time.

Hoards of journalists turned out for the large, private luncheon in the Delegates' dining room, including a photographer who shoved Madeleine Albright out of the way in order to get a better shot of Elizabeth Taylor. Madeleine, unfazed by all the fuss, retained her composure. I suspect Elizabeth found it annoying.

I met Elizabeth for the first time on the eve of my twenty-second birthday. My mother was hosting a New Year's Eve party at our home in Los Angeles, and Elizabeth's brother, Howard, was there. He and his wife Mara were friends with Thomas from Palos Verdes College. Elizabeth and her husband Michael Wilding, the British actor, arrived unexpectedly and late in the evening, after fleeing a miserable party elsewhere.

Elizabeth was nearly nine months pregnant at the time. We visited together in a quiet corner of the living room, away from the revelers. It's hard to imagine how people grow up in Hollywood, especially when they are child stars. But Elizabeth was more down to earth than people thought. Years later, when she visited Howard and Mara on Kauai, I saw their two families, complete with all the kids, enjoying a beach picnic like any "typical" American family.

In the 1980s, working with amfAR, I came to see how brave Elizabeth was. She was the first public figure to stand up and say: "AIDS is a horrible health issue that we all must address, now!" I don't know of any straight public figure—celebrity, politician, or otherwise—who spoke out before she did. Her boldness helped to humanize the disease.

Despite all the bureaucratic nonsense leading up to it, the UN event was a success. Elizabeth's presence ensured that the room was packed, and her continuing call for an AIDS vaccine made headlines. The other panelists were so knowledgeable and compelling that it was impossible to leave the room without a greater understanding of and concern about the pandemic.

I left New York in December thinking that my résumé looked pretty good. Five months later, when the Senate confirmed dozens of presidential appointees in one big batch, my name was among them.

By early 1997, the LGBT constituency was after President Clinton, demanding atonement. As part of his effort to keep the White House in the November 1996 race against Kansas Senator Bob Dole, the President signed the *Defense of Marriage Act,* a law that defined marriage as being between a man and woman. He then went on radio shows, including Christian radio, touting his "leadership" on DOMA.

At the time of the bill's lightning speed consideration, the President may have been so oppressed by the political atmosphere— the Republican fire in Congress was still at the level of an inferno— that he allowed himself to support it and sign it. But that didn't make it any easier to forgive. DOMA was (and still is[4]) one of the worst

---

[4]Fifteen years later, we are still fighting DOMA, and the spiral of state constitutional amendments that it catalyzed. DOMA almost blatantly defies the Constitution, which is why state Supreme Courts in California, Connecticut, Iowa, and Massachusetts issued carefully reasoned and crafted opinions making clear that same-sex marriage is protected in their states. In 2008, California voters invalidated their Court's decision.

pieces of legislation in the history of civil rights in America. It was an explicit, unequivocal statement of inequality, a stinging slap in the face of the LGBT constituency.

While nothing short of repeal could make up for DOMA, I and others wanted a clear sign that Clinton had not abandoned our constituency. My anger propelled me into a non-stop, night-and-day effort to secure an ambassadorial nomination. Short of cheating and stealing, I was going to do whatever it took. Nothing was more important to me in that moment.

I once again pleaded my case with Bob Nash and Marsha Scott. I pressed every openly gay White House official I knew, including Karen Tramontano, a personable and highly-regarded strategist who occupied prime real estate in the West Wing. Another was Richard Socarides, a young New York attorney serving as the White House liaison to the LGBT constituency.

Back in San Francisco, I had a new ally, Tim Wu, an Ivy League lawyer who worked at a consulting firm for nonprofit organizations. I met him years earlier at a dinner for the Lambda Legal Defense and Education Fund, a national advocacy group for LGBT individuals. We bumped into each other at events, and a friendship sprouted from our common interests, particularly politics. We started to see each other and realized how much we might enrich each other's lives. He had a lot of ideas on how to keep the pressure up in Washington.

Every time I called the 202 area code, my heart rate went up. Sometimes I boiled over in frustration. On the phone one day with Richard, he urged me to be patient.

"Hang in there, Jim," he said. "So far, so good."

I shouted back: "No, Richard, so far, *no* good—you've got to make them understand!"

Not too long after that call, I was offered the top post in Bermuda, which did not have an ambassador but a consul general. The appointment did not require Senate confirmation.

A friend in the State Department called, telling me about the glamorous residence, the golf courses, the short flight to New York—all the stuff I didn't want to hear. I was offended. How many times did I have to say that I wasn't looking for a vacation?

I knew that if I accepted Bermuda, the administration would close its case on me. People would think that they had done all they needed to do for me and, by extension, the LGBT constituency. That was when I sought guidance from Dianne Feinstein and heard her warning about the extremist Republicans trying to "eat me alive." Having witnessed her share of political atrocities, Dianne encouraged me to take Bermuda. She was trying to protect me. Too naïve to conceive of the assault the far right would launch against me, I felt driven to push ahead.

I turned down the Bermuda offer and reiterated my firm interest in an ambassadorial post.

Finally, on October 6, 1997, the White House issued a press release: "President Names James C. Hormel as U.S. Ambassador to Luxembourg."

Chapter Fifteen

THE SMEARING

I had just three weeks to prepare for my great ascent, my Everest: a hearing before the Senate Committee on Foreign Relations, chaired by the notorious Jesse Helms. *If I survive the hearing,* I thought, *I'm in. I will become Ambassador to Luxembourg.* But it seemed like a huge *if*.

Lingering in my mind was the *light of day* comment attributed to Helms three years earlier, in 1994, when he became chairman of the committee.

Many people, even the occasional Democrat, used to say that the "real" Jesse Helms was a gentleman, nothing like the ornery muckraker we saw on television. What I saw was a hatemonger who unrepentantly played to people's prejudices, particularly in his campaigns, and bore great animus toward gay people. In the 1980s, when thousands of gay men were dying, Helms steadfastly opposed federal funding for the prevention and treatment of HIV/AIDS.

Toward the end of his thirty-year Senate career, Helms said that he made a mistake about HIV/AIDS funding but he never mentioned gay people. His public relations machinery made sure that he was always seen with Bono, or African leaders, or HIV-positive children.

In 1993, my fellow San Franciscan Roberta Achtenberg was under consideration for Assistant Secretary at the Department of

Housing and Urban Development. An attorney and member of the board of supervisors, Roberta was the first openly gay person to seek Senate confirmation for a presidential appointment. I readily accepted her invitation to the confirmation hearing, both to offer moral support and to witness the historic event. As Roberta answered the Senate committee's questions that day, I couldn't help imagining what it would be like to be in her seat.

Helms attended her hearing too, even though he wasn't a member of that committee. He sat in the chair belonging to his junior colleague from North Carolina, Lauch Faircloth, with his arms folded and face drawn taut in a stony glare. He later referred to Roberta as "that damn lesbian" and told the press that she was mean-spirited. She ultimately won confirmation, but he did just about everything he could to block her.

Aside from the ongoing conversation about my nomination, my name may have been familiar to Helms for another reason. For nearly two decades, I actively supported candidates running against him, including Governor Jim Hunt in 1984 and Harvey Gantt, the mayor of Charlotte, in 1990. Astoundingly, Helms never won big; his elections were always close. But he could depend on votes from a core group who apparently shared his twisted values and would vote for him no matter what.

As I prepared for my own confirmation hearing, I had regular visions of Helms sitting in the chairman's seat, his glare fixed on me.

Before my nomination could be made public, the White House and State Department had a diplomatic hurdle to clear. As with all ambassadorial nominations, State Department officials in the Presidential Appointments Office had to seek approval, or *agrément*, from the host government. Because the process is confidential, I wasn't officially notified until after Luxembourg communicated its acceptance.

Once described to me as the high point of the lowlands, Luxembourg is a democracy with about five-hundred thousand inhabitants. A land of rolling hills and broad shallow valleys, it is roughly the size of Rhode Island. I was excited to go there because of its strategic political role in the European Union.

While Luxembourg was a leader in the political modernization in Europe, the traditions of the Grand Duchy still prevailed at home. For example, the Grand Duke, as the government's diplomatic head of state, considered all ambassadorial appointments personally. When the U.S. government brought my name before him, Grand Duke Jean gave his approval promptly.

The White House notified the Senate of its intention to nominate me on October 6. The San Francisco media reported on it, noting that I was openly gay, but there was little public reaction. The hubbub was in the State Department, where officials were as anxious as I was about the upcoming confirmation hearing. They knew what Helms was capable of.

Typically, ambassadorial nominees have a few months to prepare for a hearing, but the foreign relations committee was already scheduled to consider several designees on October 29. The consensus among strategists at the White House and State Department was that if I didn't go before the committee that day, I wouldn't get a hearing before the Senate session ended in November, and my nomination would die. So the State Department organized a rigorous program to prepare me, and I got to work.

I set up camp in the State Plaza Hotel, a clean but flavorless place stylistically reminiscent of high-end Sears but well-liked for its kitchenettes and its proximity to the State Department. After making myself breakfast each morning, I walked across Virginia Avenue for the day's briefings.

Even in the densest of bureaucratic jungles, there are people who care, and in the State Department, I felt cared for. The foreign service officers didn't treat me as just another political appointee they needed to accommodate. Instead, they saw me as the President's choice to be ambassador to Luxembourg and took it as their duty to prepare me in the best possible way.

Apparently, a few people groused in the corridors about whether a gay man was an appropriate ambassadorial candidate, but no comment or complaint ever made it to my ears. The dissension, when I found out about it later, did not surprise me, given the Department's history.

Starting in the late 1940s, the federal government undertook a broad-based campaign to purge gay men and lesbians from its service. Veiled in the fear of communism, the press dubbed the witch hunt "the Lavender Scare." The State Department was singled out particularly over fear that "homosexuals" were vulnerable to blackmail or some other coercion that would cause them to divulge state secrets. In the entire history of the U.S. State Department, no such incident was ever reported, but thousands of able, hard-working federal employees were fired nonetheless for "immoral conduct."

As late as 1968, State still reported to the congressional appropriations committees on how many "homosexuals" it had fired the year before. The dismissal of gay people in federal departments continued quietly until about 1969, when the U.S. Court of Appeals finally required the Civil Service Commission to strike "immoral conduct" from its regulations.

Despite this history, my personal experience was very positive. Nearly every time I was at State, someone would approach me, whether it was in one of the long marble hallways or in the basement cafeteria, and let me know how much my fight meant to him or her. Gay foreign service officers often spoke to me, telling me of the discomfort they experienced on a daily basis. Many of them stood up in 1992 to form GLIFAA, Gays and Lesbians in Foreign Affairs Agencies, which advocates equal treatment in the State Department and U.S. Agency for International Development.

My go-to guy at State was a man named Oscar De Soto, a senior country officer for Belgium, the Netherlands, and Luxembourg. He had a calming presence, for which I was grateful. I don't think I ever asked a question he couldn't answer. At the time, he not only had me and my last-minute preparations to deal with; he was also managing President Clinton's nominees for the posts in Belgium and the Netherlands.

With autumn leaves falling around the State Department, it seemed an appropriate time for a crash course on diplomacy. I began studying reams of material covering every conceivable subject of significance to our foreign policy and strategies, complemented by detailed briefings describing the application of those policies and strategies, and the reasons for their existence.

I sat in the hot seat during mock hearings nicknamed "murder boards" for the figurative fate of a witness who doesn't handle the questions well. Oscar and others played the role of the Senators, grilling me and challenging me on NATO, European Union enlargement, the Balkans, Kosovo, and, even then, tensions with Iraq over its weapons program. After that, I felt pretty sure I was ready. The entire three-week period felt like water rushing from a spigot, but I learned as much as I could, hoping I had an answer for every question a Senator might ask.

On October 21, Oscar informed me that Senator Helms sent a letter to Secretary Albright, raising questions about my nomination.

Here it comes, I thought.

Oscar handed me a copy of the letter and I began to read. I was amazed, and for none of the reasons one would imagine.

"Frankly, I find Mr. Hormel's nomination troubling," Helms wrote.

"However, I shall not stand in the way of his nomination—provided that you can give me the following assurances…"

Helms wanted feedback on three issues: Had the government of Luxembourg given *agrément*? Would the State Department pay any expenses for my "companion?" And last, would my "companion" have any official duties at the Embassy? The first question was an easy "yes," and the second two were easy "nos."

State Department policy at the time specified that no expenses or benefits could be paid for the unmarried partner of an employee, whether gay or straight. According to another policy, neither spouses nor unmarried partners, including those of ambassadors, could be given official duties at an Embassy.

The benefits policy was highly discriminatory—after all, gay people didn't have a choice about marriage—but it was a non-issue for me: Tim had commitments of his own and was planning to stay in the United States. Even so, some people thought I should challenge the regulations as a matter of principle.

I made a political calculation and decided that my nomination would die on the spot if I challenged the policy, making me Helms's martyr. The difficult, strategic choice—one that civil rights advocates face all the time—was whether there was greater value in fighting for the principle and losing everything, or simply accepting the status quo in order to achieve the higher goal. After considering the issue carefully, I felt sure I was doing the right thing.

What puzzled me about the three questions was that Helms, as chair of the committee, must have known the answers: all three matters related to long-standing policies. Perhaps he wanted to have an objection on the record in case he got pressure from other Republicans. I couldn't imagine that Helms was willing to be so easy on me, but I took the exchange at face value.

Secretary Albright wrote back to Helms, assuring him on all three points. The subsequent chatter between Helms's office and *H*, the bureau at State responsible for relationships with the Hill, was positive. Helms confirmed he would not stand in the way of my nomination.

Indeed, when the Foreign Relations committee hearing took place on October 29, Helms didn't show up, nor did many other members of the committee. They may have been attending official events in honor of Chinese President Jiang Zemin, who was in town that day.

The wood-paneled hearing room was filled with the families of the other nominees. We milled around, waiting for the hearing to begin. The Norway nominee, a Detroit real estate developer and philanthropist named David Hermelin, went out of his way to be friendly to me, boasting that he had eighteen family members in tow. With a playful smirk, I said, "I have twenty-two."

My contingent included all my children, their spouses, many of my fourteen grandchildren, my ex-wife Alice and her husband Jim Turner, my brother Thomas, and Tim.

Although Oscar and my other State Department handlers assured me I'd be fine, I was nervous. I had no idea what might come of the hearing. Republican Senator Gordon Smith of Oregon—the Smith who would later become one of my best allies—was head of the subcommittee on European Affairs and chair of the hearing. The other nominees were questioned without any hostility from the committee.

When it was my turn, my two Senators, Dianne Feinstein and Barbara Boxer, introduced me. Their gracious comments put me at ease. I made my statement about U.S. interests in Luxembourg. Diz told me later that my remarks confirmed for her that I was perfect for the job.

Senator Smith asked one policy question of me: could Luxembourg be a model for other European countries reforming their economies? After the weeks of preparation at State, this was a softball. I answered "yes," and elaborated on the country's evolving fiscal policies.

Walking out the bronze doors of the Dirksen Senate office building later that afternoon, my entire family in tow, I breathed in the fresh autumn air. It was the first moment I allowed myself to think and feel that confirmation was within my grasp.

Since 1992, the idea of becoming ambassador had been a suggestion, then a dream to pursue, and then an actual quest, which had lasted five years. The hearing was the first opportunity for public exposure, and it was very positive. I was there among my peer nominees being treated *exactly* the same. That was all I wanted. Jesse Helms would still vote against me, no doubt, but he wasn't drumming up the committee to oppose me. I had the impression that my nomination would be sent forward with the others.

That evening, Thomas threw a big party for the family at Kinkead's, a haunt of the Washington power elite located a few blocks up Pennsylvania Avenue from the White House. It was a wonderful, exuberant celebration. Feeling such immense relief, I was happy to be with the family. It was the first time since my fiftieth birthday cruise, fifteen years earlier, that everyone had come together in my honor.

The evening was themed "An Ode to Jesse and Jimmy," and as the guests munched on mushroom strudel and roast chicken, they took turns reciting poems lampooning Helms and me. Suffice it to say that no one in that room will be under consideration for poet laureate any time soon, but I relished every bit of mangled meter and wretched rhyme.

On October 30, my friends at home opened the *San Francisco Examiner* to read: "Hormel has Easy Time at Hearing, Senate Expected to Confirm First Openly Gay Ambassador."

The committee approved my nomination the following week, on November 4, by a vote of 16-2. Helms voted against me, as did Senator John Ashcroft of Missouri.

I was dismayed by Ashcroft's vote: as dean of students, I had admitted him to the University of Chicago Law School. I wrote to him a few weeks later, asking for a meeting. Despite repeated follow-ups on my part, I never heard back from him or his office—not even a generic form letter acknowledging my correspondence. Nevertheless, the fact that only Ashcroft joined Helms in opposing my nomination was an enormous victory for me.

My name and those of all the other nominees were sent to the full Senate for consideration. Oscar and the folks at *H* expected the Senate to approve them before adjourning in mid-November for the winter recess. The national media reported that confirmation was likely. The hardest part was over, I thought. My concentration shifted to organizing my life and assembling the information I would need to go abroad and move into the post.

State Department officials felt sure enough about my confirmation that they included me in the training program for new ambassadors, beginning on November 3, the day before the foreign relations committee even voted.

The Ambassadorial Seminar is joked about as a sort of diplomatic charm school. In reality, it is a serious nuts and bolts seminar required of all ambassadorial appointees that is part embassy management and part dos and don'ts on diplomacy and official representation. My session was led by two former ambassadors, Sheldon Krys and Alan

Flanigan, who shepherded about a dozen appointees through lectures on everything from protocol, budgets, and crisis management to arts exhibits at the embassies.

On the fourth day of the seminar, at the lunch break, one of the ambassadors pulled me aside. "There's a problem," he said.

I was completely caught off-guard. The hearing had gone so smoothly; 16-2 was a damn good vote count. Yet with each passing second, I felt a creeping sense of doom, an instinct that things were going to blow-up. A voice inside me said: *I told you something would happen. You should have expected this.*

The ambassador explained to me that some unknown senators had put holds on my nomination. A hold is a parliamentary procedure, both archaic and arcane, that allows a single senator to block a vote from coming to the floor, regardless of how the other ninety-nine Senators feel. The hold can be anonymous; it doesn't have to be publicly explained or justified.

Not sure what else to do, I returned to the seminar after lunch. I needed to collect my thoughts. By the tea break, I was back in my hotel room, making calls. The first order of business was to figure out who placed the holds.

That day was a blur—I don't even remember sleeping—but within twenty-four hours, I knew that Republican Senators James Inhofe of Oklahoma and Tim Hutchinson of Arkansas were responsible for the holds. I was furious that they waited until the last moment to raise objections.

The two men were stokers of the conservative fervor gripping Washington at the time. Hailing from the Bible belt, Inhofe was swept from the House to the Senate in 1994 with the Republican takeover. Hutchinson, a native of Bentonville, Arkansas, won his Senate seat in 1996 after serving five years in the House. He was a graduate of Bob Jones University in Greenville, South Carolina, a Christian college so socially regressive that it banned interracial dating until 2000.

Thinking we might be able to influence Inhofe and Hutchinson, Tim and I started to brainstorm a list of people we knew in Oklahoma and Arkansas. I contacted both Senators immediately, asking for a meeting to address their concerns. Meanwhile, word of the holds spread around Washington.

On the morning of November 9, Winnie Stachelberg, then the political director at the Human Rights Campaign, drank coffee with her mother in her Dupont Circle apartment. They'd been to HRC's first national dinner the night before. President Clinton, the first sitting president to address an LGBT rights group, made a statement that night, which gay equality seekers never let him forget: "All Americans still means All Americans." The two women were dissecting the evening when Winnie's cell phone rang. It was a contact from another LGBT organization, the Log Cabin Republicans, calling with news of the holds.

Winnie quickly put on a suit, bid her mother goodbye, and left for Capitol Hill, where she hoped to find out more about the Republican maneuvers. From that point on, HRC was integrally involved in the strategic and tactical aspects of my fight.

The *Tulsa World* ran an article on November 13 about Inhofe's position. The second paragraph of the story read: "Inhofe's strong anti-gay attitude is well-known in Washington and Oklahoma." Inhofe claimed that his hold had nothing to do with my sexuality but with my "agenda." He also said, according to the article, that he could not meet with me because of a family commitment, but that Hutchinson would, and that if I answered his questions satisfactorily, they would drop their holds. He made it sound as if they were giving me a chance.

In fact, as I later discovered, Inhofe had been lying in wait for me. At an October 29 strategy lunch, he reported to a group of

Christian conservatives that he planned the hold. I found a report on the meeting in a November 5, 1997 issue of an electronic newsletter called *Scoop*, a publication of the National Center for Public Policy Research. *Scoop* billed itself as "Your Inside View to the Strategies and Activities of the Conservative Movement in Washington." Inaccurately, the *Scoop* article said that I was being considered as ambassador to Norway and hoped "to influence that nation's internal debate over same-sex marriage."

What stood out to me was the premeditated nature of Inhofe's attack. Presumably, at the time he made his remarks at the luncheon, I hadn't even testified before the Foreign Relations committee.

They *were* trying to eat me alive.

In those first few weeks, I was in a state of shock. I had anticipated being grilled on European Union enlargement and the prospects for implementing the Dayton Accord. I expected that people worried about a gay ambassador would try to show that I couldn't deal with those issues. They didn't do any of that. Except for the single question from Gordon Smith, there was no discussion of my competence, background, experience, or knowledge. The only thing that seemed to be at issue was my sexual orientation.

The White House spoke up immediately, trying to focus the debate on discrimination.

"As you know, the President recently endorsed the Employment Nondiscrimination Act, which would bar workplace bias against gay men and lesbians, and it looks like we may need to apply it in the U.S. Senate," Press Secretary Mike McCurry said in the *Washington Post* on November 14.

Republican Majority Leader Trent Lott said in the November 15 *San Francisco Examiner* that my appointment was President Clinton's "pay-off to the gay community," and that he adamantly opposed it.

That meant, in all probability, that he would not pressure Inhofe and Hutchinson to remove their holds.

Before adjourning in mid-November for the rest of the year, the Senate approved about fifty presidential nominations, including all the other ambassadors who appeared before the committee with me in October.

Curiously, Senator Lott might have let my nomination die at the end of the session. Instead, he carried it over onto the Senate calendar for the next year, 1998—an election year.

In those weeks before Christmas, a few opponents of my nomination started looking into my background. Andrea Sheldon of the Traditional Values Coalition, for example, traveled to San Francisco to comb through the archives of the Gay & Lesbian Center.

The media was catching on to the story but the White House and State Department strongly encouraged me to decline all interviews. The White House took the lead in defending my nomination, and Secretary of State Madeleine Albright issued a statement strongly affirming her support. HRC played the role of attack dog lambasting the religious extremists.

Frank Rich wrote a column in the *New York Times* on November 18 headlined "Calling Perle Mesta," after the flamboyant socialite appointed by President Truman as ambassador to Luxembourg. Rich lashed Inhofe, Hutchinson, and Lott with the dry wit that I love so well. Friends in San Francisco began writing letters to the editor. One of the first, on November 19, was from Barbara Brenner, executive director of a San Francisco nonprofit called Breast Cancer Action, which I had supported for many years.

On November 30, Republican Senator Orrin Hatch of Utah appeared on *Meet the Press*. He said that he saw no reason why my nomination should not go through. I took that as a hopeful sign that Hutchinson and Inhofe were outliers trying to make a feeble point and that I would still win approval. I even mused naïvely that the hullabaloo might achieve my original goal: to open the eyes of the American people to discrimination in the highest levels of government.

At some point in the late fall or early winter, the right wing research minions unearthed something that they hoped would deliver a fatal blow: a videotape from the 1996 San Francisco LGBT Pride Parade. To this day, I have no idea who found the tape, or where it was found, or whether in fact someone in San Francisco sent it to them. But it somehow landed in Hutchinson's hands.

The tape included an interview of me during the 1996 Pride Parade in San Francisco, a huge annual event that attracts thousands of marchers and another 500,000 spectators. The parade is as ingrained in the culture of San Francisco as Mardi Gras is in New Orleans.

In 1996, a local television station, KOFY, covered it live. The station owner, Jim Gabbert, and a reporter, Ginger Casey, sat in a booth near the reviewing stand, offering color commentary as is done for the Rose Bowl Parade or the Macy's Thanksgiving Day Parade. They asked local people of interest, such as Mayor Willie Brown, to join them for short interviews. I knew both Jim and Ginger and was happy to chat with them on air.

As the co-ed ROTC, or Righteously Outrageous Twirling Corps, passed by, Ginger and Jim asked me about my life: what it was like to be married and the father of five, my experience coming out, and why I was wearing a "National Coming Out Day" T-shirt. As we spoke, Jim and Ginger noticed that a well-known local performance troupe, the Sisters of Perpetual Indulgence, marched toward the reviewing stand.

The Sisters are a predominantly male band of entertainers, who dress in nun's habits and other costumes, using satire to raise money for HIV/AIDS-related services. A charitable organization, registered as a 501c3 since 1979, the group has members with such illustrious names as Sister Ann R. Key, Sister Missionary Position, and Sister Gladys Pantzaroff. Their humor is ribald, better suited to HBO than the Family Channel, but it is by no means extreme.

When Jim saw the Sisters, dancing their way down Market Street to the tune of "Macho Man," by the Village People, he stopped the interview and turned our attention to them.

"We can't miss these girls!" Ginger said. From background notes, Ginger read: "They acquired those *genuine* habits from a convent in Cedar Rapids, Iowa. Legend has it that they told the Mother Superior that they needed them because they were putting on the *Sound of Music*."

I laughed, as did Jim.

She followed up, spontaneously: "How do you solve a problem like Maria?"

I continued laughing, heartily. That's what I did. Not a single word, just a few laughs. It all seemed like good fun.

I looked forward to the meeting with Senator Hutchinson. I assumed there had been a great misunderstanding over my views and that a one-on-one conversation would resolve his concerns.

Meg Donovan, a deputy assistant secretary of state for legislative affairs, went with me to the Hill for the December 19 meeting. She was a dynamo, so sharp she could finish your sentences for you, and extraordinarily sympathetic. I was very green at this point and a little nervous. I had this sense that Meg knew exactly what she was talking about when it came to Hill politics, and if she told me to do or say something, I did it without question.

Upon arrival, we were ushered into his personal office. Moments later, Hutchinson came in, joined by three staff people, one of whom was his communications director, Sue Hensley.

We all shook hands and exchanged pleasantries. I chatted briefly with Sue about Illinois, where she had gone to college.

Hutchinson then sat down in a chair just a few feet away from me, close enough that our knees might have touched. He held a piece of paper that, throughout the subsequent interrogation, he repeatedly lifted, peeked at, and then put face down in his lap so that I couldn't read it.

I was prepared for everything—except for what he actually asked. There was not a single question about my competence. He hardly mentioned Luxembourg.

"Mr. Hormel, will you disavow the Sisters of Perpetual Indulgence?"

"Mr. Hormel, in your opinion would it cause the U.S. government embarrassment to know that your companion Timothy Wu served on the board of an organization called Digital Queers?"

"Mr. Hormel, can you explain why the Hormel Center at the San Francisco Public Library contains materials that promote pedophilia?"

I had no idea what hit me. When he first brought up the parade day interview and the Sisters, I did not know what he was talking about. I didn't remember the exchange with Ginger, and had never seen a replay of it. Hutchinson said that the Sisters' humor was blasphemous, and that he interpreted my mirth to be anti-Catholic.

Without knowing what was on the tape, I noted that the Sisters of Perpetual Indulgence did valuable work in the community. I explained that I had never "avowed" them, and I didn't see a reason to "disavow" them. In what was surely a cherry on Hutchinson's cake, I said that I thought they were funny.

I also tried to clarify that Digital Queers was a nonprofit organization that offered technology consulting to organizations serving the gay community. I suggested that if Hutchinson knew about Tim's service on that board, then he must also know that Tim was the youngest person ever, at age twenty, to serve on the Board of Trustees of Princeton University, from which he graduated.

I stated that the Hormel Center was a repository for the history and literature of the LGBT constituency, one of four such affinity centers at the San Francisco Public Library, and that it would be inappropriate for me as a funder to influence the selection of materials for the collections.

I also mentioned something I had read about the Catholic Church in a recent *New York Times*. As I recall, the exchange went something like this:

"Just last month," I said, "a pastoral letter was sent to all parishes suggesting that the Church must open its heart to gay people and show them dignity and respect."

For the first time, Sue spoke up.

"That letter wasn't a big deal. I'm Catholic and I heard them read it in the church and it was no big deal," she said, sharply. Meg hadn't said a word until then, but her Irish came out in full force.

"I'm Catholic as well, and when they read that letter in our church it *was* a big deal. It meant something to people. It made them think," she said.

The four of us sat in silence for a moment before Hutchinson forced a smile, thanked me for my time, and ended the meeting.

I replayed the exchanges in my mind a thousand times. Hutchinson intended to catch me off guard. At first, his line of questioning puzzled me, but then it became clear that he was following a script intended to entrap me. How silly I was to expect an honest, straightforward discussion.

I doubt that anything could have changed his mind, but in retrospect, I wish I had been more direct and confrontational. For example, I could have said, "Senator, you're an alumnus of Bob Jones University, whose successive chancellors, Bob Jones, Sr., Bob Jones, Jr. and Bob Jones III, repeatedly described the Catholic Church as an instrument of the devil and said that the popes were agents of Satan. Does that make *you* anti-Catholic?"

The next day, Hutchinson told the media that I was unfit to serve and that sending me to the predominantly Catholic country of Luxembourg would be a gross insult to its people.

Over the next few weeks, a huddle emerged, consisting of a handful of staff members from the State Department and White House; HRC political and communications experts; a few other close friends, and me. We realized that Hutchinson and Inhofe were not launching random salvos; they were gearing up for a full-on attack. And we needed a strategy quickly.

I hadn't perceived the intensity of the connections between Hutchinson and Inhofe and the radical organizations that backed them. I was insensitive to the strength of their machinery.

As the year came to a close, I approached my sixty-fifth birthday. And there I was, trying to hold on to my integrity.

Chapter Sixteen

THE DANGERS OF COLORING BOOKS

Extremists in Washington politics have a formula for destroying someone.

First, they identify why a given person is not suitable for public life. Perhaps it is his or her religion, skin color, or sexual orientation. Of course they can't overtly oppose someone for these reasons—that would be discrimination—so they base their opposition on a related wedge issue.

Then, using a well-known commentator, or an advocacy group outside government, preferably one with a name that evokes patriotism, loyalty, and faith, they circulate contaminating information. They leak stories to the press. They don't worry about accuracy; in fact, they might embellish a little if the allegations aren't shocking enough. The strategy is to associate the target with an act or statement that the public will perceive as undermining "our American way of life."

That is exactly what happened to me. People cooked up stories to vilify me and turn me into a political pariah. At first, I thought the allegations so ridiculous that no intelligent or rational person would ever believe them. Even the day after my meeting with Senator

Hutchinson, when the *Washington Times* ran an article reporting that I was anti-Catholic, I didn't take it seriously. That was a big mistake.

Right after the New Year in 1998, my opponents launched a series of salvos.

On January 13, the Family Research Council circulated information packets to Members of Congress and the press with a presentation of what they deemed my "gay agenda." They highlighted my efforts to raise funds for the Servicemembers' Legal Defense Fund, a nonprofit group that supports gay and lesbian service members, along with my contribution to a documentary for teachers called *It's Elementary* about children's perceptions of homosexuality. The opening scene showed New Hampshire Senator Bob Smith giving a fire and brimstone speech about the evils of homosexuality. Not long after, Smith joined Inhofe and Hutchinson in putting a hold on my nomination. The Family Research Council billed me as a "major" contributor, while, in fact, I gave $12,000 of the $200,000 production and distribution budget. Robert Novak, the conservative *Washington Post* columnist, wrote a detailed piece regurgitating the Family Research Council "allegations."

On January 21, The Catholic League for Religious and Civil Rights, a New York City-based organization that claimed to defend the Catholic Church from "defamation and discrimination" sent a letter to all senators alleging that I "sport bias against Catholics." Their evidence: the Sisters of Perpetual Indulgence videotape.

On February 11, the same day Lott's aides told the press that the Senator had no plans to bring my nomination to a vote, Andrea Sheldon of the Traditional Values Coalition circulated a four-inch thick binder of materials from the Hormel Center at the San Francisco Public Library, insinuating that I personally selected the materials for the collection. Among the publications was a brochure from NAMBLA, the North American Man-Boy Love Association.

I thought I'd have a heart attack when I heard about that. NAMBLA is a perverse organization that usurped the call for sexual freedom in the 1970s to justify relationships between men and adolescent boys. I never had, nor would I ever have, a connection to it. But just as Hitler's *Mein Kampf* is available in most libraries across America, so, too, are materials by NAMBLA. The *San Francisco Chronicle* did a little research and found at least ten of the documents in Sheldon's folder were also in the Library of Congress.

On March 24, a group called Savior's Alliance for Lifting the Truth, or SALT, faxed an alert to the media headlined "Clinton Ignores Nominees Pedaphile (sic) Ties" and listing first among its action items: "Pray for Clinton, Hormel, and SALT's efforts to preserve the moral order." The next day, SALT, led by Christine O'Donnell (the Republican Senate candidate in Delaware in 2010), helped organize the small protest in front of the U.S. Capitol cited in Pat Robertson's April 2 segment on *The 700 Club*.

These attacks were emblematic of what I faced all through 1998. With the regularity of a weekly gossip magazine, the extreme Christian righteous inside and outside the Senate unleashed stories that were completely false and outrageous. They labeled me as "a militant activist," a "purveyor of smut," a "radical homosexual extremist," an "anti-Catholic bigot," and an "overt homosexual and pedophile" who was "well-known for keeping minors for sexual use." They said that "Jim Hormel funds pedophilia" and that my philanthropy supported activities that "denigrate Jesus Christ." In an interview with *Roll Call*, Inhofe compared me to Ku Klux Klan leader David Duke.

People said to me over and over: *Do not take this personally*. But it was *my* name associated with the dreadful distortions. I could not be philosophical about it. It was painful.

As soon as the attacks began, individuals, organizations, and newspaper editorial pages came forward to support my nomination. The White House, State Department, and HRC helped shape the information campaign. From the very start, we wrestled with whether to respond to the attacks. It was not as if the Pope was speaking, but these groups fed Hutchinson, Inhofe, and Bob Smith with justification for their holds. In the beginning, we used traditional political tactics to promote my case, believing that truth was on our side.

In early February, Democratic Senators Dianne Feinstein, Joe Biden, and Robert Torricelli, joined by Republican Senators Gordon Smith and Orrin Hatch, wrote a "Dear Colleague" letter, asking other Senators for bipartisan support for my nomination.

People and organizations from all walks of life wrote letters on my behalf, including my family. Alice wrote a letter to Trent Lott, explaining why I was qualified to be ambassador, and my son Jimmy wrote an opinion piece that ran February 5 in the *San Francisco Chronicle,* and later in several other papers.

"Those who oppose my father's nomination on the premise that sexual orientation affects 'family values' are not familiar with the strength of our family," Jimmy wrote. "My father never tried to influence my sexuality in any way. What he did teach me was kindness, acceptance of others, honesty, self-esteem, and standing up for what you believe."

Starting March 5, senators went to the floor every few days to ask for a vote on my nomination. New Jersey Senator Bob Torricelli was first, followed by Dianne Feinstein, Barbara Boxer, Ted Kennedy, John Kerry, and Paul Wellstone.

The day after SALT's protest in front of the Capitol building, HRC issued a packet that included a press release, information sheet, twelve letters of support, and nine newspaper editorials asking the Senate to vote on my nomination. David Smith, HRC's spokesperson, condemned SALT for "character assassination using the most un-Christian tactics of lying and defamation."

The letters were mainly from people whose work I had supported. Religious leaders who actually *knew* me spoke in favor of me. They included William Swing, the Episcopal Bishop of California, and Cecil Williams of Glide Memorial Methodist Church. Several influential Republicans, such as George Schultz, Ronald Reagan's Secretary of State, his wife, Charlotte, and Don Fisher, the founder and chairman of The Gap and a top Republican National Committee donor, wrote on my behalf. The editorials came from the *Arkansas Democrat-Gazette*—a paper in Hutchinson's home state—not to mention the *Chicago Tribune, Boston Globe,* and *New York Times.*

The packet included an exchange of letters between Senator Gordon Smith and me, in which Senator Smith asked seven questions asking clarification on each of the attacks. With a great deal of help from HRC, I crafted and sent Senator Smith a point-by-point rebuttal four pages long. The letter was one of the few opportunities I had to state my positions—protocol kept me from speaking directly to the press.

Senator Gordon Smith, a former bishop in the Mormon Church, was an unlikely ally given the church's view that homosexuality is a sin. "When you grow up Mormon, you know what it's like to get your teeth kicked in," he told me when I met him the morning of my confirmation hearing. Even as an adult, Smith said he found that people who told jokes about race or sexual orientation were one laugh away from making fun of Mormons.

His reasons for LGBT advocacy were both political and religious. Oregon's LGBT constituency, which he courted after losing a special election in January 1996, helped deliver victory in his November 1996 run for Senator Mark Hatfield's seat. His religious argument was rooted in the gospel story of Jesus intervening in the public square to save an adulterous woman from stoning. The comparison of gay people to someone accused of an immoral act was not apt, but the point Smith made was that Jesus would go out of his way to help someone, regardless of how society judged that person. While resolutely opposed to same-sex marriage, Smith became the Republican leader in fighting for LGBT equality on domestic partner benefits, workplace and housing protections, hate crimes, and other issues.

With a character reference from Dallin Oaks, an Apostle of the Mormon Church and former dean at the University of Chicago Law School, Smith decided to do battle for me over the holds. Republican Orrin Hatch was supportive publicly, but Smith worked hard behind closed doors to tell my story and lobby his colleagues, even when it became politically uncomfortable.

By mid April, as major conservative media such as the *700 Club* reported the controversy over my nomination, it became clear that we should have been more aggressive at the start. The lies were growing into a strangling vine. They were beginning to define me in the public's eye.

Then I was in the worst strategic position of all—on the defensive.

Throughout 1998, my supporters and I fought to present the "real" me to members of government and the public. To succeed we had to do two things: disprove the lies and get the facts in circulation. We had to make sure that the press reported on me accurately and did not parrot the opposition's stories as legitimate allegations. We also had to win the hearts and minds of Senators who had the power to act on my nomination.

At first count, we believed we had fifty-two senators on our side—forty-four Democrats and eight Republicans, among them John McCain, Alfonse D'Amato, and Arlen Specter. We created a chart with a 1 to 5 ranking of the thirty-six Republican Senators who were potential supporters. We didn't bother to include Hutchinson, Inhofe, Bob Smith, Helms, Ashcroft, or Lott; they were lost causes. Our goal was sixty, the magic number that would force a vote on my nomination and override a filibuster.

In April 1998, the White House launched another big push with a message centered on the fairness of the democratic process: *let the Senate vote*. Why should a small cabal of senators decide whether I was competent to be a U.S. Ambassador? Administration officials distributed to all Senators a half-inch thick folder with a blue ink sketch of the White House and the presidential seal. Inside were seventeen letters and thirteen newspaper editorials supporting my nomination, a detailed biography, and the exchange of letters with Gordon Smith.

I tried to meet every Senator I could. I was sure if they had a chance to talk to me, they would see why they should support me. I saw John Warner, Paul Coverdell, Phil Gramm, Kay Bailey Hutchison, and a handful of others we thought might be persuaded. Mostly gracious, none of them expressed reluctance about my service or a vote on my nomination. But in the end, it was all just talk. Not one of them publicly stated their support or pushed for a vote.

By late May, we were up to fifty-eight votes, just two short of the total we needed to break a filibuster. Increasingly, mainstream conservative media took my side. On May 21, *Wall Street Journal* columnist Al Hunt chastised those campaigning against me, noting that "overreaching and outright fabrication are ubiquitous in the ugly fight against Mr. Hormel."

As we struggled for those last two votes, the tit for tat continued. In June, HRC drafted an easy-to-read series of talking points titled, "Jim Hormel—FACT & FICTION." Within days, the Family Research Council responded with its own paper entitled, "Jim Hormel—Mythical Man."

Several weeks later, Andrea Sheldon and the Traditional Values Coalition struck again, sending every member of the Senate a box of crayons and a photocopy of a booklet she found in the Hormel Center, a feminist statement from the 1970s charmingly titled *The Cunt Coloring Book*. Despite a letter from the American Library Association to the contrary, Sheldon suggested that I myself had put the booklet in the collection. In fact, the library had acquired it two decades before the Hormel Center opened.

I strove to look at the attacks rationally. I knew in my head that they weren't fighting me personally, but rather what I represented as a gay man. A Washington friend and corporate lobbyist asked Trent Lott to meet me. He, after all, had the single-handed power to remove the holds on the vote. His response, as she quoted it, was, "Why should I do that? I might like him."

They're such hypocrites, I thought.

I had a huge network of people behind me representing the mainstream of nearly every sector of American society: the business community, religious organizations, leading academic institutions and scholars, Republicans and Democrats, even a grandmother from rural New Hampshire. But a lie that taps into a person's fear can be far more powerful than a thousand truths. I was surrounded by innuendo, however false, and a handful of powerful people were against me. With that, the Republican Senate leadership was immovable.

One mildly humid evening that September, I hoped to cheer my low spirits by visiting the year-old Franklin Delano Roosevelt Memorial. One of the many sculptures in the four outdoor rooms of the memorial depicts FDR in a big cloak, seated in his wheelchair. It humanized him in a way that he never allowed during his presidency. Seeing the memorial's depiction of all the things FDR accomplished in a time of war, I also thought about events of that time not shown, such as the

U.S. military attacks on homeless refugees of the Great Depression in Washington and the internment of Japanese Americans.

I've spent a lot of time in Washington over the years and even though I have had a few weak moments, I am rarely sentimental about it. It's always reminded me of Los Angeles—a one-industry town, where everybody is an actor. Since the days of Samuel Johnson, Washington has been the last refuge of many a scoundrel. One only need look at the false patriotism of those who show off their American flag lapel pins, as if to say, "I am a *real* American, see my flag?!"

Yet, that night, walking across the Mall toward the State Plaza Hotel, I couldn't help but feel emotional. Although I was tired, drained, and defeated, Washington still had the ability to wring idealism out of my heart. I imagined Marian Anderson on the steps of the Lincoln Memorial, singing so passionately after being kicked out of Constitution Hall by the Daughters of the American Revolution. Surely, she felt that injustice personally, but her ego did not get in the way of her public struggle for rights.

My situation was not that different. The more I was in the game, as it were, the more I saw myself as a vessel.

During the year, a New Hampshire mother wrote to me, explaining that her gay teenage son had been contemplating suicide until he saw a news story about my fight and realized that a whole universe of people was fighting for LGBT equality. Those personal experiences were the sorts of things that kept me going.

Perhaps the lowest point in the entire process for me was the day I learned that Meg Donovan had left State after being diagnosed with an advanced stage of cancer. Meg, then battling for her life, had infused me with her vitality and confidence, never losing sight of my humanity. She had dedicated herself to my fight as if it were her own.

If I had any thoughts of pulling out of the nomination process, they were fueled purely by my ego, which suffered greatly over the course of the year. Once I pushed my ego out of the way, I could see all the attacks and lies as endurable little slaps in the face. The worst thing I could have done at that point would have been to withdraw my nomination.

I had to keep visiting Capitol Hill, banging on doors, even if they refused to open.

In December, the Senate adjourned for the winter recess and ended its 105th session. And there, my nomination died.

As soon as the Senate shut down, Dianne Feinstein, Barbara Boxer, and a handful of other Senators began to lobby President Clinton to make a recess appointment. The White House offered no official response.

That was it; there was nothing more to be done. I thought about how to make the most of my martyrdom: a media blitz, a book— maybe even a movie.

Just after the New Year, I received a call from White House Chief of Staff John Podesta asking whether I would agree to be re-nominated when the new Senate session opened. At first, I said no. I had done all I could. I had nothing left.

Then I reconsidered. I said I would do it with the understanding that if, by Easter, the Senate had not voted on my nomination, Clinton would make a recess appointment. Podesta said he thought that would work.

Then President Clinton's impeachment trial, a downright horrible turn of events, started on January 7. It was bad for the president and for me as well. What else could possibly come along to derail my nomination?

The *Seattle Gay News* ran a cartoon in January 1999 depicting me as an old, long-bearded man, seated on a bench, covered in cobwebs, and surrounded by empty SPAM cans. A surprised Senator Lott walked by, saying, "James Hormel?! Don't tell me you're *still waiting* for that *Luxembourg Ambassadorship?*"

Over those months, I stayed in touch with John Podesta, Marsha Scott, Richard Socarides, and others in the White House. I heard a lot of excuses. I don't know whether they were holding out some hope that the Senate might be persuaded to vote, or whether it was just the fact that they were in the middle of the impeachment mess. And then there was Kosovo; NATO began its bombing campaign in late March.

I understood the political distractions, but I could not help but feel disappointed once again.

Chapter Seventeen

NOT DEAD YET

On Friday, June 4, 1999, I rolled out of my bed in the State Plaza Hotel, stumbled toward the door and collected my *Washington Post*. I scanned the headlines, dropped the paper on the bed, and went about the business of getting ready and making breakfast.

With my eggs and bacon on a plate, I went back to the paper. Working my way through the first section, I got to Al Kamen's column and found something unexpected: President Clinton was reportedly considering a recess appointment for my stalled nomination. While pleased, I had no idea whether there was any truth to it.

Rumors of a recess appointment had bounced around periodically, but they didn't seem credible until March of that year. By then, thanks to relentless lobbying by me and many others inside and outside the Senate, I had enough moderate Republicans on my side to win a simple yes–no vote on my nomination. Still, Senator Lott was as stuck as gum on a shoe in refusing to schedule a vote, and I didn't have the sixty Senators needed to force one. In spite of John Podesta's earlier assurance, Easter came and went, summer came into bloom, and still, the Clinton Administration promise of a recess appointment remained unredeemed. The impeachment process and its attendant wildfires had left many politicos demoralized, regardless of their leanings, and I was one of them. In moments of weakness, I let my mind wander over the broad strokes of an exit strategy.

The morning passed as I packed my bags and checked out of the hotel. Sometime after noon, Diz arrived in her black Subaru, ready to take us the two and a half hours to Charlottesville. We were off to celebrate Sarah's thirty-fifth birthday with the family, and welcome her and her three children back from Norway.

Diz and I were well across the Roosevelt Bridge and onto Route 66 in Virginia when my cell phone rang.

"Hi Jim. John Podesta here. We've been trying to get a hold of you."

I was surprised. I had spoken to the President's Chief of Staff occasionally, but I didn't get many phone calls from him.

"Question for you," he said, chuckling. "You do speak French, don't you?"

"I sure do," I replied.

"Well, then, bon voyage," he said.

I was stunned. Diz figured out what the call was about and hollered with delight as soon as I had hung up.

"Congratulations Dad! That's so great," she said. "Thank *God* it's finally over!"

By the time we arrived, the news was in the *Charlottesville Daily Progress*. Seeing the article, it finally sank in: I had won. We had won. It didn't come exactly the way I hoped—I wanted a vote so that every senator would be on the record—but still, it was a victory for me and the constituency. And, more importantly, it was a decisive blow to those who fought against us.

I was elated to be with my family that weekend. Along with Diz and Sarah, Alice and her husband Jim Turner, Alison and her husband Bernie, Anne, and several of my grandchildren were around to celebrate for Sarah, and for me as it turned out. At the Farmington

Country Club, the club manager and staff, after hearing from Sarah about my appointment, surprised us by decorating our dinner table with Luxembourg flags.

I drafted a simple statement for the media, which read: "I am very pleased and honored. I deeply appreciate the confidence President Clinton and Secretary Albright have expressed in me, and I look forward to serving."

My detractors squealed immediately. Senator Lott's spokesman, John Czwartacki, described the recess nomination as a "slap in the face to Catholics everywhere." Senators Inhofe and Bob Smith accused President Clinton of abusing his power and made it clear that they had more fight in them.

A few days later, on June 8, Senator Inhofe announced that he would place holds on all future Clinton appointees. Senator Lott was quick to distance himself from Inhofe's ploy, but the threat had an immediate effect. Harvard Professor Lawrence Summers was waiting to be confirmed as treasury secretary, and the mere suggestion of a hitch in his confirmation caused the Dow to drop and the dollar to weaken.

The conservative *Washington Times* wrote in an editorial the next day: "Mr. Hormel stands not as a presidential choice who happens to be homosexual, but rather as a homosexual activist who happens to be a presidential choice. As a symbol, then, Mr. Hormel transcends the less-than-world-shaking nature of his official role in tiny Luxembourg."

That was exactly what I was after: to be a symbol of change.

The greatest irony of my long fight was that after devoting the better part of my life trying to blend in, I was willing to stand apart from the crowd. As a young boy, I felt that I didn't have an identity. People assigned me the identity of a Hormel, whatever that meant, good or bad. I was an extension of the big brand and the accomplishments of my father and grandfather, not a feeling person with attributes of my own. And again during the nomination process, whether people were with me or against me, they evaluated me not for who I was or what I had done, but for what I represented. But this time, I was a symbol of a movement that represented me as much as I represented it.

That was a symbolism I could embrace.

The universe has ways of setting things right.

On June 14, *Roll Call* reported that staffers in Inhofe's office had downloaded so much pornography that it crashed the office computers. According to a congressional computer manager, the system was "very messed up." HRC issued a press release highlighting Inhofe's incredible hypocrisy and urging him to apologize to me.

While Inhofe remained silent on the computer crash, *Time* had something to report. In its June 28 edition, the "Winners & Losers" feature had this listing: *JAMES INHOFE Anti-gay Senator's aides caught downloading porno. Just good clean, hetero fun?*

A few weeks later, the *Arkansas Review,* a conservative political journal, revealed that Senator Hutchinson's wife had filed for divorce after twenty-nine years of marriage. She had discovered that the esteemed Pastor Hutchinson was having a prolonged affair with one of his staffers. So much for the sanctity of marriage and the virtues that Hutchinson claimed to espouse so sincerely.

In 2000, Senator Bob Smith heard from the voters of New Hampshire. After eighteen years in the House and Senate, Smith lost the Republican primary to Congressman John Sununu, who went on to become Senator.

June 29, the morning of my swearing in, felt more like late August, with extreme humidity and intermittent rain showers that did little to cool things off. I was in my hotel room, dressed in navy pants, white shirt and red tie. I have a tendency to rework my speeches up until the last minute, and this one was no exception. I took a lot of time in choosing my words. Tim was with me, as were Marcus and Ray from my San Francisco office. Out of nervous anticipation, my hands were very shaky.

Just then, Alison knocked on the door. Up that morning from Charlottesville with her family, she delivered my father's bible. I had not seen the black volume in many years and was shocked by its condition. The cover was tattered and detached from the light inner pages, which were themselves clinging desperately to a disintegrating binding. It was horrible looking. I asked Marcus and Ray for help. Marcus left the hotel and came back a short time later with an ingeniously simple solution: black construction paper. Tim went to work on a faux cover.

Watching the repair, some element of personal history came into focus for me. *Here is this book*, I thought, *that is about two decades older than me. What had it been through to get so tattered?* The first page held an inscription from Grandpa to Daddy, wishing him well. The book was a simple reminder to me of two men who had used their time on this earth to try to make a difference and leave their mark. For a moment, I missed my mother. She would have been proud that I used this bible at my swearing in.

I had seen a couple of swearing-in ceremonies, including one for Congressman Tom Foley, when he became ambassador to Japan. The proceedings, normally conducted by mid-level diplomats, tended to be low-key, apolitical affairs with no media presence.

Mine was something closer to a victory party.

Once at the State Department, I was cloistered with my family in an antechamber to the Benjamin Franklin Room, a gold and gilded space overlooking the Potomac River. Nothing could stop the ceremony from happening, but still, I was eager to have the whole thing done and over, the appointment, at long last, set in stone. Senators Ted Kennedy and Dianne Feinstein, both of whom had requested to speak, waited with us, as did Secretary Albright, dressed in a bright yellow suit. She was taking the unusual step of swearing me in. With a lot of jostling and posing for picture-taking, I felt very distracted. When the time came for us to proceed, we lined up in silence. Only then did the loud muffle of chatter from outside filter through. As the protocol officer opened the doors, dozens of cameras flashed, bathing us in light and glittering in the room's crystal chandeliers. The standing-room-only crowd of about three hundred people let out a huge cheer as Madeleine walked in, followed by the two Senators, me, Tim, and my family, who split off the parade to take up places in front of the crowd. A long row of television cameras, normally not allowed at swearing-in ceremonies, moved in sync as the remaining six of us, including the protocol officer, moved up to the podium. Bob Hattoy, an enthusiastic Santa Monica friend who in 1992 was the first person with AIDS to speak at a national political convention, ignited the crowd with a chant of "Madeleine, Madeleine." Secretary Albright got the glint of a little girl in her eyes. Some joined in, while others clapped, hooted, or whistled. It was as if we were astronauts back from space. I anticipated a large crowd, but the sea of joyful faces stretched well past my line of sight to the back of the room. Many in attendance were close friends and political soul mates; others, I later learned, were State Department employees I had never met but who had come to witness the event. The experience was literally breath-taking; I was thankful to have a few minutes to compose myself before speaking.

The protocol officer announced the order of events, beginning with the administration of the oath. "Accompanying Mr. Hormel today is Mr. Timothy Wu, who will hold the bible," she said.

In planning the event with the State Department, the question arose, as it did at every point along the way, how do we present Tim? His thoughts and ideas were integral to the whole process, but there was always a strategic question: should he be visible, or would that only provide the opposition with an additional target? While he and I generally preferred a more prominent role, we often deferred to State and the White House in keeping him off the front line. Once the appointment was a fait accompli, nobody was going to tell me that Tim couldn't hold the bible, and in fact, nobody tried. His presence was a very important statement for all of the gay men and lesbians in that room, and for anyone who saw the photos the next day.

As we gathered around Madeleine, I looked into the crowd and immediately focused on Nancy Pelosi. It was enchanting to see the joy in her face. Raising my right hand, placing my left on the bible, I took a breath as Madeleine fed me the lines of the short oath: "I swear that I will support and defend the Constitution of the United States against all enemies, foreign and domestic; that I will bear true faith; and that I take this obligation freely and without any mental reservation," I said, my upraised hand wavering slightly.

With that, I became the highest ranking openly gay person in the political annals of the United States.

The "raucous" crowd, as the *Associated Press* described it, erupted into applause. Madeleine hugged me.

Senator Kennedy took to the microphone, shouting, "Ambassador Hormel!" Cheering rocked the room. There was so much joy and warmth in the air that I could hardly process any of my own emotions.

"Jim Hormel's confirmation was resisted by the Senate for one reason only: because he is gay. That opposition was irresponsible and unacceptable," Kennedy said, eliciting a burst of clapping. "Bigotry based on sexual orientation is wrong anywhere, anytime, but it

certainly has no place in the U.S. Senate and no place in America."
The audience interrupted with more clapping, the way they do at a
State of the Union speech.

"Ambassador Hormel's opponents never had the courage of their
convictions. They never had the decency to bring the nomination to
a vote because they knew the U.S. Senate would reject opposition
based on bigotry and confirm him by overwhelming majority. To his
credit, Ambassador Hormel never wavered in this long battle."

Senator Feinstein spoke, representing the California leadership
that had fought so hard for me.

"This nation is prepared once and for all to put aside bigotry
and prejudice and judge men for what they are: their loyalty to our
country, their talent, their ability to serve, and their care and concern
as an American citizen. And Jim Hormel fulfills every qualification
that I know of to serve as an Ambassador representing this great
country abroad," she said.

Madeleine welcomed me to the team: "There is reason to celebrate
today, not just for the Hormel clan but for all of us, because today we
do send a message. And that message is that neither race, nor creed,
nor gender, nor sexual orientation is relevant to the selection of an
ambassador from the United States. The only questions that count
are whether an individual can represent our country honorably and
effectively. President Clinton believes, and I believe, and I'm sure
all of you believe, that Jim Hormel is one of those people.

"This is one of those glorious days when the nice guy finishes
first," she proclaimed.

A moment later, delivering my carefully worded statement,
I felt self-possessed. I spoke of the great honor and responsibility
of representing the United States around the world and discussed
at length the importance and promise of a strong relationship with
Luxembourg and the need to consider how our relations with other

countries affect our well-being as well as theirs. I thanked Tim, our families, my colleagues in San Francisco, and the vast array of foot soldiers and supporters in Washington and across the country.

"From Minneapolis to Tulsa, Boston to Los Angeles, St. Petersburg to Seattle, thousands of people from diverse walks of life—color, faith, creed, background, and sexual orientation—have written to the Senate urging them to bring my nomination to a vote, and to me, encouraging me to stay the course. My favorite is from a ninety-three-year-old grandmother who wrote after the announcement of my appointment to say, 'I have prayed to live to see this day.'"

Dianne Feinstein and Ted Kennedy had both mentioned the fact that I was gay, but I didn't, except to touch on the importance of equality: "I thank all of you for a moment that I hope will become but a footnote in the history of our diplomatic relations and our efforts to ensure basic constitutional equality for all citizens. I assure you, I shall do my very best to justify the confidence and trust that you have placed in me."

Following the formalities, there was a receiving line that seemed to go on forever. With a few exceptions, everyone I ever cared about was there. Like many of the San Francisco attendees, Tim's family had come in overnight on a red eye flight. My old Lakeside friend Carroll Sherer, whose husband had been an ambassador, was there, saying she wouldn't have missed it for the world. Just about the entire office of HRC attended. One of the people I met in line was Stephen Duffy, the husband of Meg Donovan from *H*. We forwent a handshake in favor of a hug. When we released and looked at each other, I could see in his eyes the affirmation of Meg's commitment to my nomination. I'm sure my eyes reflected heartfelt gratitude.

Madeleine was supposed to travel to New York immediately after the swearing in but she stayed for the reception, which meant a lot to me. It made me feel that my appointment wasn't just *my* success; it was something that mattered to her personally, something she was genuinely proud of. My sense of accomplishment was shared by the lesbians and gay men there, especially those who had worked so hard on my behalf. Yet anyone who favored equality and opposed discrimination—which must have included everyone there—owned a share of it.

Eight floors down from our celebration, at the main door of the State Department, a handful of protesters squawked. They called me a "homosexual poster boy" who was unfit to serve. Ray and Marcus had spent the better part of the morning with State Department security, ensuring that none of the protesters snuck in to disrupt the ceremony. Having gone in a side entrance, I had no idea they were there until I read about it in the papers the next day. Even if I had known, it wouldn't have bothered me—I'd been to many events that were picketed.

More importantly, they were on the *outside*. I was on the *inside*.

Chapter Eighteen

LUXEMBOURG

From the descending airplane, I marveled at the neat villages nestled among the forested hills surrounding Luxembourg City, still very green in the beginning of August, and wondered what awaited me on the ground.

In the several weeks since the swearing in, I'd divided my time between Washington and San Francisco, preparing for my upcoming duties. For the two years that the Luxembourg process dragged on, officials at the Embassy were asked regularly: "What do you think about a gay man serving as ambassador? How will your Catholic country feel about an openly gay man?" Respecting protocol, they would only say: "We've given our approval." I was not allowed to meet with the ambassador or any other representative of the government. Oscar and others at State assured me that official Luxembourg had no problem with my sexuality, and to his point, the Luxembourg Ambassador to the United States, Arlette Conzemius, hosted a lovely dinner for me at the Embassy after I was sworn in.

Yet in the moments of nervous anticipation before the plane touched down, I thought about the people of Luxembourg. What if they *are* offended by my sexuality? What if my detractors were right?

My first experience on the ground added to my concern. From the plane, I was escorted into a holding room in the airport where I was met by Ambassador Pierre-Louis Lorenz, the government's chief of protocol in the ministry of foreign affairs. He was a physically big person, about 6 feet 4 inches, and rather chilly of demeanor.

"Welcome to the Grand Duchy of Luxembourg," he said, in a perfunctory way, as we shook hands. We exchanged superficial pleasantries about the flight and the weather before he turned to business.

"I must inform you that you are not a *bona fide* representative the United States government until you present your credentials to the Grand Duke. And, of course, he accepts them," he said. "Unfortunately, Grand Duke Jean is away on holiday, and he will not be able to receive you until September."

That was four weeks away.

"In the interim, it would be improper for you, sir, to have conversations with any Luxembourg officials," he concluded.

I wondered, *Would I ever get to serve as ambassador?* It was unthinkable that the government of Luxembourg, having endured the nomination process right along with me, would balk now.

I tried not to let the message ruffle me.

"I will go about the business of making sure the Embassy is well-organized," I said, without any hint of agitation. "If I am not permitted any communication with government officials, I certainly hope that I might be allowed to travel around to acquaint myself with the country and learn how people live. That is how I would propose to use my time during this interim period."

"That is perfectly acceptable," he said.

We parted ways moments later.

Outside the holding room, a small but genial delegation from the Embassy waited, including Marie Murray, the Deputy Chief of Mission and acting ambassador. An economist by training, Marie was not far from retirement. Soft-spoken and diminutive, she was a careful observer of people, which made her a very competent advisor. As an African American in a very senior posting, she surely had her own experiences breaking through the barriers in the diplomatic service. She met me that day at the airport with someone else who played a vital role in helping me get on my feet: my driver, Bob Feller.

Although he shared a name with the famous pitcher for the Cleveland Indians, Bob was a Luxembourger who seemed to know everyone in the country. Somewhere between fifty and sixty years old, with a full head of salt-and-pepper hair, Bob dressed most often in a plain, dark suit. He took us to the Embassy in the ambassador's car, a dark blue '97 Chrysler New Yorker.

Knowing it was my first time in Luxembourg, Bob pointed out— in perfect English—notable sights along the fifteen-minute drive from the airport. One of the first things I saw was a massive sculpture by the San Francisco artist Richard Serra consisting of seven fifty- foot high oxidized steel plates. It was made for the Palace of the Legion of Honor but rejected by the City of San Francisco for being out of character with the Palace's marmoreal surrounds. Any building of consequence along the way, whether old or new, seemed to be a bank. Bob confirmed that 212 banks had offices in Luxembourg at the time, attracted by favorable privacy laws.

Marie gave me a brief overview of my obligations that day, which consisted mostly of introductions. As we approached a small, arched bridge spanning the Petrusse River, the U.S. Embassy was visible on the other side. The French classical residence and adjacent chancery were handsome, if a bit stark, in the midday light. Turning right off the bridge, we passed the Spanish Embassy, several large private homes, and a sprawling public high school. Bob eased the car into the Embassy's circular driveway, between a half moon of perfectly manicured grass and a pretty array of flowers and coiffed shrubs. Amid the greenery, the house seemed less austere.

Three stories high, with big windows and a slate tile roof green with age, the limestone building was built, according to Bob, around 1930 by a wealthy man as a surprise for his wife. She apparently found it too big and cold so the man sold it. When the Nazis annexed Luxembourg during World War II, they made the residence the home of their new mayor. After the war, the Luxembourg government appropriated the building and sold it to the U.S. government. Its first official American occupant was Ambassador Perle Mesta, who decorated it in pink and threw a party for the mayors of every town in the country. She amazed and shocked them by serving Coca-Cola in place of champagne.

Entering the grand foyer of the residence, Perle's pink walls long since painted off-white, I found a short line of smiling faces waiting to greet me. They included Dominique, the major domo of the staff, and Christian, the chef, both of whom were French. The senior housekeeper was Aurora, a first generation Luxembourger whose parents had come from Portugal. While all under fifty, each had been on the staff for at least twenty years. They had seen their share of people coming and going. The fourth and youngest staff person was a second housekeeper named Marie-Edmine, a perky woman from Madagascar. Everybody was friendly and warm, but it was clear we were checking each other out. After the welcome, I left to settle in at the residence, feeling I was in good hands.

Over time, I came to realize that I was extraordinarily fortunate to have an experienced staff who knew what to do before I even asked them. When former Prime Minister Pierre Werner came to call, before I even offered him a drink, Dominique served him a glass of bourbon from a bottle kept especially for him. At our social events, they told me who each guest was as they walked in the door. Every country has its way of doing things, and this team helped me figure out the etiquette and the routines in Luxembourg.

After a good sleep, I made the very short commute the next morning to my desk in the chancery, a three-story warren of rooms where embassy staff members worked in very tight quarters. The big event of the day was a luncheon with the Embassy staff and their spouses, a mix of Americans and Luxembourgers whom I was eager to meet. While big posts like London and Bonn had hundreds of staffers and expert advisers coaching their ambassador's every move, Luxembourg had just two dozen Americans and Luxembourgers on staff who were obliged to have general knowledge of every issue. I knew I would work closely with all of them.

Just then, the phone rang. It was Ambassador Lorenz.

"*Bonjour*," I said, picking up the receiver.

"Your Excellency, in our conversation at the airport, I mentioned to you that it would not be proper to pursue meetings or receive officials of the government at this juncture. However, I wish to clarify that if you should be *invited* by a member of the government to pay a call *on them*, then you should feel free to do so."

"Well, thank you very much. That is very helpful information," I said, a bit bewildered.

Within minutes the phone rang again, and it became apparent what was going on.

The Prime Minister was on the line, asking if I would come to his office that Saturday, the day that several new cabinet members were being sworn in. I told him that I would be honored and delighted to do so. A few hours later, Lydie Polfer, the mayor of Luxembourg City, called, asking me to see her that Friday, her last day before becoming the new minister of foreign affairs. I was eager to meet her too: she was the person in government with whom I would have the most direct contact.

On Friday morning, with Bob's help, I made my way to the Mayor's office. There, in a reception room, Mayor Polfer greeted me with a long, warm handshake. The room was devoid of furniture, except for a long table, upon which rested a bottle of *crémant*, the local version of champagne, and two flutes. We raised our glasses and toasted my arrival.

The mayor immediately treated me as a confidante, sharing several stories from her private life. *Why is she telling me all this personal stuff?* I wondered. *She must have a reason.* I concluded that she was trying to make me feel welcome, saying, in effect, *we each have our stories*, and that any judgment about mine came from America, not Luxembourg. She asked about Tim and offered to hold a dinner in his honor later that fall.

The next day, I called on Prime Minister Jean-Claude Juncker. As we shook hands, I said a few words in French about how happy I was to be in Luxembourg at long last. Lighting the first of an endless progression of cigarettes, he replied briefly that he was happy I was there too, and then jumped right into a litany of his priorities. Top on the list was his hope of meeting with President Clinton the following month at the opening of the UN General Assembly. Juncker conducted the meeting as if I were a veteran of two years and we were continuing a conversation from the prior week. I felt that was *his* way of saying *you're a part of the scene now*.

At my urging, my daughter Diz arrived in early September with her sons Nyle, who was eight, and Graeme, who was five. Recently separated from her husband, Diz thought a year abroad would offer a good change of scenery for the family. The boys went to the American School in Luxembourg, and Diz developed her own social life there. She occasionally accompanied me to events but more often served as a hostess when we had dinner and receptions at the residence.

About that time, arrangements were made for me to present my credentials to the Grand Duchy. Normally, the task of preparing me would have fallen to the protocol officer, but the woman who held the post for decades had passed away suddenly before I arrived. She never kept records—everything was in her head. Fortunately, a genteel and sophisticated Luxembourg woman who had been on the staff in the days of Perle Mesta came out of retirement to help. Like Bob, she seemed to know everyone in the country and was well equipped to instruct me on the royal meeting. We learned that I would not see Grand Duke Jean, but the Crown Prince, who was preparing to take over the title. (The Grand Duke officially announced a few months later that he would abdicate.) Crown Prince Henri was in his early forties, handsome, and very modern. He had his own experience defying the status quo when he married a Cuban student he met in Geneva, rather than another European royal.

On September 8, the day of the meeting, Bob snapped a photo of me on the embassy steps in my white tie and tails. I piled into the car along with Marie and two other embassy staff members, the three of them in normal business attire. About a half-mile from the sixteenth-century palace, Bob pulled over. Out of the trunk came a miniature American flag, which he stuck into a small hole in the front of the car. For security reasons, the flag only flew when we were near our destination, even though the Chrysler—undoubtedly the only one of its kind in all of Luxembourg—gave away the nationality of the occupants.

The ducal palace was unusual in that it sat in the heart of the medieval section of the city, with buildings right next to and across the street from it. There were no lush gardens or fish ponds, no peacocks roaming around. Rounded turrets and square gables, topped with spindly wrought iron decorations, called Rapunzel to my mind. Bob pulled the car up to the main gate, between two tall, narrow blue boxes, each of which sheltered a guard in a loden green uniform and black beret. Prepared for our arrival, the pair looked us over briefly and gave the signal to open the gate. Inside, Bob pulled up to a set of wide steps. There I was met by the presiding officer of the palace guard, a young and handsome gentleman in dress uniform, who, in the most courteous manner, whisked my colleagues and me up to the palace doors.

We paused briefly in the vast, marbled entryway, with its high ceilings and gold-leafed columns. Our escort led us up a grand staircase. If any smidge of dirt entered the building, or any finger left a print on the golden banister, it must have been taken care of immediately—the place was immaculate. The flight rose two dozen steps before splitting left and right to the second floor. Compared to places like Versailles, this building was modest, but it was a palace, no doubt about it, with glittering chandeliers, ornate ceramic urns on pedestals, and generations of soldiers and royalty captured in massive paintings on the walls. It reminded me of something Cornelius Vanderbilt, John Jacob Astor, or some other industrial baron would have built at the turn of the century in Chicago or New York.

The presiding officer took me in one direction and sent the embassy staff in another. He led me into an antechamber, which had a second set of doors at the far end. Leaving me alone for a moment, he closed the doors behind him. I took a breath and ran through my choreography. I had in hand a sealed envelope with my credentials, official correspondence from President Clinton to the Grand Duke specifying that I was his personal, official representative to Luxembourg and requesting the Duchy's acceptance of my service.

In what seemed like just a second, the two doors to the larger room swung open, and the presiding officer welcomed me in, sweeping his arm toward the crown prince. As I entered, the officer withdrew, closing the doors noiselessly.

Crown Prince Henri greeted me with a warm, open smile.

"*Votre Altesse*," I began, "I have the great pleasure of presenting you with greetings of the president of the United States." I handed him the envelope and bowed slightly, a minimal genuflection that wasn't rehearsed but somehow came instinctively in this royal context.

"You are quite welcome in Luxembourg, Excellency," Crown Prince Henri said, motioning me to sit on a seat across from him. At this meeting, there were no toasts or drinks, but he adeptly put me at ease.

While maintaining an air of dignity and solemnity, Crown Prince Henri was very genial. We talked briefly, probably no more than twenty minutes. He alluded to the "beautiful and noble relationship" between Luxembourg and the United States, which began even before the world wars, around 1900, when relatively large numbers of Luxembourgers immigrated to the United States and settled in Wisconsin, Illinois, Iowa, and Minnesota.

In 1940, the Nazis rolled into Luxembourg and took over. With the royal family in exile, the Nazis did everything possible to make the territory an extension of Germany: creating its own government, renaming streets, putting the secret police to work, and sending Luxembourg men off to fight in Russia. It was identity theft on a national scale. In September 1944, the U.S. Second Army crossed the border with Crown Prince Jean, Henri's father, driving the Nazis out and restoring both the monarchy and Luxembourg's sovereignty. In the eyes of the Luxembourg people, Americans were heroes. As Crown Prince Henri affirmed, the sentiment was still very strong more than five decades later.

We also spoke about economic and trade issues, and strategies for developing the business climate in Luxembourg. We realized that we would see each other again soon in New York at the annual dinner of the American Chamber of Commerce of Luxembourg, where Goodyear was to receive an award for maintaining its European headquarters in Luxembourg for fifty years.

I left the meeting feeling relief and satisfaction—at last, a *bona fide* representative of the U.S. government. I had reached the milestone there, truly, to represent the president. All of the horrible memories could be put behind me once and for all, and I could get on with the business of service. At the Embassy, the staff gathered with me for a little crémant and a quick toast. Then we went back to our respective desks.

It didn't take long for me to settle into a routine in Luxembourg. First thing that happened most mornings was a staff meeting at 8:30, which lasted a half hour depending on the issues of the day. The chancery was simple, functional, and so cramped that those meetings always took place in my office; I had the only room and conference table large enough to accommodate the staff. Following our meeting, I went over my schedule with Marie or Patricia, the political officer. Because we were such a barebones embassy, we also had monthly staff meetings with military and commercial attachés who came from Brussels to brief us.

The substance of our work related to the integration of the European Union. Along with lots of interaction with Washington, I met frequently with ministers and other Luxembourg officials. There were also public events, such as visits to schools or gatherings with the U.S. business community. With some regularity, I participated in commemorations of World War II events. Remembrance of the war was inescapable, in part because of the many monuments scattered across the country.

The safety of the Embassy was another big issue. The omnipresent guards in my childhood made me resist security in my adult life, but I started asking questions in Luxembourg because I felt responsible for people who worked at our Embassy. Several months before I arrived, terrorist bombings at the U.S. embassies in Kenya and Tanzania had killed hundreds of people, and there was no reason to think that we in Europe were immune to similar attacks.

The safe room in the residence was my bathroom, which had special doors that sealed it off but no phone, fire escape, or other special preparation to make it truly safe. In the chancery, the fire escape for the building was, again, through my office bathroom, and the means of egress was a collapsible metal ladder of questionable sturdiness. The basement's emergency door was broken and could not be made secure. A driveway to nearby condominiums passed right next to the embassy grounds, but there was no way to secure the road because residents of the condominiums had to have access to it. On top of everything else, the positions for U.S. Marine guards, who normally stand watch at U.S. embassies, had been eliminated two years earlier as a cost-saving measure.

The Embassy proved so insecure that Greenpeace was able to pull a dump truck up to the gate in the middle of the day and take forty-five minutes to dump tons of genetically modified soybeans into the driveway. Ironically, I was away in The Hague at a conference on the very subject of GMOs. While the protesters did their thing before television crews and other media, the Luxembourg Police stood by and watched. The Embassy was paralyzed by one massive vehicle. I was irate, firstly because of the inaction of the police, and secondly because I had supported Greenpeace as a private citizen. When I met with the police chief a few days later, he offered no more than a lighthearted apology. The protest did not weaken the U.S. government's support for GMOs, but it did provide an enterprising local farmer, who phoned the Embassy the next day, with free soybeans for planting.

Even after the Greenpeace protest, when I raised the security issues with Washington, I was met with complete resistance. The State Department was totally stretched: there were no people to oversee major improvements at the old embassies, and no money either. The department budget in 2000 was roughly the same as it had been in 1985, even though fifteen new embassies had opened in former Soviet republics and elsewhere. The Kenya and Tanzania bombings were being treated as isolated events.

(In November 2001, just two months after the September 11 attacks, I returned to Luxembourg and found that virtually everything on my complaint list was being taken care of.)

Overall, my experience in Luxembourg was extremely positive. People were gracious to me in a classic European way, and I never once sensed hostility based on my sexuality. The only blip of gay intolerance that I knew of came in the form of a letter written by a Florida man in a newsletter produced for the American ex-patriot community in Luxembourg just before I arrived. He wrote saying the appointment of an openly gay man was a disgrace. In the next issue, his commentary was answered by a Luxembourger, advising the man that the people of the country were fully prepared to accept a gay ambassador and that he should keep his bigotry to himself.

Several weeks into my tenure, the *Chronicle* sent a reporter, Peter Kupfer, to see how I was faring. Based on interviews with several government officials and other ambassadors, Kupfer wrote that my arrival had "caused hardly a stir." The German Ambassador, Horst Pakowski, told him that there were some murmurs in the diplomatic community before I arrived. "We were afraid they were sending us an *enfant terrible*," he said, but "everybody has been overwhelmed by his seriousness and charm."

Of all the countries I might have gone to at the time, Luxembourg was probably about the most pro-American. Not that people there agreed with all aspects of American policy—in fact often they didn't—but the historical bond was still very strong.

At Bob's strong suggestion, I visited the American Military Cemetery and Memorial. A retired U.S. Army colonel who ran the place met me at the bell tower near General George C. Patton's roped-off grave. He took me across an open plaza, past a small chapel. Ahead of us were rows and rows of crosses, and the occasional Star of David, rising neatly from the green carpet. The place was maintained to the last blade of grass—the complete and utter opposite of the chaos of the battlefield. The colonel walked the rows with a freshness of spirit that gave no inkling of the countless times he had done it before.

One morning at the Embassy, the Guard House called up to my office to tell me that a gentleman was at the gate with a book for me. Given the formality of embassy life, I thought it was strange the guards would call me directly about an unannounced visitor. For a moment, I considered sending a staff member to meet the man, but instinct told me to go myself. Seeing him, I instantly knew why the guards wanted me to come, and I was very grateful that I did. The visitor was a frail man in his eighties, whose watery eyes shined with the determination of someone trying to finish items on his to-do list.

I invited him up to my office and asked him to take me through the book, a scrapbook he made during the war, when he was about seventeen. It might well have been the kind of thing that I, on my side of the ocean, would have done. The collection of newspaper articles and other items covered more than the battles. There were stories about the civilians and their struggle to survive the severity of the war. It made me think of my *grandmere* and other family living in La Vernelle, about three miles south of the line separating German-occupied France from what was called Free France. Surely they lived in terror of the Nazis coming up across the line and taking La Vernelle too. I don't know whether my exchange with the scrapbook maker brought greater satisfaction to him or to me, but it gave me a vivid sense of the drama and difficulty of the privations in Europe compared to what we experienced in the United States.

What I learned in Luxembourg was that it was easy to imagine the horrors of those times, but that one could not know war without experiencing it. I don't think anyone can absorb the reality of war unless they are in the middle of it.

In 1999, Luxembourg commemorated the fifty-fifth anniversary of its liberation, including the Battle of the Bulge, which began on December 16, 1944. That day, as German forces simultaneously attacked along a line running through neighboring areas of France, Belgium, and Luxembourg, a Nazi contingent ambushed a small U.S. Army encampment in the Ardennes Forest, not too far from the picturesque village of Clervaux. All but one of the U.S. troops there were killed. Fifty-five years later, that one soldier was still alive, small and thin but sturdy and alert at eighty. He returned to Luxembourg for the dedication ceremony of a monument to mark the ambush.

Arriving at the memorial site to speak at the dedication, I was stunned by the beauty of the place. On one side was a heavily wooded hill; on the other, a vista of rolling fields made golden green in the late afternoon light. A handful of dignitaries and reporters gathered around the memorial, which was covered in cloth, preventing the American veteran from seeing that his name was engraved on it.

The pages of my speech were folded neatly in my jacket pocket, but the sensation of the surroundings was so captivating that I never pulled them out. When it was my turn to speak, I did so without notes. I said that I found it nearly impossible to imagine that spot, five and a half decades earlier, in the dead of winter—the coldest winter in many years—as a zone of casualty and death. I noted that I was a patriotic eleven-year-old boy at the time of the attack, well acquainted with the notion of sacrifice but unaware of its true meaning. I remarked at the incredible fortune of the generations after World War II—in perpetuity, hopefully—to experience that valley not as a landmark of blood and hostility but as a place of pure tranquility. U.S. and Luxembourg troops, supported by British and French elsewhere along the ranging front, had insisted with their lives that this be so.

When the cloth was pulled back from the monument, the small crowd let out a delicate "ah." The old veteran caught sight of his name on the gray stone and tears poured from his eyes. Other people, their eyes on him, started to cry. A bugler first blew Taps, and then played its Luxembourg equivalent, as I, too, wiped away tears.

On the quiet drive back to Luxembourg City with Bob, I reflected on what had transpired. It occurred to me that at the gathering, I had done exactly what I set out do as an ambassador: namely, to be the best possible representative of the United States of America without any regard to my person. I daresay that in that moment of great deference to the forces of nature and the triumph of the human spirit, no one thought about the fact that I was gay.

The people in attendance that afternoon saw me as a representative of one government to another, channeling a shared history. I was nothing more, and nothing less, than a man amid other men and women, all of us connected by the undeniable power of human relationships. All of the nonsense in Washington over my nomination, the carrying-on, the hand-wringing, and the nasty behavior, the charges, the accusations, and the dirt that didn't stick— none of it mattered. All the distinctions that had been assigned to me and used to define me fell away. There on the hillside, no one considered my race, my gender, my religion, or my sexuality. I was an honorable person representing an honorable country. I was every American.

Chapter Nineteen

THE VALUE OF ACTIVISM

Any time I catch the wonderful smell of cut grass, I remember what it meant to me as a young boy: Minnesota was in its most magnificent period—early summer. I was back in Austin not long ago, a bit into the season, but still early enough to revel in its fresh aromas.

The occasion was the town's Sesquicentennial, held over the Fourth of July weekend and marked with a concert in the band shell, fireworks, a crafts fair, and parade. All dressed up with geraniums and impatiens and banners over the streets, Austin looked very festive at 150. My home for the few nights I was there was the Holiday Inn, which put me in nice proximity of my parents and grandparents buried in the cemetery across the road. I stayed long enough to enjoy all the events and to visit family friends, play tennis, and dash across the line into Iowa for the most succulent of steaks. The parade on Saturday morning, however, was the highlight.

It was a classic small town affair, with marching bands and kids on bikes, fire trucks and ambulances, and dozens of homemade floats, all of which lined up in the early morning sun for the forty-minute trundle along Main Street. My friend Steve Nieswanger, an avid bee keeper who runs the Austin office of the department of motor vehicles, arranged for me and a few other visiting friends to ride in the parade in antique horse-drawn carriages.

Dressed in a SPAM t-shirt and straw hat, I sat up top with the driver. Two poster boards, hanging on either side of the carriage, announced *Jim Hormel* in big, black magic marker letters. The crowd ooed and aahed when we passed by, which had nothing to do with me, and everything to do with a leggy, brown foal tethered loosely to his mother and another horse pulling the carriage. The driver told us that taking the mother off the farm to the parade and leaving the baby home in the paddock would cause both terrible anxiety, so he brought the curious, wide-eyed little horse along for the two-mile trip.

From my elevated vantage point, I scanned the rows of smiling parade-goers along the route. Some were seated comfortably in lawn chairs; others stood behind them. I took note of something I had been told but that hadn't sunk in until I saw it vividly on the street: the lily-white town of my youth was no longer so. Next to Nordic-looking grandmothers with faint blonde hair, and blue-eyed kids yelling to the floats for candy, were clusters of families with considerably darker skin. They were Latino immigrants, who had come to work in the area slaughter houses and on vegetable farms, and African refugees, relocated from Sudan. Their kids, too, hollered for treats. At the parade's end, we left the carriage and walked back, joining the friends and neighbors socializing along Main Street.

Bumping into people I knew, it didn't take long to find percolating beneath the cheery veneer of the day some tension over the town's changing demographics. A retired school principal, lowering his voice as if we were backroom cronies, talked to me about "The Problem." A police officer made a remark about how the town was not as safe as when I was a boy.

Toward the end of the day, I met Julie Craven, the vice president of corporate communications for Hormel Foods, and then Bonnie Rietz, who was mayor at the time. In separate conversations, both told me about an organization called The Welcome Center, created by the town in 2000 with support from the Hormel Foundation to help the new arrivals acclimate. The center provided people from Mexico, Sudan, Vietnam, Bosnia, and Eastern Europe with language classes and medical, housing, and immigration assistance. In subsequent years, other community agencies and foundations joined the effort, helping to sponsor an annual Ethnic Festival. Over time, the Center became a place where the cultural traditions of *all* Austin's residents were celebrated.

What I heard from Julie and Bonnie reminded me of the power that individuals have to open their minds and look at things from someone else's point of view. Exposure makes an incredible difference. When one group of people gets to know to another group of people, the preconceptions—however intimidating or scary they might have been—tend to fall away. The mystery becomes a familiarity. Perhaps those in Austin who took the time to consider the position of the new arrivals discovered a perspective similar to that of their ancestors, who, under an earlier immigrant circumstance, had some of the same difficulties adjusting to a new place.

In his own memoir, my grandfather George Hormel recalled with great enthusiasm the day that Main Street was paved for the first time, and I couldn't help but wonder how he would have perceived my view from the carriage. I wanted to think that both he and my father would have seen nothing but hope and opportunity in the diversity of the parade-goers. But they lived in different times, and I can't be sure that anything in their early twentieth century experience could have prepared them for the Austin of the twenty-first century.

Grandpa finished his manuscript, called *Three Men and a Business,* just a few months before he suffered heart failure at the age of eighty-six. In re-telling the story of our immigrant family, the beginnings of the company, and the growth of Austin, he re-created an almost unbelievable world. He described food sellers pushing their carts along unpaved city streets, with planks across the open sewers and street lamps powered by kerosene. They were lit one-by-one at dusk by a lamplighter trailed by a gaggle of ragged-clothed kids.

He opens the narrative in Toledo in the mid 1870s, during the period of economic desperation that followed the Wall Street panic of 1873. Thirteen at the time, Grandpa describes starving horses— their ribs sticking through their thin coats—brought to my great-grandfather to settle debts. He was struck by the air of desperation and the way in which the faltering economy leveled both of what he called "the big trees" and "the little trees." Our family was deeply affected by the times.

When my great-grandfather's small tannery eventually failed, Grandpa was obliged to leave the sixth grade and go to work. The family ate less meat and reinforced old shoes with cardboard rather than replacing them. For Grandpa, the greatest indignity of those times was not the physical suffering but that the recession deprived men of an opportunity to work. In his mind, the chance to work hard, to prove oneself, to be an entrepreneur large or small, was everything that a man was meant to be, and everything that the country stood for. Success was almost incidental—the reward was in the effort itself. That was *his* American Dream.

Yet Grandpa was not overly idealistic. He was aware that the playing field was not completely even and that some people were treated differently than others. He saw in his own meat-packing business that cultural differences often translated into economic disadvantages: "In summer, when seasonal layoffs took place, the first men to lose their jobs were those who belonged to a racial or national group that differed from the foreman's...so it didn't matter how hard a man worked or how well qualified he was to maintain his position—he lost it due to factors beyond his control."

Never published, the book was forgotten until someone found it in a filing cabinet shortly after my father's death. I knew Grandpa in his late seventies and early eighties, when he lived in retirement in California with servants whom he addressed by their last names. Because I was just thirteen when he died, his book was a great revelation. In a way, Grandpa seemed more enlightened than my father, which may be the result of the enormous difference between their childhoods. Grandpa grew up in a big, poor family in a big, dirty city, surrounded by struggling immigrants from the far corners of the world. My father, by contrast, was an only child, coddled and protected, who lived in a homogenous little town in a well-to-do family.

Even so, my father inherited a certain sensibility and sensitivity. The notable difference in Daddy's version of the American Dream was that he had a sense of scale about it. He wasn't averse to making money, but he didn't do it for the sake of building his own empire— he wanted prosperity to be possible for everyone in his sphere of influence.

He, too, saw in the monumental downturn of his lifetime, the Great Depression, that big business often wasn't fair to the "little trees." He concluded that workers bore the brunt of bad times and didn't profit enough during good times. That's what inspired his ideas of profit-sharing, pensions, and guaranteed annual wages. Whenever possible, if my father could do something that was good for the business and also for the workers, he did it. Those practices stabilized the workforce and increased profits while also improving the standards of living for all Hormel employees.

My father and grandfather did so well in living the "American Dream" that, for many years, I saw no way to live it myself. It seemed that I had nowhere to go but down. As a young man, I worried that my life would be a manifestation of the Peter Principle: I would rise to the level of my own incompetence. I feared that if I did become involved in the company, I might unwittingly drive the family business into financial ruin, fulfilling that old adage of *shirt sleeves to shirt sleeves in three generations.*

In my early days, I was run by fear. I was run by guilt. I was run by convention. I spent most of my time dreaming not about what my life could be, but of how I was failing to meet the goals that others had set for me. After my father died, the inevitability of corporate succession faded in my mind. After finishing law school and settling into my life with Alice and the kids in Chicago, a sense of possibility gradually replaced my feelings of obligation. I still worried about whether I could survive on my own, but I felt less guilt about not returning to run the company. It would do just fine without me.

Little by little, as I opened up, opportunities presented themselves. I found over time that there were things *I* wanted to do, things *I* wanted to achieve. They were a far cry from running a company or kindling the entrepreneurial spirit that had defined the lives of the Hormel men before me. My early objectives were simple and immediate, such as admitting more women and people of color to the University of Chicago Law School. But with life experience generally, and the admission of my sexuality specifically, my aspirations grew.

I became occupied by the imperatives of tearing down racial barriers and, eventually, eliminating discrimination based on sexual orientation and identity. What came to me after many years of self-exploration and reflection was a mandate to devote my human faculties and financial resources to building a better world, one in which equality and personal freedoms were extended to all.

My ability to make any real progress toward those goals was a big uncertainty. But in finally figuring out what I wanted out of life, I came several steps closer to living my own American Dream.

I was born in a world without television, where half of the men and women who married had grown up within walking distance of each other. I, like my grandfather, tell my story against the backdrop of a lifetime of change. Never mind the Internet and the iPhone, it was unfathomable to me as a young man that I might ever walk down the street holding hands with a man I called my partner, or see any manifestation whatever of society acknowledging or accepting same-sex relationships. There was no way for me to conceive of gay couples living in the open, or of actors one day dramatizing such relationships in movies and soap operas. I could not imagine that I would watch two women, Del Martin and Phyllis Lyon, life partners for fifty-five years, marry at San Francisco City Hall on a June day in 2008.

Not more than twenty years ago, there were members of Congress who claimed that they didn't have any gay people in their districts. Today, such a statement would be laughable—something a zealot in a foreign dictatorship might claim. The sweeping shift is thanks to LGBT people in big cities and small towns who, over the last few decades, were brave enough to be out. And that includes countless AIDS sufferers, whose presence cannot be denied. The soldiers of our movement waved placards in front of government buildings, marched in gay pride parades, unfurled a quilt larger than a football field on the Mall in Washington, and held candlelight vigils whenever one of us was beaten or killed. We waged political warfare in the courts, in the halls of Congress, and in the media.

But the greatest mind-changers among us were the thousands of fameless people—the lesbian police officer in seaside New Jersey, the gay Wall Street banker, the gay lawyer in Oxford, Mississippi, and the transgender hairdresser in Peoria—people who lived steady, even predictable lives, true to the desires of their hearts. Whether, as a price for their honesty, they were thrown out of their father's house, mocked at the office water cooler, or subjected to kicks and punches on an unlucky, dark night, their fearlessness was persuasive. As they went to work, did their grocery shopping, mowed their lawns, and paid their taxes, they showed those around them that in pretty nearly all respects, they were just like everyone else. They sent a message, which, regardless of its popularity, got through to most Americans: *we're here, and we're not going away.*

Today, even with all the progress we've made, the single most important thing a gay person can do to advance the cause of equality is to come out and be out to friends, to family, and in the workplace. The decision to be open about one's sexuality is healthy on a personal level, and it tells people: *This is who I am. And I'm the exact same person I was before you knew I was gay (or lesbian, or bisexual, or transgender), except that maybe now, I will be an even better person because I won't have to hide who I am.* Until the day that everyone in our constituency is out, others will still hold power over us. No one can expect an ounce of sympathy over discrimination and injustice if they are not willing to tell the rest of the world who they are.

On that propitious June day in 2008, Del, white-haired and dressed in a lilac pantsuit, rose from her wheelchair to clasp hands with Phyllis, her dark-haired, bespectacled partner, vibrant in turquoise. With Mayor Gavin Newsom presiding, the two exchanged vows. The sixty or so of us crammed into his office, along with the hundreds waiting in the city hall rotunda with cake and champagne, knew that the marriage would be challenged.[5] But for the moment, the polemics were parked outside. Nearly every breathing body around City Hall was swept up in the sweet, bittersweet force of two

---

[5]Proposition 8, which was on the California ballot that November, eventually revoked the right to same-sex marriage, though unions that took place prior to the vote, such as that of Del and Phyllis, were allowed to stand.

soulmates being joined *legally* before all who knew them and loved them. As Phyllis gently bent to kiss Del on the cheek, a sense of utter, divine completion filled the room.

No human being could witness that scene and not be moved. Tears poured from the eyes of the guests. People cry at every wedding, but this one was different. It was long, long overdue.

Several weeks later, Del died at the age of eighty-seven.

While I am mindful—and very grateful—that times have changed, I'll be the very first to say that they haven't changed enough. The contemporary equality movement is at least as old as Phyllis and Del's relationship, and in those many years, I've had plenty of time to visualize a country in which gay, lesbian, bisexual, and transgender people enjoy every single right and freedom afforded to every other American citizen. *When* will it happen?

Huge numbers of us are treated as second class citizens, not protected from job discrimination or, in most places, able to marry the person they love. I feel compelled to note that these are not benefits or privileges. They are *rights*, outlined in our Constitution and upheld by courts over the years as the just due of any American. Yet they are still being denied to LGBT people in this country.

Rights are the manifestation of our values, and whether we afford them to others speaks volumes about what we really believe. History has shown that everybody wants rights, but nobody wants to share them. Back in 1958, if the people of Virginia were asked to decide whether Mildred Jeter, an African-American woman, and Richard Loving, a white man, could be married, how would they have voted? In their prescience, our founding fathers gave the courts power to decide such matters, as they did in 1967 in *Loving v. Virginia*, which held that bans on interracial marriage were unconstitutional.

We as a nation spend an incredible amount of time, human capital, and money to maintain inequality. *Don't Ask, Don't Tell*, for example, resulted in the removal of more than 13,500 U.S. soldiers between 1994 and 2009. At least fifty-five of those discharged were linguists whose Arabic and Farsi skills were desperately needed to combat terrorism. A blue ribbon panel of military experts, convened by the University of California Palm Center, projected in 2006 that the U.S. government spent $364 million between 1994 and 2003 to keep gay people out of the military. That figure is estimated now to have topped $500 million. That's enormously wasteful. The expense alone should have been enough to persuade cost-conscious Republicans to join in the 2011 repeal of DADT. Since President Barack Obama took office, wasting federal dollars is their number one complaint about government.

Sadly, hypocrisy dates back to the founding of the country. Since America's early days, we have abided by a constant tension between the ambitious values to which we aspire and those that we practice. The first few sentences of the Declaration of Independence speak so elegantly about equality, yet the very authors of that document, drafting the Constitution and Bill of Rights a few years later, could not agree to forbid the enslavement of human beings. As Americans, we acknowledge a certain set of values and truths, but not all of us want a society that is 100 percent faithful to them.

This tension is not only relevant in terms of national policy but also in terms of personal politics. Washington's unofficial registry of sexual dalliances is chockablock with politicians whose public rhetoric centers on ideals of family, fidelity, and heterosexual love but whose private affairs include deception and adultery. And political and religious leaders who, in some cases, are divorced, once, twice, sometimes even three times, audaciously claim to defend the sanctity of marriage. I've talked at length about Senator Tim Hutchinson, who falls into this category, and I could go on to discuss the almost yearly revelations of others. Nevada Senator John Ensign resigned in April

2011 after revelations of an affair with a campaign staffer and former California Governor Arnold Schwarzenegger revealed in May 2011 that he fathered a child with his housekeeper. It must not be forgotten that former House Speaker Newt Gingrich, now trying to breathe life into a 2012 presidential bid, admitted to having an affair with an aide while leading the effort to impeach President Clinton. And of course, there's Idaho Senator Larry Craig, arrested in 2007 for "lewd conduct" in an airport bathroom. All four of these men decried and ultimately opposed same-sex marriage even as they violated their own marriage vows.

I don't really care about politicians' private conduct, except when those same people wrap themselves in moral superiority, and deprive the LGBT constituency of rights on the grounds that *our* behavior is somehow perverse. Millions of voters are content, apparently, to accept the spin and live with these deceptions. Or perhaps they are so detached from politics that they have not noticed. Ultimately, though, the voters sustain inequality and hypocrisy at the ballot box.

I took part in a panel discussion in Philadelphia not too long ago on the state of gay politics, which involved a great deal of discussion on same-sex marriage and political will in Washington. The session was held in the Constitution Center, just a six-minute walk across two lush, grassy blocks to Independence Hall. During the question and answer period, a red-haired woman stood up from the audience.

"Do you consider yourself a patriot?" she asked.

"Yes, I do," I responded, without a moment's hesitation.

My response was quick because my heart is unwavering: I am a patriotic person. Whether or not I put an American flag pin in my jacket lapel on a given morning, my devotion to my country is unshakeable.

During my nomination process, the rightists did everything they could to make me seem un-American, as they do to anyone with whom they disagree. In the run-up to the 2008 elections, political baiters accused President Obama of removing an American flag from his campaign plane (it was in fact a stylized red, white, and blue graphic, the corporate logo of the previous owners) and refusing to place his hand over his heart during the national anthem. These are the cheapest and most base of tactics.

A true patriot, I believe, is devoted to his or her country, but not to the point of blind acceptance. Carl Schurz, a German-born senator from Missouri who served in the late 1800s, did not say, "My country, right or wrong." He said, "My country, right or wrong; if right, to be kept right, and if wrong, to be set right." That is the essence of patriotism and the motivation for activism. If gay people had no hope of becoming first class citizens, I'd consider moving to Canada or some other place where I would be treated equally. But I do have hope. I believe that all laws discriminating against the LGBT constituency will be repealed one day. I live for, and fight for, that day. That's what makes me a patriot.

There is a prevailing belief in our society in rugged individualism and the notion that our country was built on individual opportunity and ingenuity. It is a gross oversimplification of our history. Families on the Great Plains helped each other with their farms, and Andrew Carnegie had no empire without his steelworkers. The fact is that we are, and always have been, interdependent.

My grandfather was an entrepreneur with lots of ideas, who slaughtered the hogs for several years until he could afford to hire more men. Neither he nor my father, who kept his desk alongside those of dozens of middle management employees, had any illusions about their importance relative to their thousands of workers. For as ingenious as he was about new products and advertising and production, my father knew that Hormel would only succeed with hard work from all involved in the company. He knew that it was the dedication of the workers, including the women who took over the jobs of men who were drafted, that enabled the company to meet the demand of World War II.

My father and grandfather learned—and shared with me— the idea that we live as individuals but depend on others and our environment for survival and growth. As a means of protecting our own welfare in the world, it is incumbent on us to be concerned about each other.

It's been more than a decade since I served in Luxembourg, and my Senate battle feels like it has become, as I wished at my swearing-in ceremony, a footnote in history. The question of my life now, as I near my eightieth birthday, is: *Did any of it matter?*

I don't like to think about the meaning of life, at least the meaning of *my* life. But it's in my nature to do so. The cynic in me wonders: Is the meaning of life to kick back until you get old and then expire? I certainly could have chosen that path; I'd probably still be living on Kauai. But the cynic is overwhelmed by the idealist, who is compelled to say: Isn't the meaning of life to follow the direction of your inner compass, and stay the course until your dying breath? To leave this world a better place than you entered it?

In 2001, a second openly gay man, a career diplomat named Michael Guest, was nominated as an ambassador by President Bush and received Senate confirmation without public debate over his sexuality. It was only at the swearing-in ceremony, after Secretary of State Colin Powell graciously introduced Guest's partner, that the extremists on the right became aware that this ambassador had a man as a partner. They made a small ruckus, but Guest was already on his way to Romania.

Ambassador Guest pushed the issue of domestic partner benefits for LGBT diplomats but resigned in frustration in 2007. "For the past three years, I've urged [Secretary Condoleezza Rice] and her senior management team to redress policies that discriminate against gay and lesbian employees. Absolutely nothing has resulted from this. And so I've felt compelled to choose between obligations to my partner—who is my family—and service to my country. That anyone should have to make that choice is a stain on the Secretary's leadership and a shame for this institution and our country," he said. In June 2009, Secretary Hillary Clinton ended the lengthy conversation by extending domestic partner benefits to gay and lesbian employees.

I can look at these circumstances and see that life for gay employees at the State Department has become more equal. I can say, *yes, my efforts were a step along the path to achieving that outcome.* I must acknowledge that my efforts forced me, too, to make some difficult personal choices and left some of my children feeling that I neglected them. I regret that. But I take heart in thinking that I did make a difference.

On jury duty recently in San Francisco, in a high-ceilinged room drowning in fluorescent light, a clerk called names to confirm the attendance of prospective jurors waiting before her in orderly rows of chairs. When she read my name, I called out, "Here." A moment later, a man sitting behind me tapped me on the shoulder.

"You don't know me, but I just want to tell you that I really appreciate all you've done," he said. "The world needs people like you."

What a surprise, a decade later, to hear some stranger thanking me for fighting for what was right.

Every time I have one of those sorts of exchanges, I hope the person I see before me represents hundreds of others I'll never meet. I hope that my experience has inspired people to look into their hearts and ask: *What can I do to make the world a better place?* And then, find the courage to act.

Martin Luther King, speaking of his own American Dream at the Lincoln Memorial on August 28, 1963, mentioned "the promissory note to which all Americans were to fall heir." That note was nothing more and nothing less than the protections and guarantees of our Constitution and Bill of Rights. Dr. King spoke on behalf of a people who were dragged from their homes, sold as chattel, and very often treated as chattel, or worse. That collective experience is far uglier than that of LGBT people in America but there's no difference in our respective desires for equality and full representation. As MLK also said, "We may have come on different ships, but we're all in the same boat now."

And it's true. There's nothing different about the screaming anger and frustration of seeing men like me beaten and left for dead in the Wyoming outback, or stabbed fatally in a Los Angeles high school, or decapitated along a roadside in Puerto Rico. All just for being who they are—for being what God made them. When a country has different laws for different citizens, the damage to the soul is immense. It relegates those citizens to an imprisonment of the mind and encourages suicide, repression, and duplicity. That's why I say that our society is "relentlessly" heterosexual—it is so unremittingly focused on straight people that it encourages all others to hide and deny who they are.

The persecution of African Americans was based on a clearly identifiable physical trait, and their inability to change their skin color prevented them from hiding. It also inclined them toward hope, comfort, solidarity, and mutual strength. By contrast, the LGBT constituency, with no ethnic commonality or identifying physical features, has the ability to hide. That is our Achilles heel. Within the constituency, there is racism, sexism, homophobia, and a tendency toward fractious behavior. But worst of all, too many of us deny who we are. Until every one of us has the courage to be out,

we will not enjoy a common bond. Rather, we will endure unequal
treatment.

On November 4, 2008, in the packed ball room of the St. Francis
Hotel, I held hands with my partner, Michael Nguyen, as we waited
for the election results. About an hour after California's polls closed,
a television network anchor on a huge screen made an announcement
that caused me, Michael, and nearly everyone around us to hug,
cry, clap, whoop, dance, and otherwise overflow with joy. Illinois
Senator Obama, campaigning on a message of change, had made
history by being elected President of the United States. Michael,
an accomplished dancer, choreographer, musician, and Swarthmore
grad, is also a Chicago native—he was particularly proud that night.

President Obama inspired people to engage in public life in a
way that I hadn't seen since the Kennedy era. He promised an end
to the barbarism in Washington politics that turned my nomination
process into a sick parlor game, and I bought what he was selling.
Perhaps naïvely, I imagined bipartisanship on the order of what I saw
as a boy growing up after World War II, when political cooperation,
particularly on international affairs, was a natural outgrowth of war
unity.

Despite my ardent support of Obama, I could not immerse
myself in the joy of the moment—we still didn't have an answer
about Proposition 8, the measure revoking California's constitutional
right to same-sex marriage.

Michael and I spent several months working on the *No on 8*
campaign, an effort scarily reminiscent of *No on 6* exactly thirty years
earlier. My favorite slogan of the campaign was one that I saw on a
T-shirt, which read: "When do I get to vote on YOUR marriage?"

When the television anchor announced a few hours later that
Prop 8 had prevailed narrowly, I was crushed. I was in a state of

utter desolation. We had lost again. The extremists, with an infusion of out-of-state volunteers and some $20 million from the Mormon Church, had won.

A desperate tug of war is taking place across the country. Every time a state takes a step toward approving a gay equality measure, extremists mobilize to prevent it. In California in 2008 and then Maine in 2009, voters revoked measures allowing same-sex marriage. In 2009, the Iowa Supreme Court unanimously invalidated a ban on same-sex marriage. A majority of Iowa voters, inflamed by a campaign bankrolled by out-of-state political interests, voted out three Supreme Court judges in November 2010—the first such removal of a judge in Iowa since 1962.

To me, it was the most dangerous outcome of the 2010 elections. Do we live in an America that does not respect the independence of the judiciary? Are we going to say that judges are independent so long as they do the will of the majority of voters? Our system has judges to make judgments, and it's too bad if we the people don't like them. The removal of judges by a popular vote is a nightmare come true, the unraveling of our democracy.

Desperation is the motive of those who sully our republic in this way. Their movement against LGBT rights is taking its last gasps. The polls consistently show that younger generations support full equality in large percentages. And the 2011 passage of a landmark marriage equality law in New York was made possible by senators of both parties who anguished over the issue and then reversed their 2009 "no" votes. They demonstrated that those of other generations are increasingly concluding that inequality is untenable.

But I can't wait for *eventually*. My time is running out, and I don't see any reason why anyone—whatever his or her age—should have to wait for fairness and justice. My partner Michael, two generations younger than me, feels the same way. Age has nothing to do with it—our time has come.

So I say, to myself and others: We must keep pressing forward. The snake, while dying, is still venomous. People are losing jobs for being gay. People are still being killed in the meanest and most humiliating ways because of their sexual orientation and gender identity. We must focus the public on the injustice of it all and get their support to repeal DOMA, pass the Employment Non-Discrimination Act, and change federal laws and regulations that bar same-sex partners from enjoying the medical, tax, and financial benefits that heterosexual couples enjoy.

An important question about patriotism is whether it is possible for any patriot to sit on the sidelines and not be involved. For gay people, my answer is no. We have to be out. If not, we are complicit with the old order, the one that would have us remain invisible. We have a perfect opportunity now to fight for the Respect for Marriage Act, introduced by Dianne Feinstein in July 2011, which would repeal DOMA and open the door to full marriage equality. We must not miss this chance.

In his manuscript, my grandfather wrote, "Perhaps man's inability to gauge his true self-interest is the only stumbling block to his progress on this earth." He was suggesting that a person's true self-interest is in humanity and a world that is kinder to more people, but that too many of us cannot or choose not to recognize that interest.

My progress on this earth was stymied until the time in my life when I chose to follow my heartfelt instincts and desires and live openly as a gay man. I had to clear away truckloads of psychic garbage in order to free the real me from a self-imposed prison. Only then was I able to see that my genuine interest was in finding a way to help build a better world. That awareness yielded a new sense of self, which in turn gave me the strength to hold fast to my goals, even in the face of hideous personal attacks.

Nothing about a human being's psyche is ever completely resolved, and I will be the first to say that I struggle continuously to be true to myself. I contend daily with the specters of my past and lingering guilt over things I wish I had done differently. And the universe is ceaseless in presenting new tests and challenges. My relationship with Michael is a perfect example.

We met in May 2006, at the annual Equality Forum dinner in Philadelphia. I had donated a table to Swarthmore for LGBT students and Michael—a sophomore at the time—was among those invited by the Dean's office to attend. When we met, there was magic. He looked dazzling in a suit that he told me he borrowed from the college Drama Department. Our conversation sparkled. I gave him my card and, when he saw that I was from San Francisco, he said, much to my delight, that he would be at Berkeley in two weeks for a study program. Soon after he arrived, I gave him a tour of San Francisco. We began seeing each other frequently. And we fell in love.

Over the next several months we called each other every day and met up in San Francisco, Chicago, and on the East Coast. I wrestled privately with my own ageist preconceptions about how we could possibly be together—Michael had just turned twenty-one. Our running joke was that when he was a sophomore, I was a senior.

Michael's faith, passion, and openness were so clear and compelling that he brought me to realize that what we shared was genuine, special, and precious. He enabled me to listen to my heart and honor our mutual feelings of commitment and devotion, no matter what the world around us might say.

The day of his graduation in 2008, Michael moved to San Francisco to live with me and pursue further studies in dance and music. Through our rich and varied experience together, I have learned more about myself and how I have unconsciously managed my world. Michael has made me a more honest person, and I'm very proud of that.

For trusting my heart, I was rewarded with true love and a rich, fresh insight into who I am. What greater gifts are there for a man in the eighth decade of his life?

About the Authors

JAMES C. HORMEL, a native of Austin, Minnesota, is a businessman and philanthropist dedicated to social justice and equality. Active in Democratic politics for decades, Jim served as U.S. Ambassador to Luxembourg from June 1999 to December 2000. Jim has five children, fourteen grandchildren, and five great-grandchildren. He lives in San Francisco with his partner Michael Nguyen.

ERIN MARTIN, a native of Thomaston, Connecticut, writes both fiction and non-fiction. A former newspaper reporter and deputy press secretary to U.S. Senator Christopher J. Dodd, Erin spent seven years working on democracy assistance programs in post-Apartheid Namibia and South Africa. She lives in New York City with her husband Frank Schaefer.

ACKNOWLEDGMENTS

Fit to Serve was conceived as a travelogue through political peaks, precipices, and gullies of our national government and a reflection on some of those who seek to influence its actions. It has become more of a biographical memoir of an individual who traveled that terrain, and in so doing, came to discover much about integrity and, well, himself. That different course was the result of my friendship and association with Erin Martin.

Although this book is written in the first person singular, it is in fact a collaboration. It was Erin who continually pushed and prodded me to reveal details, not only of my adventure but also of my development as a person. She probed my memory and my sensitivity. She called forth my weaknesses and my vulnerability. She caused me to examine my motivations and to notice times and places that reflected on my integrity or lack thereof; my altruism and my egotism. She questioned, commented, challenged, and listened as countless words poured from my mouth. She sorted them, edited them, and brought order to them. She interviewed and researched and checked facts. And she absorbed my perspective about my life.

That is how *Fit to Serve* came to be. Erin and I have produced what we hope you will find interesting, entertaining, and thought-provoking. Without Erin, however, my writing screen would still be blank.

I met my life partner Michael Nguyen in 2006. He has given me unconditional love, and in loving him unconditionally, I have discovered the spiritual and emotional fullness of caring completely and selflessly for another. Our relationship is one of mutual commitment and devotion. Although two generations separate us, the challenges we face together strengthen our bond. Michael empowers me to clear my thoughts of self-doubt and self-concern, to notice my tendency to judge myself and others by superficial standards, and to focus instead on principles of love and caring. He has given me guidance and imparted wisdom beyond his years. Michael has taught me that to live is to grow. And it's never too late to learn.

I am indebted to many special people for helping me through the ambassadorial process.

How I love my family! My children have loved me no matter how I tested them. I am very grateful to them and their spouses/partners: Alison Hormel Webb and Bernie Webb; Anne Hormel and Matt Bixby; Elizabeth Hormel and Ted Vlach; James Hormel Jr. (Jimmy) and Kathleen Hormel; Sarah Hormel Everett and Tommy Everett; Falk von Quillfeldt; and their brother Andrew Kramp. My grandchildren have brought tremendous joy to my life. They are (in family order): Ira David Miller, Harry Webb, Georgia Webb, Heather Hormel Miller, Aven Hormel Kinley, Tristan Magee, Nyle Leddy, Graeme Leddy, Ryland Hormel, Ella Hormel, Anniken von Quillfeldt, Anders von Quillfeldt, Mats von Quillfeldt, and Kobi Everett. And my great-grandchildren are the delightful dividends of a long life. They are (to date): Stella Magee, Roman Miller, Jude Miller, Sawyer Kinley, and Margaret Miller. I'm especially grateful to Alice Turner for a profound friendship made evident by her forgiveness and more than five decades of abiding love and support. Heinz Kramp and Jim Turner have always been great allies. Simone Scharff, my former sister-in-law, has been at the heart of our family since 1952. Simone

Meignan, always more sister than cousin, taught me so much about finding strength in times of trouble. My brother Geordie, who died too young, was the most talented person I ever knew. I didn't realize how much he influenced me until after he was gone. And to my brother Thomas, thank you for the many times you've been my guide in living. You are my most trusted friend.

Deepest thanks to my dear colleagues at Equidex: Kenner Foote, Paul Grippardi, Marcus Guerrero, and Ray Mulliner, who, working with Jimmy and me, have exceeded the call of duty both professionally and personally, transcending the normal workplace relations with their unwavering friendship and loyalty. My appreciation extends to Jimmy, who has responsibly relieved me of responsibilities, and to our recently retired attorney, Meriel Lindley. What a gift it has been to work with such devoted, caring individuals. I also wish to mention Ken Burkhardt, Maria Miranda, Gisele Oakes, and Margaret Stangl, who have been devoted caretakers of me and my homes.

Political leadership was indispensible to all aspects of my ambassadorial fight. I am grateful to President Bill Clinton for sticking by me all those years and taking the heat for the recess appointment. Secretary of State Madeleine Albright was also a staunch ally and strong voice on my behalf. My success was the direct result of dogged public and behind-the-scenes advocacy and lobbying by Senators Barbara Boxer, Joe Biden, Alan Cranston, Dianne Feinstein, Ted Kennedy, Bob Kerrey, John Kerry, Chuck Robb, Gordon Smith, Robert Torricelli, and Paul Wellstone, as well as Congresswoman Nancy Pelosi. Along with my former partner Tim Wu, a core group of Washington movers and shakers was unstoppable in fighting for my nomination: Elizabeth Birch, David Smith, and Winnie Stachelberg of Human Rights Campaign, and lobbyist Hilary Rosen. I am thankful for all their efforts.

In Congress, Senate and House staffers worked diligently and strategically to keep my nomination alive, including: Rob Epplin in Senator Gordon Smith's office; Mike Epstein on Senator Kennedy's staff; Jim Molinari in Senator Feinstein's office; and Brian Wolff on Congresswoman Pelosi's staff.

I am very appreciative of the efforts of White House staffers including: John Emerson, Bob Nash, John Podesta, Leon Panetta, Marsha Scott, Wendy Sherman, Richard Socarides, Tracy Thornton, and Karen Tramontano. Anne Bartley, a staffer to First Lady Hillary Clinton, was a great supporter.

In the State Department, Oscar de Soto, Meg Donovan, Peter Yeo, and many others were masterful in handling the nomination process and gracious even in its most challenging moments. I am thankful for the dozens of other staffers in Congress, the White House, and at other Washington organizations whose support got me to Luxembourg.

Across the country, many people raised their voices to press my case with elected leaders and the American public. They include: Roberta Achtenberg, Art Agnos, Nancy Bechtle, Barbara Brenner, Willie Brown, Kevin Cathcart, Kenneth Dam, Doris and Don Fisher, Sako and Bill Fisher, Matt Foreman, Wade Henderson, Frank Jordan, Mark Leno, Cindy Testa McCullough, Tim McFeeley, Carole Migden, David Mixner, Mary Morgan, Ralph Neas, Rick Phillips, Deb Price, Louise Renne, Frank Rich, George and Charlotte Schultz, G. Rhea Serpan, Walter Shorenstein, Merv Silverman, Karen Strauss, Cissie Swig, Rt. Reverend William E. Swing, Andy Tobias, Martha Whetstone, and Reverend Cecil Williams. Thank you, all.

I was extremely humbled by and grateful for the thousands of letters of support that people wrote to me, to their members of Congress, and to newspaper editorial boards. They came from across the country—giving me comforting assurance that my nomination had national support—and they poured out from friends, neighbors, and people I did not know in my hometown of San Francisco. These thoughtful, persuasive words sustained me and gave me hope in the darkest hours.

Many people were very kind in sharing experiences and recollections for the book. They include: Mary Bitterman, Chuck Forester, Hildegarde and Chuck Golden, Bruce Knotts, Tom Nolan, and Jim Van Buskirk. Charity Lifka and Gretchen Ramlo were very helpful in finding old photos. I'd like to give special recognition to my dear friend Bob Sass not only for his encouragement but also for his dedicated record-keeping of political activities in San Francisco over the last four decades.

Both Erin and I are also deeply grateful to Kevin Bentley, Ann Marsh, and Deb Swift for their keen editorial guidance on various drafts and chapters of the book.

I have countless friends who have shared their love and their lives with me over many years. Their confidence during the confirmation process boosted my own. They include Don Angus, Samira Baroody, Vic Basile, Al Baum, Terry Bean, Linda Blackmore, Peg and Al Bloom, Stuart Burden, Sally Carlson, Tony Chase, Karl Christiansen, Dudley Clendinen, Kate Clinton and Urvashi Vaid, Mark Cloutier, Matt Coles, Christian de la Huerta, Q. Todd Dickinson, Gloria Duffy, Dorothy Ehrlich, Milton Estes, Helene Feingold, Ruth Felt, David Smith Fox, Jeffrey Fraenkel, Ellen Friedman, Phyllis Friedman, Bill Glenn and Scott Hafner, Marcia and John Goldman, Daniel Goldstein, Marya Grambs and Jan Montgomery, Jim Gregory, John Hall, Bill Hayes, Lance Henderson, Paul Herman, Sandra Hernandez, Bob Hill, Fred Hochberg, Brooks Holton, Jim Holton, Karl Keesling, Kate Kendall and Sandy Holmes, Nancy and Dick Knowlton, Hael Kobayashi, Mathilde Krim, Jeff Leiphart, Gordon Murray, Steve Nieswanger, Dixon Osburn, Laura King Pfaff, Liza and Drummond Pike, Geoff Stone, Larry Soule, Steve and Mary Swig, and John Vasconcellos.

I would also like to thank the staff of the United States Embassy in Luxembourg for their excellent counsel and considered care during my eighteen months of service. Marie Murray and Gerald Loftus served as deputy chiefs of mission during my term, providing me with outstanding support and guidance.

A special word of gratitude goes to the Government of Luxembourg and its genial citizens, who so cordially welcomed me to their country. Particular thanks go to Pierre Dillenburg and Roland Hubsch, and Luuk Jacob and Pierre-Yves Rahari.

I am deeply appreciative of my agent Gillian MacKenzie for her determination and pluck in getting this book into the marketplace, and my editor at Skyhorse, Julie Matysik, for her fine eye.

Finally, to countless others whose names belong here but whose generous deeds are not recorded in my files: please forgive my faulty memory and accept my very sincere thanks for your invaluable assistance.

SOURCES

This book is based on the recollections of James C. Hormel and correspondence, newspaper clips, and other materials contained in his extensive personal files covering the period of 1993 to 2001. This information was supplemented by twenty-three interviews with individuals relevant to the story, as well as a range of secondary sources that include, but are not limited to:

Newspapers, magazines, and other print media: *Arkansas Democrat-Gazette, Arkansas Review, Associated Press, Austin Daily Herald, Bay Area Reporter, Boston Globe, Charlottesville Daily Progress, Chicago Tribune, Human Events, Los Angeles Times, New Haven Register, New Republic, New Statesman, New York Review of Books, The New York Times, Pacific News Service, Philadelphia Inquirer, Political Science Quarterly, Roll Call, San Francisco Chronicle, San Francisco Examiner, Scoop, newsletter of the National Center for Public Policy Research, Seattle Gay News, Sun-Sentinel, The Daily Oklahoman, The Hill, Time, Tulsa World, USA Today, Wall Street Journal, Washington Blade, Washington Post*, and *Washington Times*.

Reports, documents, and correspondence: the Congressional Record, presidential papers of William J. Clinton, correspondence, and other materials in the files of James C. Hormel; correspondence from the White House, State Department, and various senators; press releases, action alerts, and other distributed materials from Human Rights Campaign, Savior's Alliance for Lifting the Truth, Catholic Alliance, and Traditional Values Coalition; official United Nations records; "Don't Ask, Don't Tell: How Much Does the Gay Ban Cost," a Blue Ribbon Commission Report, 2005.

Books: *In Quest of Quality: Hormel's First 75 Years* by Richard Dougherty; *The Lavender Scare* by David K. Johnson; *Out for Good* by Dudley Clendinen and Adam Nagourney; *Policy Issues Affecting Lesbian Gay Bisexual and Transgender Families* by Sean Cahill and Sarah Tobias; *Three Men and a Business*, unpublished manuscript by George A. Hormel.

Electronic media: KOFY-TV interview with James C. Hormel at San Francisco's 1996 Lesbian, Gay, Bisexual, and Transgender Pride Parade, and Christian Broadcasting Network's April, 1998 broadcast of *The 700 Club*.

Websites: www.cnn.com; www.fbi.gov; www.impeachclinton.com; www.hivinsite.ucsf.edu; www.hrc.org; www.eclipse.gsfc.nasa.gov; www.equalityforum.org; www.state.gov; www.un.org; and www.who.int.

INDEX